Contemporary Growth Therapies

Resources for Actualizing Human Wholeness

Howard Clinebell

Howard Clinebell

ABINGDON
Nashville

CONTEMPORARY GROWTH THERAPIES:
Resources for Actualizing Human Wholeness

Library of Congress Cataloging in Publication Data

CLINEBELL, HOWARD JOHN, 1922-
Contemporary growth therapies.
Companion volume to the author's Growth counseling.
Bibliography: p.
Includes index.
1. Psychotherapy. I. Title.
RC480.C55 616.89'14 80-24368

ISBN 0-687-09502-6

MANUFACTURED BY THE PARTHENON PRESS AT
NASHVILLE, TENNESSEE, UNITED STATES OF AMERICA

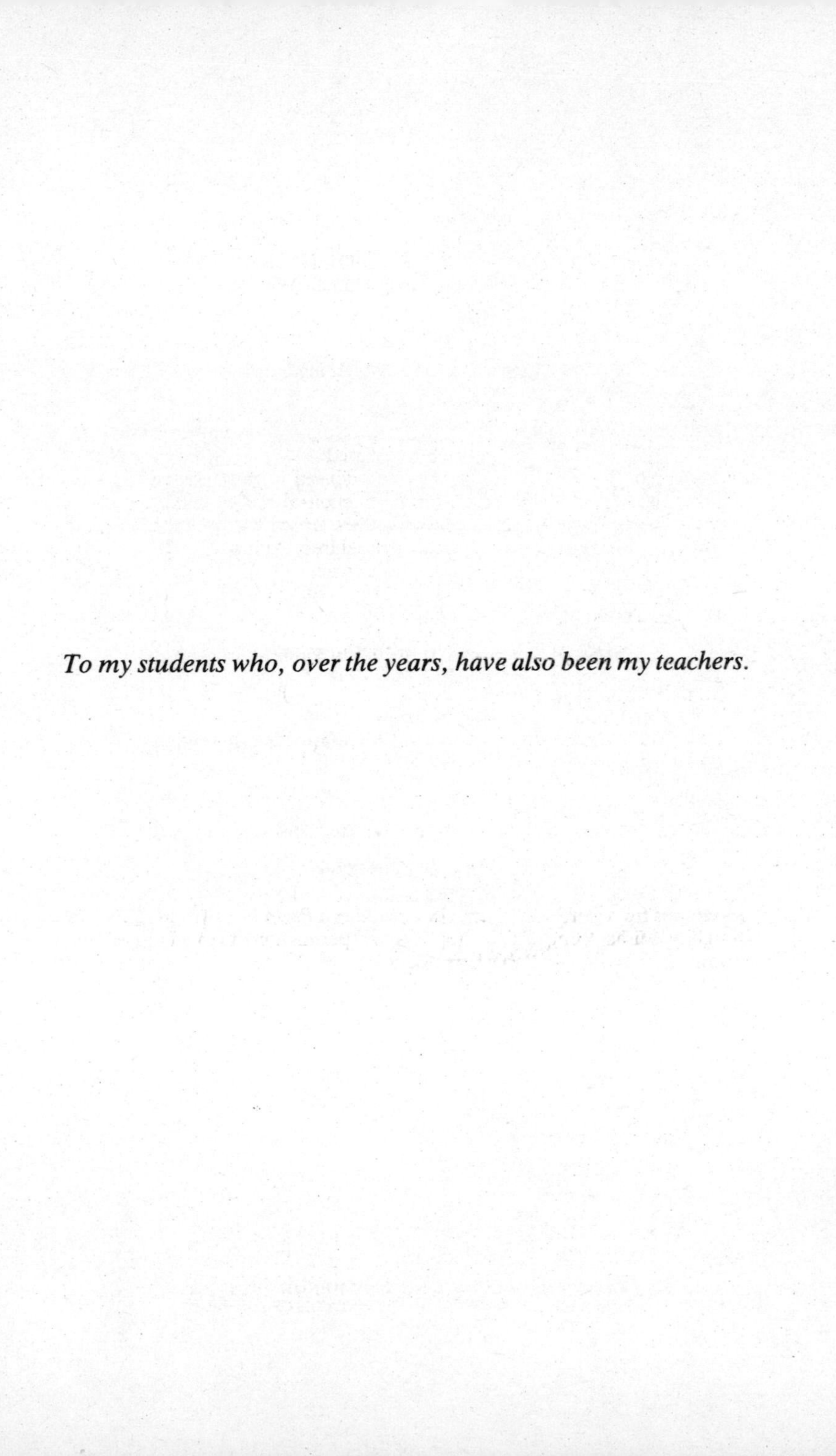

To my students who, over the years, have also been my teachers.

Contents

Some Personal Reflections About This Book

As I get in touch with my feelings about the subject of this book, an image forms in my mind. I see a beautiful mountain meadow in the high Sierras in early summer not long after the last snow has melted. The meadow is filled with wildflowers. It is a riot of breathtaking colors! We who do counseling and therapy are fortunate indeed to be living in a time when new methods of healing and growth are blossoming as never before. New innovative therapies and fresh developments in older therapies are springing up like the flowers in a mountain meadow. Many of these therapeutic approaches offer rich resources for nurturing growth toward wholeness in ourselves and in others.

The purpose of this book is to highlight and make readily available in one place the resources for personal and relational growth in a variety of contemporary psychotherapies. Each chapter will seek to open a window through which the growth insights and methods of a particular therapy or cluster of therapies can be seen, understood, and appropriated for use in counseling and therapy, in growth groups and creative education.

No attempt will be made in these pages to give a comprehensive exposition of the theories and methods of any of the therapies. Such in-depth discussions of these therapies are readily available elsewhere. Because of space limitations, several of the early chapters will present only a few key growth insights or tools from each approach in a cluster of related therapies. I do not expect that my discussion of any of the therapies will seem fully adequate to those who are strongly attracted to a particular therapy.

As you encounter (or reencounter) certain therapies in the chapters that follow, you'll discover that your energy level rises sharply. You'll feel attracted to them because you sense that they are of special relevance to your own continuing growth needs or to the needs of those with whom you have the privilege of working as a growth enabler. As you experience this surge of energy I hope that you'll decide to explore the rich terrain that lies beyond what can be covered in the brief space devoted to each therapy here. At the end of each chapter I'll annotate some books "for further exploration" of that approach. Happy exploring!

In my experience, the most growth-enabling counselors and therapists are those who are open to learn from and use the resources of a variety of therapies. The intent of this book is to encourage such creative eclecticism. The book is, by its format, an invitation to enrich your resources for nurturing growth by opening yourself to a wide spectrum of contemporary therapies.

In this book I will highlight the insights and methods I have found useful in my personal growth work, in doing counseling and therapy, and in teaching and leading growth groups and workshops over the last two decades. In each chapter I will seek to answer two questions. First, what *insights* from this therapy can illuminate our understanding of the nature and process, resistances and resources for helping persons move toward greater wholeness? Second, what *methods* does this approach offer that can be used to nurture growth in oneself and others? The answers to the first question will seek to help you enrich the working concepts out of which you function as a growth facilitator. The answers to the second will seek to enhance your practical tools for facilitating growth work. Because I regard spiritual growth as the key to all dimensions of human potentializing, each chapter will focus on resources from that therapy for nurturing growth toward spiritual wholeness. In each chapter I will also comment briefly on what I regard as the limitations and weaknesses of that therapy, when viewed from the growth-hope perspective.

This book is a companion volume to *Growth Counseling: Hope-Centered Methods of Actualizing Human Wholeness* (published by Abingdon in 1979). That volume spells out the goals, working principles, basic methods, and theological-biblical resources for doing Growth Counseling (which includes both short-term counseling and longer-term therapy). This present book builds on the earlier companion in the sense that the resources described here are valuable for doing effective Growth Counseling. But these resources should be useful to any counselor, therapist, pastor, chaplain, teacher, or lay caring team member who desires to make his or her work more growth-enabling. In this sense, the book is designed to stand on its own feet without reference to the Growth Counseling approach or the other book.

As a pastoral counselor-psychotherapist I am keenly interested in the relevance of the insights and methods described in these pages to the work of pastoral counselors. The growth-hope orientation is remarkably energizing and liberating of the rich potentialities inherent in *pastoral* counseling. In the early decades of the modern period in pastoral counseling, the pioneers in this field drew very heavily on the therapies developed by Sigmund Freud and Carl Rogers. Both these therapies, in my view, have much to offer growth-oriented counselors, including pastoral counselors. But taken either alone or together, they are less than fully adequate as a conceptual basis for pastoral counseling. There is a pressing need to broaden and enrich the conceptual resources of my discipline. It is my experience that the growth orientation is the most effective conceptual framework within which to integrate resources from various therapies in a uniquely pastoral way.

Although I view the therapies discussed in this book from the professional perspective of a pastoral counselor, I'm aware that the growth resources discussed here are relevant and useful to counselor-therapists from other professions. I trust that the emphasis throughout this book on *spiritual* growth resources will enable these persons to increase their effectiveness in facilitating healing and growth in this crucial dimension of being human. I hope that this may be a significant contribution which a person with theological as well as therapeutic training can make to some persons in the other counseling and therapy professions.

To get the most from the precious time you'll spend reading this book, I recommend that you keep a *growth journal,* a log of your journey through its pages. Jot down in your journal your responses to what you read, your questions and criticisms, your thoughts and plans for using various insights and techniques. Or you may prefer to underline those things that strike you as useful or important, jotting your comments and questions, your criticisms and insights in the margins of the book. If you use the margins for your growth journal, I hope that you'll write a resounding "Yes!" or "Right on!" beside the things that seem valid and important to you, and a "No way!" or "?" beside the things that seem inaccurate or questionable. By the use of either of these approaches (or another that fits your own style of encountering a book) make this *your* book! Record or underline the things on which you want to reflect further. Argue with my understandings, my interpretations, and my evaluations of various therapies. As particular insights and methods touch your "relevance button," perhaps you'll stop and decide how these can be applied in your own growth or in working more growthfully with others. Perhaps you'll plan a strategy for trying certain methods in your work with particular persons. In this way you'll be rewriting the book to fit your unique life experiences, insights, and needs.

In the last seven chapters there are experiential exercises designed to take you "inside" some of the newer growth methods from contemporary therapies. As a busy person you'll probably be tempted to skip these. I hope that you'll resist this temptation and take time to try the exercises. You'll find, I suspect, that doing them will both increase your grasp of the methods and also serve as the best preparation for using them creatively with others.

This book has been developing for a long time through a variety of experiences. For nearly twenty years I have taught a graduate seminar at the School of Theology at Claremont on Contemporary Psychotherapies and Pastoral Counseling. The lively interaction with the scores of theological students, graduate students in pastoral counseling, and clergypersons who have taken the seminar through the years has been rich indeed. I have learned much from their probing questions and illuminating insights. What I have learned from them has helped to make it essential for me to revise the contents of the seminar repeatedly over the years. During this same twenty years I have been using many of the insights and methods from the therapies discussed in this book, in my counseling, therapy, and growth groups. During approximately half of these twenty years, I served as clinical director of what is now called the Pomona Valley Pastoral Counseling and Growth Center. Each week we struggle as a staff to integrate therapeutic theories and methods in seeking ways of working more growthfully with the persons who came for help with their crises and problems. As I look back, I am grateful for what I learned about certain therapies from experiencing them as a client, both during my graduate training and subsequently during periods of personal need. I have a consumer's perspective on and appreciation of psychoanalysis, client-centered therapy, gestalt therapy, and psychosynthesis. Experiences as a client can bring particularly valuable learnings.

I have been planning and struggling to finish this book for the last decade. I realize now that *some* of my resistances to completing the task were constructive resistances stemming from a subconscious awareness that I wasn't really ready to do so. It was only as the growth-hope perspective emerged more clearly in my thinking and practice that I saw that this was the motif I needed to use as the unifying theme of the book.

My heart is warmed as I think of the friends who helped me with this book—Scott Sullender, who did much of the detailed research on the contemporary therapies; Clare McKeever and Linda Herbert, who helped me in so many ways with the final revision including Linda's preparation of the index; Ginny Becker, Sharlene Jensen, Elaine Railey, and Phyllis Weldon, who typed and retyped most of the manuscript; those who gave me helpful feedback on various chapters—John Adams, Hunter Beaumont, Barbara Loy, Myron Chapman, Gordon Jackson, Rod Hunter, Noel Phelan, Erma Pixley, Doug Russell, Edith Stauffer, Nelle Morton, and Charlotte Ellen. To these friends, to all the clients and to the participants in training workshops on Growth Counseling in various parts of the world, I feel warm gratitude for all I have learned from you.

It's good now to share this book with you, the reader, after its long gestation. My hope is that it will challenge you and expand your horizons; that it will reinforce your hope-for-growth (in yourself and in others); that it will enhance your awareness of the complexities and the continuing mysteries of human growth; that it will affirm and strengthen your commitment to doing everything you can to increase wholeness in your own life and in those whose lives touch yours. I send this book forth with the warm energy of hope and caring.

Shalom
HOWARD CLINEBELL

An Overview: Growth Counseling and the Five Streams of Psychotherapy

The basic assumption that undergirds this book is that the fundamental goal of all counseling and all psychotherapy (as well as of all creative education) is to maximize human wholeness! The various short-term counseling methods are understood as means of enabling people to handle life crises growthfully. The techniques of psychotherapy are essentially ways of helping people whose growth has been deeply diminished by painful early-life experiences or by multiple crises, to free themselves for continuing growth. Creative education and growth groups are means for enabling those who are living "normal" lives to use more of their potentialities and thus to increase the creativity, zest, joy, and significance-for-humankind of their life-styles. All these growthing arts are ways of enabling people to use more of their unfolding strength and possibilities. The central task of counselors, therapists, and growth-oriented teachers is to awaken realizable hopes for creative change in persons and then to help them actualize these hopes. The process by which persons grow is called "potentializing" or "growth work."

It's important to spell out more fully the perspective from which the various therapies will be viewed in this book. I call this perspective Growth Counseling. This is an approach to perceiving and understanding people, and to helping them grow through counseling and therapy. Here is an overview of the working principles of Growth Counseling:[1]

—Most persons possess a wealth of undeveloped strengths, assets, and capacities. Most of us use only a small percentage of our physical, mental, spiritual, and relational potentialities.

—There is a gentle, often suppressed, but persistent striving in persons to keep developing their evolving potentials. The process of activating this growth *elan* is at the heart of all effective education, counseling, and therapy.

—People need to develop their unused gifts in the six interdependent dimensions of their lives—in their bodies and minds, their relationships with other people, nature, institutions, and God. Genuine "happiness" is a by-product of continuing potentializing in these six dimensions.

—The growth drive is diminished in many persons by a variety of factors including emotional malnutrition, toxic relationships, economic deprivation, social oppression, and their own fear of and resistance to growth.

—Adequate physical wholeness (resulting from good nutrition, exercise, and health care) is a valuable foundation for full development of the other five dimensions.

—Each life stage offers new growth resources and possibilities as well as new problems and losses. Wholeness is a lifelong journey of becoming.

—Health or wholeness is much more than the *absence* of gross pathology. It is the *presence* of positive whole-person wellness resulting from continuing growth.

—Psychopathology is essentially long and severely diminished and distorted growth. A low level of potentializing makes people very vulnerable to developing mental, emotional, physical, psychosomatic, interpersonal, and spiritual illnesses.

—When one's growth is deeply diminished for a long time, the growth energies and potential creativity often become distorted into malignant destructiveness, which hurts oneself, others, and often society.

—Counseling and therapy are means of helping people to overcome diminished and distorted growth, by developing their potentialities through moving intentionally toward their own growth goals.

—Counselors, therapists, and teachers are essentially growth-enablers who must themselves continue growing if they are to nurture the growth of others.

—Growth-enabling therapy and education involve helping people activate their intuitive, imaginative, right-brain capacities and integrate these with their rational, analytical, left-brain capacities.

—The growth-enabler's seeing and affirming the hidden strengths and capacities in others helps them to discover and develop those potentialities.

—Creative education and counseling-therapy are complementary diversions of one growth-enabling process.

—Spiritual growth, the enhancement of one's values, meanings, "peak experiences," and relationship with God, is central to whole-person growth.

All growth is a gift of Spirit, the source of all life, to be received and developed. In a profound sense, human growth is a joyful mystery to be celebrated.

—The gift of growth is received when we choose to develop our options intentionally. The process of growth, though deeply fulfilling, often involves pain and struggle.

—Laughter (particularly at oneself) and play are inherently healing and growth-enabling.

—Life crises, both accidental and developmental, can be used as opportunities for growth, if persons encounter them in a context of meaning and within the loving support of a network of caring.

—The futures that people expect, image, and work toward can pull them forward toward those futures. Hope, a future-oriented expectation, is the essential energy for constructive change. The effective counselor-therapist-teacher is an *awakener of realistic hope for growth* in persons.

—The present moment is the arena of potentializing. Only within the present can the painful and the enriching experiences of one's past and the call of one's future be integrated growthfully.

—Growth occurs in relationships. The quality of one's closest relationships and one's wider community of caring determines, to considerable extent, whether and how rapidly one grows.

—Relationships in which both love-acceptance-empathy, on the one hand, and openness-congruence-confrontation, on the other, are experienced (this is the "growth formula") tend to energize the growth *elan* of persons within those relationships.

—Reaching out to others with caring, to encourage and nurture growth, is essential for the continuation of one's own growth.

—Individual, relational, institutional, and societal change are deeply interdependent. Institutionalized injustice and social, economic, and political oppression diminish human potentializing on a wholesale basis, while teachers, therapists, and parents strive to facilitate it on a retail (individual) basis. Working to change the wider systems that diminish people's growth often is essential to sustain growth within them and their close relationships. Rather than adjusting people to growth-crippling institutions, constructive counseling and therapy seek to *empower* people to work with others to change the institutional and societal roots of individual problems.

—Our people-serving institutions (especially churches, schools, and health agencies) should redefine their purposes and revise their programs to become better human wholeness centers devoted to helping people maximize growth throughout the life journey. Every community needs a network of such wellness-growth centers. To increase their effectiveness in nurturing wholeness, these institutions need to develop a variety of nurture-growth groups.

—Churches and temples should become better *spiritual* wholeness centers, places for facilitating holistic health centering in spiritual growth.

The Five Streams

The abundance of therapies available today poses a perplexing problem for those who are convinced that no one approach has all the therapeutic answers. The issue is how to develop an *integrated eclecticism* that utilizes insights and methods from a variety of sources coherently and in ways that maximize the unique personality resources of the practitioner. The difficulty that stems from just assembling therapeutic components from different sources is that this approach usually produces a kind of *hash eclecticism*—a theory from here, a technique from there—with no integrating structure, no internally consistent core of assumptions about the nature, process, and goals of therapeutic change. Those who practice the growthing arts on such a shaky conceptual foundation run the risk of unwittingly using concepts and methods that work against one another and thus diminish the effectiveness of the process. Their approach lacks the power-for-growth that can come from using a consistent coherent conceptuality.

For a number of years, I used the psychoanalytic, neo-Freudian system as such a unifying conceptual framework. I now find the basic principles of Growth Counseling as summarized above to be a more change-producing conceptual framework. This orientation offers a framework of assumptions and principles within which a counselor-therapist-teacher can develop her or his unique, integrated approach to the practice of the various healing-growthing arts.

There are various ways of categorizing contemporary psychotherapies. I find it most meaningful to divide the many approaches into five major categories or streams.[2] Each stream includes a variety of different therapies. The streams overlap at many points. Some of the therapies can be placed logically in more than one stream. But in spite of these problems, I see this schema as a useful way of identifying the major thrusts within contemporary therapies.

Growth Counseling draws on insights and methods from all five streams but more heavily from the last three. Viewing all five streams from the growth perspective heightens awareness of how they complement, balance, and enrich one another in many ways as well as how they are in conflict in other ways. Here, then, is an overview of the five streams that will be explored from the growth perspective in this book.

Stream 1: *Traditional Insight-oriented Therapies.* This stream includes the vast majority of therapies developed before the last fifteen years. The stream began with the seminal work of Freud, around the turn of this century, and includes the many variations on the psychoanalytic-insight model of therapy. Many of these traditional therapies are "contemporary" in that they are still used widely today. Strictly speaking, they are not "growth therapies," but they must be considered in this book because they provide crucial insights that illuminate the dynamics of the depth dimension of personality and of deeply diminished growth. In the first four chapters of this book I will highlight some growth resources from a variety of these traditional therapies.

Stream 2: *Behavior/Action/Crisis Therapies.* This stream includes a cluster of diverse therapies linked by the common assumption that maladaptive learning is the cause of problems of living and that behavioral and/or cognitive relearning is the heart of effective therapy. In chapter 5, I will highlight some growth resources from several behavior therapies.

Stream 3: *Human Potentials Therapies.* This stream includes those therapies whose explicit goal is the actualizing of persons' full potentialities. From among these therapies I will discuss (in chapters 6, 7, and 8) three that have influenced my understanding and practice most—transactional analysis, gestalt therapy, and the body therapies.

Stream 4: *Relational/Systems/Radical Therapies.* This stream includes a variety of therapies that focus on changing social systems so that all their members will be freer to grow toward wholeness. The stream includes therapies utilizing ad hoc therapy groups, growth groups, and self-help groups as well as those which seek to enable healing and growth in natural groups such as families. From among this cluster of therapies I will highlight growth resources from family therapies (in chapter 9) and from feminist therapies (in chapter 10). Feminist therapies are "radical" therapies in that they aim at both personal growth and social change.

Stream 5: *Spiritual Growth Therapies.* This stream consists of those therapies which regard spiritual growth as central and essential in all healing and growth. The Jungian and existentialist therapies (see chapter 4) are a part of this stream. From this stream, I will explore (in chapter 11) the remarkable growth resources in psychosynthesis, which is also a human potentials therapy. The stream also includes pastoral counseling and psychotherapy (which incorporate healing-growthing resources from the Hebrew-Christian tradition) and the Eastern approaches to enhancing consciousness which have many parallels with Western psychotherapies.

For Further Exploration of Growth Counseling

Clinebell, Charlotte H.* *Counseling for Liberation.* Philadelphia: Fortress Press, 1976. Explores counseling and consciousness-raising as methods of liberating women-men relationships.

Clinebell, Howard. *Growth Counseling: Hope-Centered Methods of Actualizing Human Wholeness.* Nashville: Abingdon, 1979. Discusses the theory, methods, and theology of Growth Counseling.

———. *Growth Counseling: New Tools for Clergy and Laity.* Nashville: Abingdon Press, 1973, 1974. Fifteen do-it-yourself cassette training courses for learning Growth Counseling techniques. Part I—"Enriching Marriage and Family Life"; Part II—"Coping Constructively with Crises."

———. *Growth Counseling for Marriage Enrichment: Pre-Marriage and the Early Years.* Philadelphia: Fortress Press, 1975. Applies the growth counseling approach to marriage enrichment, particularly during the preparation and early stages.

———. *Growth Counseling for Mid-Years Couples.* Philadelphia: Fortress Press, 1977. Marriage enrichment and counseling methods for the mid years.

———. *Growth Groups.* Nashville: Abingdon, 1977. Spells out the growth-group approach and applies it to marriage and family enrichment, creative singlehood, youth work, women's and men's liberation, social problems.

Goble, Frank. *The Third Force: The Psychology of Abraham Maslow.* New York: Pocket Books, 1971. A systematic overview of Maslow's basic theory.

Gould, Roger L. *Transformations, Growth and Change in Adult Life.* New York: Simon & Schuster, 1978. Describes growthful ways of coping with adult life crises.

Maslow, Abraham H. *The Farther Reaches of Human Nature.* New York: Viking Press, 1971. Explores health and pathology, creativeness, values, education, and transcendence.

———. *Religions, Values and Peak Experiences.* Columbus: Ohio State University Press, 1964. Discusses transcendental experiences, the split between science and religion, hope and values in education.

———. *Toward a Psychology of Being,* 2nd ed. New York: Van

* This was the author's name when she wrote this book. Subsequently she chose a new name, Charlotte Ellen.

Nostrand, 1968. A classic statement of Maslow's growth-oriented psychology.

Miller, Jean Baker. *Toward a New Psychology of Women.* Boston: Beacon Press, 1976. Describes how growth is stifled by sexism and how sexism can be overcome.

Otto, Herbert A., ed. *Human Potentialities: The Challenge and the Promise.* St. Louis: Warren H. Green, 1968. A collection of papers by Gardner Murphy, Abraham Maslow, Charlotte Buhler, Clark Moustakas, Alexander Lowen, Herbert Otto, and others exploring human potentialities.

———, and Mann, John, eds. *The Ways of Growth: Approaches to Expanding Awareness.* New York: Viking Press, 1968. A collection of nineteen papers describing a wide variety of methods for facilitating growth.

Schultz, Duane. *Growth Psychology: Models of Healthy Personality.* New York: Van Nostrand Reinhold, 1977. Discusses the nature of wholeness in the thought of Allport, Rogers, Fromm, Maslow, Jung, Frankl, and Perls.

Shostrom, Everett L. *Actualizing Therapy.* San Diego: Edits Publishers, 1976. A synthesis of growth concepts and methods from various psychotherapeutic approaches.

Chapter 1

Growth Resources in Traditional Psychotherapies

Sigmund Freud and the Ego Analysts

For a variety of reasons, it is important for growth-oriented counselors, therapists, and teachers to know the traditional psychoanalytic therapies well. Although their central focus is on psychopathology and its treatment, many of the traditional therapies have growth thrusts that provide valuable conceptual tools. Some of the insights from these therapies can correct and complement the understandings of persons and their growth presented in more recent therapies. Knowledge of the historical roots of most contemporary therapies (in the psychoanalytic tradition) can help growth-enablers to evaluate and use the current therapies more critically and growthfully.

The growth contributions of the traditional therapies are, for the most part, concentrated in two areas—their illumination of the depths and complexity of human personality, and their insights about the nature and dynamics of deeply blocked growth (pathology). These insights are invaluable particularly when one is working with persons whose growth has been diminished deeply for many years. In my experience, the traditional therapies provide many valuable working concepts but relatively few growth methods that are as effective as those in some of the more recent therapies. In the first four chapters I will highlight the conceptual tools from traditional therapies that I have found useful for facilitating growth in the lives of those with whom I have worked as counselor, therapist, growth-group facilitator, and teacher.

Generic Growth Resources from Sigmund Freud

Sigmund Freud was born in Freiberg, Moravia, a small town in what is now Czechoslovakia, May 6, 1856. When he was four, the Freud family moved to Vienna, where he lived until one year before his death. When he entered the University of Vienna, he chose to study medicine, mainly because he was moved by a deep curiosity about human beings, a curiosity that had been stimulated by reading Darwin and Goethe.[1] Throughout his life, his consuming professional interest was his search for greater understanding of the depths of the human psyche.

Following medical school, Freud did research in physiology for a while. He entered private practice reluctantly, in order to have enough income to allow him to marry. He worked as a surgeon and then in general medicine before taking a course in psychiatry. A travel grant allowed him to study in Paris with Jean Martin Charcot, who was using hypnotic suggestion to treat hysterical symptoms. Following this he explored the dynamics of hysteria in more depth, working with an older physician, Joseph Breuer.

Freud first used the term "psycho-analysis" to describe his methodology in 1896. His first and probably his most significant book, *The Interpretation of Dreams,* was based to a considerable extent on the self-analysis of his own dreams. When it was published in 1900, it was almost ignored by the medical community. But a group of young physicians were attracted to Freud's ideas and they began to meet weekly at his home to discuss them. This circle, which eventually included Alfred Adler, Carl Jung, Otto Rank, Ernest Jones, and others, established a professional society and began to publish a journal, thus launching the psychoanalytic movement. The influence of Freud's ideas gradually expanded. In 1910 he came to the United States, accompanied by key members of the Vienna Psychoanalytic Society, to lecture at Clark University.

Freud's consuming passion was to develop a system for understanding human beings that would live after him and would eventually reorient all of psychiatry. He spent his professional life doing psychoanalysis with patients, developing his theories (which he continued to change throughout his life) and writing voluminously. Freud's ideas drew intense criticism from the medical and scientific communities of his day. He rigidly tried to control the direction of developments within the movement and rejected most of those who radically challenged his views. When the Nazis invaded Austria in 1938, Freud was allowed to move to London, where he died the next year, after a long, painful struggle with cancer of the mouth. He continued to do analytic work until less than two months before his death. He refused to take pain-deadening drugs, except occasional aspirin, preferring "to think in torment to not being able to think clearly."

My training in psychotherapy was strongly influenced by psychoanalytic concepts and methods. Although I have become increasingly aware of the limitations of these methods for facilitating growth and of the gaps and inaccuracies in Freud's vast conceptual system, I retain a profound appreciation for the way his pioneering discoveries illuminate the depths and darkness of the human psyche. All of us who practice the healing-growthing arts owe a tremendous debt to this brilliant adventurer into the unconscious, this courageous explorer of the hiddenness of the human psyche. In this chapter I will give an overview of Freud's major contributions to growth-oriented work with people and then identify some inadequacies of his system, when viewed from the growth perspective.

Many of Freud's key concepts have become a part of the common heritage of Western thought and of our general psychological understanding of persons. In this section I will describe six of these generic concepts that have been accepted by most traditional therapies, concepts that are a part of our legacy from Freud.

The *first* generic concept is what can be called the *developmental perspective*[2]—the view that human personality develops through a series of stages each with its inherent conflicts and growth potentialities. This understanding of human personality as a process is taken for granted by most therapies today. There are significant variations among traditional and contemporary therapies regarding the nature and importance of various stages. But that there *is* such a growth journey is a part of their common understanding of human beings.

For obvious reasons, the developmental perspective is fundamental to all growth work. This perspective is invaluable as a resource for understanding and facilitating healthy development through lifelong education and growth groups as well as for doing growth-oriented counseling and therapy. For example, when working with children in the grammar school period and with their parents, it is important to understand the general growth issues and needs that are typical of the particular life stages of the children and of their parents. To be aware of these growth themes is to be in touch with the broad *context* of the unique individual problems and potentials of particular children and their parents.

The *second* generic concept from Freud is the *blocked-development view of pathology*. Psychological disturbance is understood as being caused by blocked development at a particular early life stage when the developmental conflict of that stage is not resolved satisfactorily. This "fixation" of growth at that stage results in a diminution or distortion of development at all subsequent life stages. Freud helped to make us aware of the profound destructiveness that occurs when the orderly process of growth is seriously blocked.

The basic psychoanalytic aim—to provide opportunities to complete in a healthier relationship the unfinished growth tasks from the past which continue to distort the present—is still viable and important. This concern should be a basic goal of all therapy and all growth groups, whatever their other goals. Use of the long-term, regressive methods of psychoanalysis, however, is not the most efficient or effective way to accomplish this re-growthing in most cases.

The *third* generic concept is the emphasis on the *crucial influence of experiences during the earliest life stages* on all subsequent development and functioning. As Freud persisted in asking the searching question "Why?" concerning the problems of his patients, the answers he got pointed further and further back into the early years of their lives. He discovered that the foundation of the building of personality is created during the first six years of life by the quality of a child's close relationships with need-satisfying adults. Freud's heavy emphasis on the profound influence of the earliest years is seen as extreme by several of the traditional therapies. But there is general agreement among them (as among developmental psychologists generally) that, for better or for worse, human growth is most rapid and crucial during these foundational years.

This emphasis on the early formative years has profound implications for growth-oriented approaches to people. To illustrate, the realization that parents of young children literally have the future at their fingertips is an awesome awareness pregnant with potentialities. It is essential for society to provide an abundance of growth-nurturing classes, workshops, and seminars for youth and young adults so that they will become more capable of satisfying, in personality-nurturing ways, the basic heart-hungers of the children they have or will soon have. Nothing could have a greater impact on the wholeness of the next generation than providing in every community a network of readily available growth and growth-repair (therapy) opportunities for parents of young children and parents-to-be. Members of all the counseling-therapy professions should take active leadership in developing such a network in the churches, high schools, colleges, adult education programs, and in all health care and counseling agencies of their communities!

The *fourth* generic concept from Freud is that *the unconscious has a powerful influence on all aspects of our lives.* The existence of the unconscious was discussed by more than fifty writers between 1680 and 1900. Freud's great achievement was to explore its structure and contents and to demonstrate how it influences our thoughts, feelings, fantasies, beliefs, and behavior.[3] By so doing he changed irrevocably the basic self-understanding of humankind. It was his illumination of the unconscious that makes Freud the conceptual grandparent of all "depth psychologies." As he discovered, it is through the repressed memories, wishes, conflicts, and impulses in the unconscious that painful experiences and unfinished growth from the early years continue to cripple the ability of many people to live creatively in the present. He demonstrated that bringing these repressed elements into the light of conscious awareness often facilitates healing and growth.

The idea of the unconscious is threatening to many people because it implies that we human beings are not in complete control of our own personalities. Yet, there is clear evidence that there *are* memories, wishes, and feelings that we cannot recall at will that *do* influence our behavior. As many people are at least dimly aware, there *is* a stranger within us. From both the psychoanalytic and the growth perspective, the inner stranger is a potential ally and friend. Until we begin to get to know the stranger, our unconscious resistances to change will tend to sabotage our conscious growth intentions. Bringing these defensive resistances to growth into the liberating light of consciousness can be a necessary part of the process of helping some people free themselves to grow. The more we establish open communication with our unconscious, and hear its messages (e.g., by understanding what our dreams and daydreams are telling us about ourselves), the greater our ability to live choicefully in the present and thereby move more intentionally into the future. Freud's view that dreams are the "royal road to the conscious" contributes a valuable awareness that can be used to help people develop the hidden growth resources of their psychic depths.

The psychoanalytic heritage has led to the discovery that the mind is like a vast house with many rooms on many levels. Our minds are much more powerful, intricate, and potentially creative (as well as destructive) than our conscious self-understanding can even imagine. The depth discoveries of psychoanalysis constitute an invaluable resource for understanding how our potentials for wholeness are imprisoned and how they can be liberated.

The *fifth* generic concept from Freud's thought is *the*

principle of psychological causation (often called "psychological determinism"). This view holds that all human behavior has a cause or, in most cases, multiple causes. As Freud demonstrated, the most trivial and the most bizarre behavior is meaningful if we learn to understand its unconscious causes. Strange thoughts, fantasies, dreams, slips of the tongue, the jokes we think are funny, the place we sit in church, the way we feel when someone is angry, the things we remember, the people we like or don't like—all make sense when we understand their hidden meaning. The fact that the human psyche is an orderly, cause-and-effect realm is what makes psychology as a science possible. This fact also makes it possible for psychotherapy to facilitate growth by enabling people to change the causes of their life-constricting feelings, thoughts, beliefs, and behavior. For growth-crippled people it can be tremendously energizing to discover the hidden dynamics of their diminished potentializing. By illuminating the causes of their repetitive, self-damaging patterns, therapy with a depth dimension can help them move toward liberation from the tyranny of the past, which continues to operate through these patterns.

The *sixth* generic insight from Freud's thought (closely linked with the fifth) is the recognition that *all behavior is motivated by drives and needs.*[4] Deeply disturbed people are torn by unconscious conflicts between different needs and drives. The findings of psychoanalytic research reveals that even the self-damaging and crippling behavior of severely disturbed persons is somehow functional. It serves some defensive need of which they are consciously unaware. For example, the functional paralysis of a middle-aged man's arm expressed the immobilizing conflict between the unconscious desire and the fear of striking out in rage at a person on whom he felt passively dependent. The paralysis served the purpose of blocking the acting out of his long-repressed rage, which would have led to overwhelming guilt (from his superego) and probably resulted in retaliation by the other person. Psychoanalytically informed growth therapies aim at helping people face and resolve their energy-depleting inner conflicts and satisfy their appropriate needs in ways that are constructive for themselves and others.

Other Growth Resources from Freud

What is often called Freud's "tragic vision" is an accurate and valuable (though painful) perception of the dark, irrational, destructive side of human life. Freud's remarkable tough-minded realism enabled him to become aware of the truncated freedom, entrapment by the past, profound inner conflicts, resistances to change, ambiguity, and paradoxes in the human psyche. Like many great thinkers, he grappled with the absurdity and tragedy that are a part of the human situation. Freud saw that we cannot have everything we want in life—e.g., that in order to develop our full capacity to love we must lose in our first love affair (the so-called Oedipal and Electra conflict). Freud identified the universal tendency to self-deception in human beings, showing that human motivation is seldom as simple or as pure as it may seem on the surface.[5]

Freud's tragic vision, though incomplete from the growth perspective, reveals a dimension of human reality that cannot be ignored by anyone who wants to facilitate growth. Our effectiveness as growth enablers will be enhanced if we see and understand persons through the *glasses of growth.* These glasses must be bifocal![6] The psychoanalytic therapies make a significant contribution by providing the bottom lens for these bifocals. This is the lens that enables us to see and understand the psychopathology and unresolved conflict that are present in "normal," functional people, as well as in dysfunctional people. Our work with people will be growthful only if it is based on an open-eyed awareness of the reality, depth, complexity, and tenacity of human brokenness. Approaches that perceive persons only through the upper lens of the bifocals (which enables one to see the strengths and positive potentials in everyone) sabotage their own effectiveness by their incomplete vision of human beings. Freud was accurate when he insisted that we must look at the truth about ourselves, whether we like it or not, if we are to grow. His realism is a salutary corrective for any tendencies we may have toward easy optimism. Respect for reality, including its tragic dimension, is the only solid foundation for human potentializing. It is important to recall that there is a heroic quality about Freud's commitment to helping people salvage all that they could of productive living in the midst of life's trappedness and tragedy. When asked about the central goal of his therapy, he responded that it was to enable people "to love and to work."

Freud's discoveries concerning the parallelism and interaction between psychological and sexual factors in human development have profound implications for understanding blocked growth. Many of his insights concerning the power and pervasiveness of human sexuality from the beginnings of life are useful for growthful parenting as well as for therapeutic repair work later in life. We can be grateful for the courage it must have taken to continue exploring the taboo-shrouded area of infantile sexuality, in spite of bitter attacks from the scientific and medical communities of his day. The healing and growth insights that are available from the psychoanalytic understanding of psychosexual development through adolescence, particularly as these insights have been extended by Erik Erikson and corrected by feminist psychologists, offer valuable conceptual tools for understanding and facilitating human growth. The recognition of the vital role of sexual crippledness and diminution in general psychological and interpersonal problems (and vice versa) is, in itself, a crucial concept for helping people develop their wasted potentials for fulfillment, ecstasy, and joy.

Freud's concepts of transference and countertransference are valuable growth resources.[7] In psychoanalytic therapy, transference is understood as the projection of repressed wishes and feelings from early-life relationships onto the analyst. The "transference neurosis" thus established is used as an opportunity for the person to relive and redo the unfinished growth work from the past. As one becomes aware of the transference projections and lets go of them, the grip of the past on the present is gradually diminished. Countertransference is the unconscious projection by therapists onto their clients of unconscious material from their own early relationships. Transference and countertransference factors are present to some degree in all therapeutic and teacher-student relationships. If therapy is to be growth-enabling, therapists must become aware (through their own therapy) of their countertransference projections so that they can withdraw these and relate to clients authentically in the present. Transference is a way of trying to continue past relationships by recreating present relationships in their image. It also serves to block awareness of the newness present in today's relationships. As Freud made clear, effective therapists must frustrate the transference needs of their clients so that they can become aware of and change the growth-inhibiting way in which they are attempting to live in past relationships. Transference dynamics also operate in other close relationships. For example, the most common unconscious growth-blocking factor in marriages is what has been called "parentifying one's spouse"—i.e., seeing one's spouse as a good or bad mother or father figure. Chronic problems with bosses, ministers, and other authority figures often root in unconscious transference projections. (People often project infantile, magical transference feelings about God onto ministers.) All of us who work closely with people need to be aware of transference dynamics so that we can facilitate growth beyond them.

Though not the first to do so, Freud viewed religious behavior, attitudes, and beliefs as legitimate objects of psychological investigation. Thus he helped to lay the foundation of the contemporary discipline of psychology of religion, an essential resource in counseling on spiritual issues. He made a profound contribution to our understanding of the many forms of pathogenic, growth-diminishing religion that constrict the wholeness of so many people today. Recognizing that our religious ideas and feelings are deeply influenced by early experiences with need-satisfying adults, he saw accurately that we tend unconsciously to project our need for a perfect parent figure onto the universe as we create our perception of deity. Freud pointed to the magical, infantile feelings and longings that continue to dominate many people's religious lives long after the reality principle has gained ascendancy in other areas of their lives. He saw the obsessive-compulsive dimension that is very prominent in many conventional religious practices. He threw light on the growth-crippling effects of such unfree, infantile, reality-denying religion. All of us who are committed to nurturing spiritual growth as an essential dimension of human potentializing stand in Freud's debt for these contributions.

Freud accurately identified the process by which the conscience is developed and its initial contents determined. He saw how the values of a culture, as these are incarnated in the attitudes and behavior of parents, are internalized by children as they experience these values in the rewards-punishment, praise-blame responses of their parents. When dealing in counseling and therapy with problems of immature or distorted conscience—e.g., neurotic guilt or lack of appropriate guilt—these insights, as they have been refined and developed subsequently by other psychoanalytic thinkers, are invaluable working concepts.

Some Inadequacies in Freud's Thought

In spite of Freud's enormous growth contributions, there are serious weaknesses, gaps, and inaccuracies in his thought when viewed from a growth perspective. The fundamental inadequacy from which the other weaknesses are derived is his impoverished view of the nature of human beings. He saw human personality in biologically reductionistic, pathology-centered ways. He illuminated psychopathology in brilliant ways, but he neglected the healthy dimensions that are present in all persons, even the most disturbed. When he attempted to create a general psychology of personality, based on his findings from studying neurotic patients, he did not see that health is much more than the absence of gross pathology.

Freud helped to provide the pathology lens of the growth

enabler's glasses, but he was not aware of the need for another lens. He failed to see fully the profound strivings and resources for growth that people can use to transcend or transform their brokenness. This fundamental gap in his perception of people reinforced his deep pessimism. From the growth perspective, the pathology lens functions most therapeutically when the other lens is present to enable us to see pathology in the context of the people's potentials for wholeness. The pathology lens prevents shallow optimism, while the top lens allows one to see strengths and growth possibilities in persons who otherwise appear hopeless. The two lenses together function in ways that energize a reality-based hope for creative change.

Freud's instinctivistic and biological reductionism led him to a mechanistic model of human beings reflecting nineteenth-century Newtonian physics. He viewed the ego as a puny being caught between powerful instinctual drives and id impulses, on the one hand, and the harsh demands of society, internalized in the superego, on the other. This conception left little room for seeing the possibility of a strong, unifying self that can enable persons to orchestrate their own conflicts and growth struggles effectively. Freud's understanding of psychological causation smacks of hard determinism. He rightly emphasized the unconscious trappedness of human beings. But he did not believe that people have the capacity to increase their self-awareness significantly on their own, or to function out of the "conflict-free" areas of their personalities. The working concept of psychological causation can be retained, however, without surrendering to rigid determinism, by showing that the self, the center of our being, can become the most important cause of behavior. Growth in inner freedom consists of becoming more self-causing, more free to rearrange constructively the unchangeable givens of one's life.

Freud accurately described the primitive, impulsive, and destructive aspects of the unconscious. He did not emphasize (as did Jung) the potential riches and creativity that are also available in the depths of the psyche. He dichotomized the rational and the nonrational, mythic and intuitive sides, and invested reason (divorced from these resources) with an exaggerated faith. His fascination with origins caused him to exaggerate the influence of the past. He rejected the notion that the future can energize human intentionality by luring people (teleologically) toward new possibilities. Freud reduced all the cultural achievements of humankind—art, philosophy, religion, and so forth—to sublimated sexual energy. This reductionism implied a rejection of any *height dimension* in human personality having its own inherent integrity in the functioning of personality.

The hyperindividualistic, instinct-centered view of Freud reduced human development to what is essentially the intrapsychic evolving of the instincts. He underestimated the powerful influence of interpersonal relationships in all human growth. This error was compounded by the paucity of cross-cultural studies which led him to assume inaccurately that he could extrapolate from the characteristics of mid-Victorian Viennese patients in describing a universal psychology. Many of his generalizations about psychosexual development have been challenged and corrected by subsequent developmental, feminist, and cross-cultural studies.

Because of his intrapsychic focus, Freud's depth psychology lacks a breadth dimension, which would have allowed him to see that we human beings are also interpersonal in our very essence and that therapy must also deal with the interpersonal systems that nurture or starve our growth. His individualism and his pessimism apparently caused Freud to misunderstand the relation between the individual and society, seeing these as essentially antagonistic. He rejected Adler's view that people have a basic striving to satisfy their needs for power and worth in ways that do not alienate them from others. Consequently Freud was not interested in developing an ecological ethic based on the awareness that, in the long run, the real good of individuals requires cooperation, not conflict and competition. Today, our ultimate welfare and even survival depend on developing such an ethic and discovering the basis for such cooperation in personal and intergroup relationships.

Because Freud's understanding of human beings reflected a

nineteenth-century energy theory, he did not see that interpersonal transactions are different, in some basic ways, from the exchanges of physical energy. His view that self-love (narcissism) somehow depletes the energy available for loving others caused him to miss the key insight (developed by Erich Fromm and others) that genuine self-love, self-respect, and self-caring provide the only firm foundation for genuinely loving others. Chronic narcissism, rather than being self-love, is really a symptom of self-doubt, self-rejection, and lack of ego strength.

With all his brilliant insights into pathogenic religions, Freud was unaware of the fact that growth-nurturing, salugenic (wholeness-fostering) religions even existed. He generalized on his appropriate critique of the infantile, obsessive-compulsive, wish-dominated religions (with their roots in tribalism and totemism) that he encountered in his patients, assuming that he was describing all religions. He was unaware of the fact that human beings are inherently transpersonal and that we cannot fulfill our basic potentialities fully unless we develop the spiritual dimension of our lives. His world view was derived from nineteenth-century scientific rationalism which made reason his god. Freud's understanding of the superego, the immature, authority-centered conscience, stopped short of recognizing that there are other stages of moral maturing beyond this early stage. Persons who continue to grow in this area gradually learn to evaluate and partially transcend the values of their parents and culture, which they internalized during early childhood. Freud does not help us understand the more mature, autonomous conscience, whose values are based on the ego's perceptions of what is authentically good for oneself *and* for others, rather than on the dictates of one's superego.[8] His use of the "death instinct" as an explanation of all human evil and destructiveness prevented Freud from understanding the complex and varied sources of this negative side of human life.

Freud's enormous blind spots regarding women produced major inaccuracies in his psychology of women. These distortions reinforced the sexism in most psychotherapy during and since his times. He assumed that what he saw in neurotic women patients (masochism and nonassertiveness, for example) was normative for women generally, rather than the consequence of the crippling effects of the patriarchal culture in which they lived. His unconscious sexism caused him to exaggerate the role of fathers and underestimate the role of mothers in the growth of children. As feminist psychologists are now showing, many of his theories about "normal" psychosexual development are actually descriptions of the ways in which boys and girls develop in a patriarchal culture. Unwittingly, by his assumptions, Freud reinforced the norms and values of a patriarchal culture in ways that have tended to increase its destructiveness for both women and men.

Some of the traditional psychoanalytic methods for opening up blocked communication between the unconscious and the conscious mind, e.g., free association and analyzing the transference neurosis, are unnecessarily time-consuming and expensive and their therapeutic effectiveness does not seem to be confirmed by empirical research evidence. The use of psychoanalytic methods is justifiable mainly as instruments of depth research into the human psyche. As is true of all long-term intrapsychic, nonsystemic approaches to therapy, psychoanalysis has little relevance to the task of healing the brokenness of the masses of humankind. Freud himself was aware of this but saw no basis for a wider hope.

Growth Resources from the Ego Analysts

A movement toward more growth-centered understandings of human beings and of therapy has occurred in many traditional as well as contemporary therapies. The most creative thrust in psychoanalysis since Freud—the work of the ego psychologists or ego analysts—introduces a robust emphasis on health understood as growth.[9] This thrust has produced a radical, growth-centered metamorphosis within psychoanalytic thought, which has corrected many of the weaknesses in Freud's thought.

Ego psychology has developed on two fronts, the first represented by Anna Freud (Sigmund's daughter), and the second by Heinz Hartmann, David Rapaport, and Erik Erikson. In 1923 Freud introduced his "structural hypothesis,"[10] which stated that the personality is organized into three basic energy systems. The *id* is the seat of the primitive, instinctual sexual and aggressive energies, which provide the raw material out of which the entire psyche develops. The id is ruled by the pleasure principle rather than by logic, sense data, or moral considerations. The *ego* is developed from the id energies to allow the organism to cope with external reality and obtain maximum satisfactions. The ego is governed by the reality principle. The *superego,* a subsystem of the ego, develops by internalizing the culture's values in order to guide the organism's behavior in ways approved by that particular society. The id is entirely unconscious; major functions of the ego and superego also operate unconsciously. Freud concentrated his major efforts on understanding the id and the unconscious. Since he saw the ego as derivative from and the servant of the id, he believed that it was extremely vulnerable to id impulses and control. The ego psychologists, as the name suggests, have focused their attention on understanding the functioning of the ego. As a result of their research, the ego is now seen within psychoanalysis as having a central and dynamic place in determining the psychic health of the whole person.

In her book *The Ego and the Mechanisms of Defense,*[11] Anna Freud explored in depth the ego's unconscious defenses against anxiety (described originally by her father). She gave the ego a new status by showing how the ego defenses are the key to understanding both healthy and disordered personality dynamics.

From a growth perspective, knowledge of the dynamics of the ego's defenses is a valuable resource because it clarifies the ways in which people unconsciously isolate themselves from painful reality and from the growth that is possible only by dealing more openly with this reality. Among the defenses frequently encountered in counseling and therapy are *repression* (of painful memories into the unconscious); *fixation* (at a safer-feeling growth stage); *regression* (to an earlier, safer-feeling stage); *projection* (onto others of the feelings or impulses eliciting anxiety); *rationalization* (giving oneself and others reasonable excuses for unreasonable behavior); *denial* (of threatening aspects of reality); *introjection* (seeking protection by identifying internally with a feared person or idea); *reaction formation* (denying a threatening impulse by going to the other extreme in one's behavior—e.g., denying repressed rage by behaving in super "loving" ways); *intellectualizing* (avoiding threatening feelings by chronic "head-tripping").

All of us have and need defenses to cope with the pressures and crises of our lives. When failure feelings become too intense in me, my response is rationalization or projection of responsibility onto circumstances or other people. If my ego is relatively resilient at the time, my defenses relax as my self-esteem recovers. I gradually become aware of my own responsibility in causing or contributing to the failure experience, and eventually decide what I must do about it.

In growth-enabling work, it is important to remember that people *have* defenses because they still *need* them, or believe they do, because they once needed them desperately to maintain even minimal feelings of worth and power. The problem with ego defenses is that they often function in compulsive, life-constricting ways, long after the original threat is gone, rather than being temporary defenses when self-esteem is too threatened. When they operate in rigid compulsive ways, the energy they consume is unavailable for growth. Growth can occur when people cope with painful reality by using and thus strengthening their personality's coping "muscles." People let go of energy-squandering defenses not when those defenses are attacked, but when their self-esteem and confidence grow stronger. Only then can they risk living more openly, vulnerably, and authentically.

The research of Heinz Hartmann and Erik Erikson moves far beyond Anna Freud's focus on the defensive functions of the ego to examine the ego's many capacities for constructive coping. In their thought, the ego is seen in ways that are very similar to the "self" in contemporary therapies—as the potentially effective coordinator of the overall integration and development of the whole personality. Hartmann focuses psychoanalytic thought on the healthy, conflict-free dimensions of personality.[12] He sees the ego as having a growing autonomy and strength of its own. Rather than being derived from the id, both the ego and the id develop from the more fundamental bio-psychic resources of the organism. The infant is born with resources that gradually mature into "ego apparatuses," basic tools for handling both the inner instinctual drives and the demands of the external world. These developing apparatuses include thinking, perception, memory, language, and all the other psychological and neuromuscular skills of a growing person. Hartmann integrated psychoanalytic insights with developmental studies in psychology, showing that the human organism has a built-in timetable for the development of the ego's potential abilities. This developmental timetable is influenced but not determined (except in case of extreme pathology) by unconscious, instinctual forces.

The implications and applications of this newer psychoanalytic understanding of growth are many and profound. For example, children learn to walk and talk according to their own neuromuscular developmental timetable. This process can be delayed or disrupted only by severe unconscious conflicts fostered by severely depriving relationships with parents. Once children have learned to walk or talk, they have acquired ego skills of enormous value for coping with their physical and interpersonal environment in ego-strengthening ways. This principle can be used in doing re-educative, action-oriented counseling and therapy. Shy, socially inept adolescents may be helped to increase their self-esteem and sense of competence by being coached and encouraged in basic social skills that will allow them to experience success in peer relationships. Youth who feel trapped in vicious cycles of repeated failures may be helped to interrupt the cycle by being coached and supported as they accomplish modest realistic goals. Acquiring practical skills for effective action (rather than insight) is the key to the growth that occurs in such counseling. Ego psychology illuminates the growth that occurs in crises and in supportive relationships within which new coping-with-life skills are learned. I have been impressed repeatedly with the remarkable growth I have seen in many alcoholics who, with no formal therapy, found in AA an ego-strengthening, growth-nurturing environment.

As a result of the more dynamic conception of the ego derived from the work of the ego analysts, Sigmund Freud's tripartite model of personality has become more valuable as a resource for facilitating growth. It can be used as a shorthand way of understanding the therapy that is needed to overcome some common types of growth blockages. To illustrate, some people (called "psychoneurotics" in traditional psychiatric nomenclature) are tyrannized by cruel superegos (hairshirt consciences), which produce neurotic guilt and anxiety. They need to develop more accepting consciences, guided by what they genuinely value rather than by fear of punishment. Persons who are easily pushed around by the demands of others need to develop a stronger sense of their own worth and power so that they will not be manipulable. These two types of growth often occur as such persons experience the acceptance of and then gradually identify with the more robust self-esteem and accepting conscience of the counselor-therapist.

People with very weak egos and rigid defenses that cut them off from perceiving major areas of reality but do not protect them from feeling flooded by raw impulses from the id, need a different type of help. Such people (called "psychotics" or "borderline personalities" in traditional psychiatric nomenclature) often need a long-term supportive relationship that reinforces the effectiveness of their less reality-denying defenses and allows them to gain ego strength by coping better with everyday realities. Uncovering, insight-oriented therapy is usually contraindicated because it is too anxiety-producing. Within the safety of warm, supportive individual or small-group counseling relationships, growth in coping-with-life ego skills often can occur.

Persons with immature or malformed superegos (called "character disorders" or "psychopathic personalities" in traditional psychiatric language) need a different type of growth and therefore a different approach to therapy. Such persons act out their inner conflicts with little insight or guilt. To help them the therapist needs to use behavior modification or "reality therapy" approaches aimed at helping them learn to control their destructive acting out.

Growth-enabling counseling and therapy must include two essential experiences—acceptance and caring, on the one hand, and confrontation with reality, on the other. I call these two ingredients together the growth formula.[13] A crucial decision in applying the growth formula involves deciding what balance between the two ingredients will be most likely to activate the growth *elan* in a particular person. Ascertaining the relative ego strength of clients is a prerequisite to making this decision. In general, the greater the degree of ego strength, the more confrontation can be accepted growthfully by persons. The weaker the ego, the more support and acceptance are needed as the context of even gentle confrontation. When persons come for help, here are some of the questions counselors should ask themselves to gain a sense of their current ego strength:

> What is the nature and quality of their ego defenses? Are they using heavy defenses (e.g., denial or extreme projection) or light defenses (e.g., rationalization or mild projection)? Do their defenses feel compulsive and rigid or relatively flexible? Do they have any self-awareness that they may be denying aspects of reality by their defenses? As the counseling relationship develops, do they gradually relax their defenses and become more open to awareness of reality?

> What is the quality of their pattern of relationships? Is trust, mutuality, continuity, or commitment present in them? Are they able to develop trust within the therapeutic relationship?

> How constructively do they handle everyday crises and frustrations? How quickly do they begin to mobilize new coping skills? How do they cope with the normal responsibilities? How well (including how flexibly) do they organize their lives as they cope with their situation? To what extent does their behavior reflect a sense of self-esteem, competence, and power?

In general, persons who use heavy, inflexible defenses, are unable to sustain relationships of trust and mutuality, cope ineffectively, become disorganized or regress quickly when confronted with everyday crises and responsibilities, and are very dependent on others for sustaining their necessary sense of worth and power, suffer from ego weakness and dysfunction. Ego weakness is present in many chronic alcoholics and drug addicts, persons with multiple psychosomatic problems, delinquents and criminals, and people whose lives seem to consist of one (or several) crisis after another. Social oppression and deprivation deplete the ego resources of many women and members of minority groups in our sexist and racist culture. One's degree of ego strength changes constantly. Under sufficient internal or external stresses, anyone will show temporary ego dysfunction.

Ego psychology has given supportive counseling, in its various forms, a new importance. The greater the degree of ego dysfunction, temporary or chronic, the more need there is for using supportive methods in counseling and therapy.[14] Growth in the ability to cope constructively can occur in supportive relationships as the counselor or the support group helps persons gratify their dependency needs; drain off powerful, ego-paralyzing feelings (e.g., guilt, failure, anxiety); review their situation more objectively; and plan and implement realistic ways of coping constructively with their situation. Confrontation must be gentle, and the need for ego defenses must be respected until the need for support diminishes.

Erik Erikson's many-faceted ego psychology has enriched the developmental thrust in contemporary psychoanalytic thinking and practice tremendously. With his growth-centered vision of what it is to be whole, and his profound respect for the ego's creative capacities, he has redefined many of Freud's working concepts. As Don Browning says: "Erikson believes that the ego, in contrast to the superego and id, is the human counterpart of those regulatory capacities of animals which assure their ecological integrity. It is the ego which is the real servant of evolution, adaptation, and the cycle of the generations."[15] Like Freud, Erikson understands health developmentally. But he corrects Freud's myopic view that most if not all major growth changes occur before the end of adolescence (unless one undergoes extensive psychoanalysis). Erikson extends the developmental view of wholeness throughout the life cycle. Each of his eight stages has its new growth tasks, conflicts, risks, and new ego strengths that develop as growth tasks are accomplished. To illustrate, adolescents are "healthy" to the degree that they are developing a strong sense of identity with the accompanying ego strength, fidelity. Mid-years persons are healthy to the degree that they are creating a life-style of generativity with its ego strength of care. In the companion volume to this one, I have suggested a variety of growth-enabling ways of using a modified version of Erikson's growth schema with fourteen stages.[16]

Erikson adds an essential sociocultural dimension to Freud's psychosexual understanding of human development, integrating the two with the light touch and sensitivities of an artist (which was his background before becoming a psychoanalyst). He thus provides the relational-institutional-cultural context of individual development. Unlike Freud, Erikson does not see individual strivings as *inherently* antagonistic to the demands of society. He shows that there are vital resources for nurturing human growth in all cultures, even though there is also some necessary sacrifice of individual instinctual strivings. Individuals can become and remain strong only in the supportive context of their culture's institutions, the interdependency of the generations, and "a widening radius of significant individuals and institutions"[17] throughout their lives. Erikson criticizes Western culture because it provides an impoverished environment for nurturing the ego in its task of integrating experience and gaining mastery of one's life situation.

One of the vital resources for growth-enablers in Erikson's thought is his emphasis on the power of the future and of hope. Like Hartmann, he sees the infant as being born with a built-in ground plan and the necessary resources for growth in all the life stages. He calls this the "epigenetic principle" and regards it as the energizing motif of all human growth. He reverses Freud's attempt to explain the present by the past, making the pull of one's growth potential toward the future the explanatory principle.[18] Hope, a basic orientation toward the future, is the most indispensable strength of the ego. Hope is nurtured in small children when faith and trust pervade their parents' pattern of caring.

Erikson makes invaluable contributions to our understanding of spiritual growth. With the touch of an artist, he describes psychoanalysis as a Western form of meditation—a way of getting in touch with vital inner processes. Faith, like health, is understood developmentally. To be alive, faith must continue to grow.[19] The foundation of faith (and the cornerstone of healthy personality), is basic trust, the growth goal of the first life stage. In adolescence, faith must grow to include a meaningful ideology; in the mid-years, to include generativity; and so on throughout life. Erikson sees religious institutions as an important means of helping parents renew their inner trust regularly so that their children can experience and internalize trust from them. "Trust, then, becomes the capacity for faith—a vital need for which man *[sic]* must find some institutional confirmation. Religion, it seems, is the oldest and has been the most lasting institution to serve the ritual restoration of a sense of trust in the form of faith while offering a tangible formula for a sense of evil against which it promises to defend man."[20]

In his studies of Luther and Gandhi, Erikson has illuminated the role of dynamic religious leaders whose personal and existential conflicts reflect the central conflicts of their age.

Their resolution of these conflicts becomes a kind of universal drama that gives meaning to many people in their cultures. Such a spiritual leader becomes "a cultural worker who creates out of the conflicts of his time, a new identity for his age."[21]

Erikson calls for the creation of a growth model of ethics. The golden rule, he suggests, could well be reformulated "to say that it is best to do to another . . . what will develop his best potentials even as it develops your own."[22] He points to the need in our modern world for a universal ethic in which nurturing and caring for the growth of others (generativity) becomes the guiding motif: "The overriding issue is the creation not of a new ideology but of a universal ethic. . . . This can be advanced only by men and women who are neither ideological youths nor moralistic old men [or women], but who know that from generation to generation the test of what you produce is the care it inspires."[23]

One significant weakness in Erikson's thought is his psychology of women. As feminist psychologists have shown, his views of "inner space" reflect sex role stereotypes, even though they are far less blatant than Freud's sexist biases.[24] In spite of this serious limitation, Erikson represents psychoanalysis in its most open, free, and growth-enabling expression.

For Further Exploration of Growth Resources in the Therapy of Freud

Fadiman, James, and Frager, Robert. "Sigmund Freud and Psychoanalysis," *Personality and Personal Growth.* Harper, 1976, chap. 1. A succinct overview of Freud's major concepts.

Freud, Sigmund. *Introductory Lectures on Psychoanalysis,* vols. 15-16, in *The Standard Edition of the Complete Psychological Works of Sigmund Freud.* London: Hogarth Press, 1953–66. A series of lectures to students at the University of Vienna.

———. *The Interpretation of Dreams* (Standard Edition of Freud's *Complete Works,* vols. 4-5). According to Freud, contains "the most valuable of all the discoveries it has been my good fortune to make."

———. *New Introductory Lectures on Psycho-Analysis* (Standard Edition, vol. 22). Includes Freud's structural hypothesis.

Fromm, Erich. *Sigmund Freud's Mission.* New York: Harper and Bros., 1950. An evaluation and analysis of Freud's personality and influence.

Jones, Ernest. *The Life and Work of Sigmund Freud.* New York: Basic Books, 1953, 1955, 1957. The standard biography of Freud in three volumes. Vol. 3 includes a historical review of Freud's thought on a variety of topics.

Rothgeb, Carrie L. *Abstracts of the Standard Edition of the Complete Works of Sigmund Freud.* New York: Jason Aronson, 1973. Brief synopses of all Freud's writing with an introduction to reading Freud by Robert R. Holt.

For Further Exploration of Growth Resources in the Therapy of the Ego Analysts

Browning, Don. *Generative Man: Psychoanalytic Perspectives.* Philadelphia: Westminster Press, 1973. A depth study of Erikson, Fromm, Hartmann, Robert White, Norman Brown, and Phillip Rieff and their views of wholeness and society.

Clinebell, Howard. "Ego Psychology and Pastoral Counseling," *Pastoral Psychology,* February 1963, pp. 24-36. Discusses the basic concepts of ego psychology as resources for strengthening the effectiveness of supportive counseling.

Erikson, Erik H. *Childhood and Society,* 2nd ed. New York: W. W. Norton, 1963. A groundbreaking book that sets forth his eight stages of growth.

———. *Identity, Youth and Crisis.* New York: W. W. Norton, 1968. Explains the identity crises of adolescents in contemporary America.

———. *Insight and Responsibility.* New York: W. W. Norton, 1964. Essays on the ethical implications of psychoanalytic insights.

———. *Young Man Luther.* New York: W. W. Norton, 1958. A psychoanalytic study of Luther's developmental crises and their impact on his times.

———. *Gandhi's Truth.* New York: W. W. Norton, 1969. Shows how Gandhi's childhood and youth prepared him to be the revolutionary innovator of militant nonviolence.

Gleason, John J., Jr. *Growing Up to God: Eight Steps in Religious Development.* Nashville: Abingdon Press, 1975. Applies Erikson's stages to religious development.

Hartmann, Heinz. "Ego Psychology and the Problems of Adaptation," David Rapaport, ed., in *Organization and Pathology of Thought.* New York: Columbia University Press, 1951, pp. 362-98. A basic statement of Hartmann's perspective.

Parad, Howard J., ed. *Ego Psychology and Dynamic Casework.* New York: Family Service Assn. of America, 1958. A series of papers on the implications and applications of ego psychology in working with various types of clients.

Chapter 2

Growth Resources in Traditional Psychotherapies

Alfred Adler and Otto Rank

Growth Resources from Alfred Adler

Alfred Adler was born in a suburb of Vienna in 1870. He trained in medicine at the University of Vienna and practiced general medicine for a while. His relationship with Freud began in 1902, when he wrote a defense of Freud's book on dreams after it had been ridiculed in the press.[1] Freud invited him to join a small psychoanalytic discussion group that met at his home each week. From the beginning the two had disagreements over dream analysis and the role of early sexual trauma in mental illness. In 1911, after a series of disagreements, Adler left Freud's circle, taking nine of the group's twenty-three members with him. A year prior to this split, Adler gave up general medicine to practice psychiatry full time. Within a year after the split he named his theories "Individual Psychology" to emphasize the distinctiveness of each individual's experience and growth.

After World War I, Adler set up the first child-guidance clinic in cooperation with the Vienna school system. Adler was fun-loving and affable, enjoyed good food, companionship, and music, particularly opera. He abhorred technical jargon. He believed in the application of insights from therapy to the everyday life of people and spent much of his professional time writing and lecturing to nonprofessional persons. In 1935 he left Vienna because of the fascist wave that was sweeping over Europe. He settled in New York, where he practiced psychiatry and taught medical psychology at the Long Island College of

Medicine. He died in Aberdeen, Scotland, in 1937 while on a lecture tour.

Adler believed that human beings possess remarkable positive potentials *and* the ability to mold their heredity and their environment intentionally and creatively. His system offers much to growth-oriented counselors, therapists, and teachers. It is noteworthy that Abraham Maslow includes Adler among the pioneers of the "third force," the human potentials approach to psychology.

In contrast to Freud, Adler saw human beings as essentially creative (rather than impulse driven and destructive). He emphasized the active, integrating self (rather than the frail, victimized ego); held to a "soft" (rather than a "hard") determinism; had a strong interest in future, goal-directed strivings (rather than origins); emphasized the organism as a whole centered in the self (rather than a conflict view of personality); regarded the striving for worth and power (rather than sexual striving) as the central dynamic in mental health and illness; emphasized the possibilities for continuing change in the later years (rather than regarding the early years as utterly decisive).[2] It is clear from these motifs in Adler's thought that his vision of human beings was positive and growth-centered.

Adler believed that everyone has a will-to-power as a result of the early experience of being a helpless infant surrounded by powerful adults. He declared: "Just to be human is to feel inferior."[3] In the struggle to master one's environment, issues of worth and power become central. A great variety of compensatory devices—healthy and unhealthy—are developed by persons in their struggles to overcome feelings of powerlessness and inferiority. In facilitating growth work in counseling and therapy there is something reassuring, even liberating, about Adler's view that everyone suffers, to some degree, from inferiority feelings. This awareness can help free persons from the fallacious assumption that most other people have no self-esteem problems, while they themselves suffer from feelings of low self-worth.

Early in life each individual, according to Adler, learns a particular *life-style*—a structured pattern of behaving and responding, the aim of which is to maintain the minimal self-esteem and feelings of power that everyone must have to cope with life. The life-style of persons is the key to understanding all their behavior—dreams, attitudes, actions, perceptions, memories, fantasies, feelings, and so on. Behind one's life-style is one's *life goal.* Adlerian therapy aims at identifying the malfunctioning life goal, reeducating the person toward a new, more constructive goal, and thus making the life-style more constructive. Adler's emphasis on the functioning of the person-as-a whole is a valuable perspective in counseling and therapy. Watching for patterns in counselees' ways of feeling, perceiving, behaving, and relating to others often allows one to identify the pattern by which persons are sabotaging their own lives.

Adler believed that all human beings have and need to develop the germ of the capacity for loving, cooperative relationships. (This contrasts sharply with Freud's view that individual strivings are essentially selfish and antisocial and that all adjustments to society are concessions by the instincts to the demands of social reality.) All people have a striving for superiority, to overcome ubiquitous feelings of inferiority, but they also have a deep need for human togetherness and cooperation. Adler called this need *Gemeinschaft-gefühl,* usually translated "social feeling" or "social interest." The German word expresses a passionate need for relationships of closeness, mutual caring, and active social concern. (This concept is close to what I have described as the will-to-relate, which is *the* fundamental human drive since it is only in relationships that people can satisfy most of their basic psychological needs.)

In Adler's understanding, the healthy means to compensate for feelings of inferiority and satisfy the human need for power and esteem are ways that include the welfare of others. Adler stated: "Finding an avenue through which he can struggle toward objectives of social as well as personal advantage is the soundest 'compensation' for all the natural weaknesses of individual human beings."[4] Social interest first appears in the early interaction with the mother. It grows as a person matures. Neurosis occurs when, because of defects in parental attitudes (pampering or rejection) or physical defects, a child's social interest is distorted or stunted. In such persons, the striving for superiority becomes grandiose. They try to satisfy their need for power at the expense of others and in ways that isolate them from others. Adler called this an "erroneous solution"[5] to feelings of inferiority. Self-centeredness, aggressions, and sadism are not inherent in human nature; they are learned responses to unfortunate early-life experiences that produce a maladaptive life goal and life-style.

Adler's emphasis on the human need for feelings of worth and power is very useful in facilitating growth work. Feelings of powerlessness and low self-worth are present in nearly everyone who seeks therapeutic help, though often these feelings are well hidden behind their defensive "pride." As trust develops in therapeutic relationships, people usually begin to relax their defenses, revealing their underlying feelings of self-rejection. The chronic, mutually damaging power struggles that bring people for marriage counseling almost always stem from hidden feelings of powerlessness and low self-esteem in both persons. Only as they can learn new ways to satisfy their legitimate need for power and worth in ways that support rather than stymie the other's feelings of power and worth will the destructive cycles be replaced by more mutually satisfying marital relating. To do this they must discover how to use power *with* and *for* (the other and themselves) rather than *over* or *against*. More often than not, the presenting problems that bring a couple with a dysfunctional marriage to counseling—money, sex, child-rearing conflicts, and so on—are power struggles stemming from underlying feelings of impotence and self-deprecation.

The awareness that compensation for handicaps, losses, and feelings of inferiority *can* be constructive is a potentially growth-enabling insight. Enabling troubled people to "own" their feeings of inadequacy and then use them as a challenge to develop personally and socially useful compensation is a healthy way to help them transform minuses into partial pluses.

One of Adler's significant contributions was his illumination of growthful ways to parent children. He recognized that the general attitudes and feelings of parents and the relationships among the siblings determine the growth climate of a family. He helped parents see that discipline and training should have a positive, not a repressive character. Through his lectures, books, and work in child guidance centers, he encouraged parents to nurture their children's budding social interest, self-confidence, responsibility, and concern for others. A close collaborator of Adler in the child-guidance clinic movement in Vienna was child psychiatrist Rudolf Dreikurs. Later he became director of the Alfred Adler Institute of Chicago. Through his writings (see *Children: The Challenge*), he has made Adler's approach to children readily available to parents.

Adler anticipated by several decades some of the key insights of feminist psychologists and therapists. He saw that our male-dominated society saddles women generally with an additional burden of inferiority by treating them as inferior. To compensate for this, some women adopt what Adler called a "masculine protest," rejecting their special strengths as women and joining the male success rat race in an effort to feel worthwhile. Adler held that compulsive goal-striving (on the part of both women and men) is directly related to the polarization of the sexes. It was clear to Adler that rigid sex-role stereotyping is a way of keeping women in a less powerful place in relationships and in society. Forcing human beings into narrow, rigid categories impoverishes self-actualization for both women and men.[6]

Adler's belief that inappropriate power strivings are involved in personal, relationship, and institutional problems makes him an ideological foreparent of what eventually became radical therapy. His concept of social interest carried him into the arena of concern for social and institutional change. Adlerian Heinz Ansbacher declares:

> An exploration of Adlerian psychology always comes back to social interest and to society. Man *[sic]* is inextricably imbedded in society and cannot be considered apart from it. . . . Social interest is Adler's criterion of mental health and it does include growth, expansion or self-transcendence. . . . When Adler speaks of . . . well-adjusted human beings, he is speaking of adjustment to the ultimate benefit of mankind. Adjustment to contemporary society and automatic conformity limit the individual and are not indicative of mental health. Adler consistently associated social interest with courage and with independence. The mentally healthy person cooperates for a better future for all and in the process gains the independence and courage to fight present evils. Adler would have applauded Martin Luther King's call for the establishment of an international Association for the Advancement of Creative Maladjustment.[7]

With his concern for social justice, Adler worked actively to change oppressive institutional practices and structures, particularly in education and through the creation of a network of child-guidance clinics. He was an ardent socialist. His Russian wife was a friend of Trotsky, who visited their home frequently. Adler is a refreshing example of a therapist who refused to focus exclusively on intrapsychic factors, ignoring the relational and societal context that mold intrapsychic development.

I find many of Adler's major insights useful for understanding pathogenic religion and for facilitating spiritual growth.[8] To illustrate, Carl, a young adult in a growth-oriented therapy group, struggled to resist the nostalgic attraction that he felt for the rigid, authoritarian, but comfortable religion of his childhood. Although he no longer found most of this belief system intellectually acceptable, he still felt pulled back toward it emotionally. In the group, he gradually became aware of the crippling impact that his old religion had had on his spiritual life. He discovered the ways in which the old beliefs had given him a sense of undeserved and derivative (from God) worth and power to compensate temporarily and ineffectively for his personal feelings of unworthiness and powerlessness. As he grew he gradually claimed more of his own real strengths and developed more of his competencies. As his awareness of his inner power and value increased, his spiritual life also changed. He reported feeling more in touch with people and with a Spirit who affirmed him as a valuable person.

The break between Freud and Adler was unfortunate for both sides. Each tended to ignore important dimensions of the truth about people and therapy that the other had discovered, while overemphasizing and overgeneralizing his own insights. Much of Adler's approach seems to have developed as an antithesis to Freud's. He rejected Freud's valuable findings regarding infantile sexuality and the unconscious. He rejected the very concept of inner conflicts, seeing all conflict as being between environmental forces and inner strivings for superiority. All this impoverished his understanding of the complexities of the human situation. His refusal to admit that the house of the human psyche is often divided against itself resulted in intellectual contortions, particularly when he tried to give a cogent explanation of the dynamics of psychosis. His important emphasis on the growth-oriented, freely responding side of human beings often seems like superficial optimism because it is not balanced by awareness of the dark, trapped, destructive forces on which Freud had concentrated his attention. Freud likened the ego, as described by Adler, to "the clown who claims to have himself accomplished all the difficult feats of the circus."[9] Adler is a vivid illustration of the need for any viable growth approach to have a depth dimension that includes a robust awareness of the powerful resistances to change and growth within persons. In spite of these serious limitations, Adler is a significant foreparent of contemporary growth-oriented therapies who contributed valuable insights that deserve to be rediscovered by teachers, parents, counselors, and therapists.

Growth Resources from Otto Rank

Otto Rank was born in 1884 in Vienna, the son of an emotionally absent, alcoholic father and a gentle, responsible mother. When he first encountered Freud's writings in 1904 his response was as if he had had a religious revelation. He said, "Now I see everything clearly. The world process is no longer a riddle."[10] Rank was a brilliant engineering student when, in 1905, he first met Freud. His creativity, talents, and enthusiasm impressed Freud greatly. Rank became one of his closest associates for nearly twenty years, apparently forming a strong but ambivalent transference relationship with Freud, as a substitute father figure. Rank became an outstanding lay (non-medically trained) analyst. In 1921 Freud hailed him as the greatest living analyst.

In 1924 Rank published *The Trauma of Birth,* which made birth (a mother-centered event) rather than the Oedipus complex (a father-centered experience in Freud's thought) the key to anxiety. The book was dedicated to Freud, but its main point constituted a devastating attack on Freud's thought. With an intense interest in mythology, art, and literature, Rank came to reject Freud's biological reductionist understanding of human personality. He found classical psychoanalytic theory therapeutically inadequate, so he began to experiment with more active and briefer methods. He called his approach "psychotherapy" and eventually "will therapy" rather than "psychoanalysis." He came to understand neurosis as a philosophical and moral problem rather than as a medical problem. The troubled person needs a new *Weltanschauung,* a new world view. The unorthodox development in his concepts and methods eventually led, when Rank was forty, to a painful break with Freud. Beginning in 1926, Rank lived in Paris. He commuted frequently to the United States for lecturing until he moved to New York in 1935. He died of an infection in 1939 a month after Freud's death. The timing of his death was probably not a coincidence.

Rank's views had, as Ruth Monroe makes clear, "profound influence on the development of psychiatric social work, psychotherapy, counseling, education and other non-medical fields in which deep psychological insight is required."[11] Rank anticipated thrusts that eventually became central in client-centered therapy, reality therapy, and assertiveness training. In a sense he was a foreparent of the whole growth trend in contemporary psychotherapies. I feel drawn to Rank by his dynamic concern for human potentializing, his emphasis on intentionality, and his awareness of the strong, healthy side that is in persons generally, even the most disturbed.

There are rich resources in Rank for use by growth-oriented teachers, counselors, and therapists. Like Adler, he emphasized the healthy dimensions of personality. His understanding of persons was essentially hopeful. He highlighted human freedom and potentials. With Adler, Jung, and Horney, he understood the self holistically. According to Rank, there is in all persons a positive striving toward wholeness, which he called the "will-to-health."[12] Rejecting Freud's determinism, Rank, like Assagioli (the creator of psychosynthesis), regarded *will* as the very core of human personality. Rank wrote, "I understand by will a positive guiding organization and integration of the self which utilizes creativity as well as inhibits and controls the instinctual drives."[13] As the creative expression of the total personality, the will distinguishes each person as unique from all others.

The neurotic suffers mainly from an inability to function as an integrated, asserting, purposeful self. The goal of therapy (and personal growth in general) is to activate and strengthen the will so that people learn to live intentionally. Effective therapy puts us in the driver's seat of our own life! In reflecting on the power of the will as it relates to the concept of the unconscious, Rank observed: "It is astonishing how much the patient knows and how little is unconscious if one does not give him this convenient excuse for refusing responsibility."[14]

Rank describes a variety of ways in which human beings evade responsibility. In animism, responsibility is avoided by projecting human will onto the physical world, peopling nature with spirits. Theists escape responsibility by projecting a part of their will onto an all-powerful deity to whom they must submit. Similarly, scientists introduce determinism into their understanding of persons, to escape from affirming the responsible will. Thus animism, religion, and science can all be used to evade the responsible exercise of will. According to Rank, many people use psychoanalysis, focusing on explaining behavior by probing the past, to avoid living responsibly in the present. In a viewpoint that anticipates by several decades a similar emphasis in Fritz Perls, Rank points out that explanations are about as helpful in psychotherapy as in appendicitis.

Will, in Rank's understanding, is ambivalent from the beginning. Birth, the loss of a perfect union between mother and child, is the basic source and prototype of all subsequent anxiety. All anxiety is separation anxiety. The trauma of birth is more than being ejected from the pleasure and safety of the intrauterine garden of Eden; it is the feeling of no longer being whole in oneself. But birth is also the prototype of all experiences of *rebirth,* of dying to the safety and integration of one life stage or experience to be reborn into the next. The will motivates persons to strive toward autonomy and independence, but this is in conflict with their "life fear," the fear of independence and nonunion. The fundamental human polarity is between separation and union, between the risk of moving into the future to become one's potential self and the risk of returning to the womb of the past and of conformity. Constructive living involves satisfying the need for both separation and union. Positive will has the capacity to integrate these two dichotomous needs. Rank uses the term "artist" to describe the person who achieves creative integration of these two poles.

Most people, according to Rank, achieve a dull quieting of this basic conflict by conforming and thus renouncing their striving toward creative autonomy. Rigid conformists may function satisfactorily in a stable society but in a period of lightning-fast social change (like ours), their security and their virtues may evaporate almost overnight. Neurotics cannot conform like most people, nor can they move ahead purposefully. Rankian therapy aims at helping people overcome their womb-returning tendencies through strengthening their wills by actively exercising them (as in assertiveness training). Psychotherapy focuses, as it does in Adlerian and gestalt therapy, mainly on the present. The problems that bring people to therapy have to do with their inability to deal intentionally with the present. Too much involvement with either the past or the future can be used to avoid responsibility in the present.

The therapist is seen as a warm human being whose task is to accept and affirm the wills of persons until they can develop strength in exercising their own wills. The therapist seeks to create a permissive atmosphere within which persons have the space to exercise and strengthen their own wills. The responsibility of changing themselves into self-directing persons must stay with them. If persons are to grow, the therapist must resist their efforts to project responsibility by saying, in effect, "I am weak, confused, helpless. Tell me what to do or do it for me." To yield to this request is to reinforce their basic problem. The will is only strengthened as it is exercised! Therapy is seen as a microcosm of life. Therapists must stay flexible and in tune with the struggles and creativity of their clients, but also they must be willing to engage clients in a confrontation of wills that can strengthen the clients' wills. There is an egalitarian thrust in Rank's view of the therapist-patient relationship. "The therapeutic experience is characterized by the fact that both patient and therapist are at once creator and creature. The patient may not be only creature, he must also become creator; while the therapist plays not only the creator role, but at the same time must serve the creative will of the patient as material."[15] There is in Rank a deep respect for the personality of the disturbed person, conflicts and all. Their conflicts, as expressions of will, are affirmed. Therapy does not eliminate all conflicts but rather enables persons to live creatively and intentionally *with* the conflicts that are a part of everyone's experience.

The central Rankian theme—the primacy and ambivalence of the will—is relevant and useful in both educational and therapeutic growth work. All of us have experienced the powerful conflicts between the striving toward becoming the unique, authentic selves we potentially are and the pull toward safe, comfortable belonging and conformity. We all know the "life fear," the anxiety about nonconformity and assertiveness. The dependence-autonomy conflict often is strongest during adolescence, but it continues in different expressions throughout all the life stages. The seductive pull of the past is powerful, particularly during times of insecurity. There are many "wombs" around, inviting comfortable escape from growth. The search in many marriages today (including my own) for a mutually acceptable balance between autonomy and growth, on the one hand, and relational growth and closeness, on the other, is a variation on the same theme. How can couples maintain a creative relationship within which the needs of each of us for distance, autonomy, and personal growth are balanced with our need for intimacy? The key to transcending the dependence-independence polarity is creative interdependency.

Rank's central working concept, *separation anxiety,* is very useful in coping with grief. As the French proverb put it, "Every parting is a little death." All growth work also includes grief work. Each new stage of our growth requires leaving the security of the past stage, within which we have learned to cope with some comfort and competence. Rank emphasized *rebirth* as the key to growth in loss experiences. Thus, growth becomes a series of deaths and rebirths.

One practical application of the concept of separation anxiety is Rank's discovery that end-setting, early in therapy, allows people the opportunity of dealing, in the therapeutic relationship, with their ambivalence about separation and union, dependence and autonomy. Setting a tentative time for terminating a counseling or therapy relationship has a variety of growth-enabling effects, in my experience. It tends to diminish dependency and encourage development of clients' own strengths and will by reminding them that the counselor-therapist is available only for a limited time. Awareness of the ending, even if it is still several weeks or months off, tends to motivate more responsible growth work by clients. As the agreed-upon termination approaches it is not unusual for clients to become aware of unfinished grief work associated with previous losses. The ambivalence toward being in therapy—wanting the security and dependency of the relationship and yet wanting to be free and autonomous—is resolved growthfully when it is confronted and resolved in favor of purposeful autonomy. Tentative termination dates can always be renegotiated, of course, if it becomes evident that further therapeutic work is essential for the person's growth.

One of the strengths in Rank's thought was his view that human beings are inherently social. Of the inner world and the outer world of relationships, he wrote: "The harmonious balancing of the two spheres needs to be the presupposition of therapy so that both spheres are worked upon simultaneously. Both worlds are real or unreal. What we seek in the outer world is what we have found in the inner."[16]

Rank criticized Freud's patriarchal assumptions and his view of women as derivative from and inferior to men. By making the mother-child relationship the key to human development and therefore to the psychic life of persons, Rank moved away from Freud's father-centered psychology of persons. In his description of the psychological differences in men and women he observed that men have sought their strength in creating and in controlling by their masculine ideology and by their wills. Rank believed that women find power and a kind of immortality in motherhood. Many men, he held, have not accepted their mortality and therefore have never really accepted themselves. Because women have accepted patriarchal ideology, they need constant reassurance that they are acceptable to men and are living up to their ideals. Women conceal much of their psychology both because they need it as a weapon against the male world, which dominates them, and as a refuge for their injured self.[17] In a discussion of the meaning of equality between women and men, Rank declared that the only real equality is "the equal right of each individual to become and to be himself, which actually means to accept his own difference and have it accepted by others."[18]

The main thrusts of Rank's theory are particularly useful when counseling with persons caught in severe independence-conformity conflicts (such as some adolescents); those who are paralyzed by anxiety about finishing a project or a chapter of their lives (e.g., pre-graduation anxiety attacks) and in danger of sabotaging the successful completion of something they really value; those who are afraid to make decisions or try something new which they want but which may mean giving up old securities; couples who are struggling to find satisfying closeness without either of them losing their identity and autonomy.

For counselors and therapists interested in facilitating spiritual growth, Rank offers a variety of resources. His writings deal extensively with the psychology of religion. His insights about how religion can be used to foster conformity and avoid personal responsibility can help identify pathogenic, growth-blocked religious beliefs and systems. There is a constant temptation to use religion as a comfortable womb rather than a stimulus to rebirth. Dependency-creating ministers, childish belief systems, and exclusivistic conceptions of religious truth ("My way is *the* truth") can all function as seductive, growth-inhibiting wombs.

The death-rebirth theme in Rank has obvious affinities with the dying-resurrection motif in the New Testament. In working with persons going through the deep waters of painful mid-years crises, it is often growth-enabling to help them face the fact that the values and priorities by which they have been living are no longer viable. Their old philosophy of life will not provide creative guidelines for the second half of their lives. A rebirth is urgently needed. Such an awareness can lead to a painful but freeing revision of their guiding values. Religion is growth-enabling only if it encourages continuing rebirth to new dimensions of oneself, one's relationships, and one's experience of nature and of spiritual reality.

Although I resonate to Rank's positive emphasis on human strengths and potentialities, the depth dimension found in Freud and Jung is underemphasized in his thought. In spite of his interest in myth and art and his exploration of the psychic life in some depth (for example, in *The Myth of the Birth of the*

Hero) there seems to be little awareness of the "demonic" or the "shadow side" in personality. The important resources of his approach, to be used most growthfully, must be integrated with complementary resources from the depth therapies.

For Further Exploration of Growth Resources in the Therapy of Alfred Adler

Adler, Alfred. *The Individual Psychology of Alfred Adler,* ed. L. Heinz and R. R. Ansbacher. New York: Harper, 1956. Two persons who studied with Adler did what he himself was unable to do—systematically organized his thoughts on critical issues. The book consists of direct quotes from Adler, with comments by the Ansbachers interspersed.

Dreikurs, Rudolf. *Children: The Challenge.* New York: Hawthorn Books, 1964. Presents a practical application of Adler's insights and approach to creative parenthood.

Fadiman, James, and Frager, Robert. "Alfred Adler and Individual Psychology," *Personality and Personal Growth.* New York: Harper, 1976, pp. 92-110. A succinct overview of Adler's major concepts and his understanding of human growth.

For Further Exploration of Growth Resources in the Therapy of Otto Rank

Rank, Otto. *The Trauma of Birth.* New York: Harcourt, Brace, 1929. Rank discusses birth both as the origin and prototype of the fundamental dependence-autonomy struggle.

———. *Will Therapy, and Truth and Reality.* New York: Alfred A. Knopf, 1945. A description of Rankian therapy.

Chapter 3

Growth Resources in Traditional Psychotherapies

Erich Fromm, Karen Horney, Harry Stack Sullivan

Resources from Erich Fromm

Erich Fromm was born in Frankfurt, Germany, in 1900. He studied sociology and psychology at the universities of Frankfurt and Munich and Heidelberg, and was trained in psychoanalysis at the Psychoanalytic Institute in Berlin. He came to the United States in 1934 and was affiliated with the International Institute for Social Research in New York until 1939. In 1941 he joined the faculty of Bennington College. In 1951 he became a professor at the National University of Mexico. For a number of years Fromm lived and wrote in Cuernavaca, Mexico. His death in March, 1980, at his home in Muralto, Switzerland, ended the career of one of the most creative thinkers and prolific psychoanalytic writers of our times.

When I was a student at Columbia University in the late 1940s, Fromm was a resource person for a small cross-discipline group of faculty and graduate students who met regularly to discuss papers on the relationship of religion and health. I recall the excitement that I experienced when he presented his ideas and interacted with members of our group on two occasions. Through the years, my thought and practice have been influenced repeatedly by the insights of this therapist-theoretician.

Fromm's major contributions to growth-oriented teachers, counselors, and therapists are his understanding of the ways in which cultures constrict or nurture human individuation (Fromm's term for potentializing) and his discussion of the importance of existential-philosophical-religious factors in all human growth. Fromm gives psychoanalysis a broad philosophical and cross-cultural orientation that provides a fresh context for growth work.

His discussion begins with a description of the existential dilemma that we human beings face. Humans are animals who have lost our instincts (our fixed, inborn patterns of response) and have developed reason, self-awareness, and autonomy to replace them. We are freaks of nature. Deep within us there is a nostalgia for our "lost Edens," the primitive unity with nature and the herd that we have lost in our evolutionary development. Thus there is a two-way pull within us—toward autonomy and individuation, on the one hand, and toward conformity and merging our identity with the group on the other. This creates a continuing conflict between the need to become our autonomous selves and the need to feel a part of the larger whole.

In Fromm's thought, as in Adler's, Horney's, and Sullivan's, human beings are essentially social. Our culture molds our basic personal pattern and determines our degree of wholeness. Each society tends to produce what Fromm calls a "social character," a common personality core that is required to cope with that society. This pattern is created in individual children by the way they are reared.

Our self-awareness, though it helps define what is unique and precious about being human, also renders us prey to guilt and to the anxiety stemming from our existential aloneness and our mortality. The inherent dichotomies of the human situations—e.g., autonomy vs. belonging, life vs. death—are bearable only within a sense of meaning and a sense of community with others who share our existential fate. When people are alienated from a community of shared meanings, as countless millions now are, the inescapable human dichotomies become unbearable. They produce a variety of destructive problems and nonproductive life orientations. Many people try to escape from the existential dichotomies by embracing one side and rejecting the other. When the mass insecurities fostered by a society in rapid transition reinforce the feeling of vulnerability derived from personal autonomy, people tend to "escape from freedom"; they lose their anxiety but also their freedom by overidentifying with some authoritarian ideology, leader, or system, political or religious. Fromm analyzes the social psychology of Nazi Germany (from which he fled) and of Reformation Calvinism to illustrate how people escape from freedom when it becomes too threatening.[1]

The goal of growth and of therapy is what Fromm calls the *productive person.* Such persons develop their unique potentialities and thus become capable of genuine love, creativity, productive work, and participation in a community of shared meanings. In this way, the productive person is able to cope constructively with the inescapable existential dilemmas. If this maturing does not occur, four types of nonproductive life-orientations (and character structures) develop in the attempt by persons to defend themselves from feelings of existential insignificance and aloneness. *Receptive* type persons require constant approval and reassurance from others. *Exploitative* type people take what they want or need from others. *Hoarding* type people center their lives on defensively saving and owning. They try to possess others by behavior that is often disguised as love. *Marketing-oriented* people experience themselves as commodities whose value is limited to their value for use by others. They say, and mean, "I had to *sell* myself to that prospective employer." The marketing orientation is the pervasive social character produced by a capitalist society like ours. All four of these nonproductive personality types represent an alienation from our potential for real love, self-esteem, and creative living.

Fromm provides important resources for facilitating spiritual growth. With Jung and Assagioli, he sees religion (broadly defined) as a fundamental need of all human beings. He points to the crucial distinction between growth-inhibiting and growth-enabling religion: "There is no one without a religious need, need to have a frame of orientation and an object of devotion. . . . The question is not *religion or not* but *which kind of religion,* whether it is one furthering man's *[sic]* development, the unfolding of his specifically human powers, or one paralyzing them."[2] He describes neurosis as a *private* religion (which reverses Freud's view that religions are a *collective* childish neurosis of humankind); he sees neurosis as a regression to primitive forms of religion.

Fromm's critique of authority-centered religions as inherently growth-limiting is a valuable contribution to the spiritual growth work of individuals and to their development of growth-enabling religious beliefs:

> When man *[sic]* has thus projected his own most valuable powers onto God . . . they have become separated from him and in the process he has become alienated from himself . . . His only access to himself is through God. In worshipping God he tries to get in touch with that part of himself which he has lost through projection. . . . But his alienation from his own powers not only makes man feel slavishly dependent on God, it makes him bad too. He becomes a man without faith in his fellowmen or in himself, without the experience of his own love, of his own power of reason. As a result the separation between the "holy" and the "secular" occurs. In his worldly activities man acts without love, in that sector of his life which is reserved to religion he feels himself to be a sinner (which he actually is since to live without love is to live in sin). . . . Simultaneously, he tries to win forgiveness by emphasizing his own helplessness and worthlessness. Thus the attempt to obtain forgiveness results in the activation of the very attitude from which his sin stems. . . . The more he praises God, the emptier he becomes, the more sinful he feels. The more sinful he feels . . . the less able he is to regain himself.[3]

Fromm sees clearly that for many people Christianity is a thin veneer over the idolatrous worship of power, success, and the authority of the marketplace; or it is a cover masking their idolatrous fixation on their clan, religious or ethnic group, or nation-state. Fromm's insights about the dynamics of our modern idolatries illuminate many of the growth-blocking religious beliefs, practices, and institutions one encounters both in doing therapy and in society.

In his books *Psychoanalysis and Religion* and *Psychoanalysis and Zen Buddhism,*[4] he spells out his understanding of growth-enabling religion. This is essentially a religion in which people do not give their power and freedom away to external deities or to idolatries such as those mentioned above. It is a rational, nonauthoritarian religion. Fromm's analysis of authority-centered religions and of their ethical systems is a critique that all religious leaders and pastoral counselors need to take seriously and use to exorcise the growth-inhibiting beliefs and practices of their own religious systems. One can learn from his critique without necessarily agreeing with his underlying nontheistic metaphysical assumption.

In a time when more and more people are rejecting old authority-centered standards of right and wrong, truth and falsehood, Fromm's contributions to a humanistic, psychologically informed ethic (in *Man for Himself*) offer valuable resources for growth work. In contrast to approaches to the good life which derive their criteria from external sources of authority, Fromm looks for criteria in the depths of persons and in society. He asks the key question for any growth-centered ethic—which ethical guidelines contribute to the growth of creative, loving, productive people? The good is defined as that in individuals and in social institutions which makes for the unfolding of full human possibilities. The bad is whatever blocks growth toward full humanness. The massive collapse of old authority-centered value systems provides humankind today with an unprecedented opportunity and necessity to grow up morally. This can happen only as we develop self-validating ethical guidelines to help us maximize the full potentialities of persons. Fromm's understanding of ethics can offer valuable insights concerning how a planetary ethic-of-growth can be developed. He makes it clear that our moral problem today is that we have become alienated from our real selves, that we treat ourselves, and therefore others as things. Ethically speaking, our period of history is "an end and a beginning, pregnant with possibilities."[5] The outcome of this period of transition will depend on whether human beings have the courage to become their potential selves—loving, creative, and productive.

Fromm's understanding of human evil provides an approach that can help human potentials approaches to education and therapy avoid superficial optimism. In *The Heart of Man* and subsequently in *The Anatomy of Human Destructiveness* he rejects both sentimental optimism and the view that human beings are inherently evil. He sees our greatest problem as our individual and collective destructiveness and points to the crucial importance of discovering ways to resolve it. He identifies a variety of types of destructiveness in persons and in society. There is *playful aggressiveness* motivated by the display of skill, not by destructiveness per se. There is *reactive or defensive violence* motivated by fear when individual or collective life, freedom, property, or dignity are threatened. Much destructiveness of this type results from our incestuous tribal ties to family, clan, culture, and nation. If the collective narcissism of such limited circles of concern is threatened or wounded, defensive violence results.

Another contemporary form of violence which is very prevalent results from the shattering of *old faith* systems. Another form of violence is *compensatory*. A person "who cannot create wants to destroy. He thus takes revenge on life for negating him."[6] Compensatory destructiveness is a negative substitute for making a creative impact on the world. The only cure for this form of evil is the fuller development of love and reason, autonomy and creativity.

Destructiveness and violence can also be *malignant,* as in sadism. We human beings apparently are the only animals who become driven by the *lust* to hurt, torture, and kill others of their own species. This form of violence today is threatening the very survival of humankind. It is motivated, according to Fromm, by a distorted religious need, the passion to have absolute, unrestricted control over another being, as a way of attempting to overcome existential anxiety. "The experience of absolute control over another being, of omnipotence so far as he, she or it is concerned, creates the illusion of transcending the limitations of human existence, particularly for those whose lives are deprived of productivity and joy. Sadism . . . is the transformation of impotence into the experience of omnipotence; it is the religion of psychical cripples."[7] The extreme forms of malignant destructiveness are labeled "necrophilous" by Fromm. The necrophile is a lover of death and destructiveness. Hitler is an example of a pure necrophile who was passionately fascinated by force, mechanical things, killing, and death.

More than any other therapist, Fromm has brought the searchlight of depth psychology to bear on the historical and societal roots of individual problems. In *The Sane Society* and elsewhere, he describes factors in our society which make for widespread alienation of persons from their powers and potentials. He shares his vision of a sane society in which human possibilities will be maximized. The road to such a society is the creation of an economic system in which "every working person would be an active and responsible participant, where work would be attractive and meaningful," where every worker would participate in management and decision-making.[8] The sane society would be one that is organized to serve the basic need of all human beings—for relatedness and love, for a sense of inclusive identity, for creativeness, for a frame or meaning, and for a satisfying object of devotion.

From the growth perspective, there are several weaknesses in Fromm's approach. His nontheistic belief system renders his religious orientation two-dimensional. He lacks awareness of a Source of inspiration and creativity that is both *beyond* and within human beings. Only such an awareness can give depth and height dimensions to what Fromm calls one's "frame of orientation and object of devotion." Although I find his critique of authority-centered ethics convincing in the sense that it is clear that we *must* find moral criteria that are self-validating in human experience, his orientation here also seems two-dimensional. There is no sense that what is best for human potentializing is somehow undergirded by ultimate spiritual Reality.

Fromm has a tendency to demonize authority in general. This tendency is partially offset by his recognition of the need for "rational authority," the authority of competence, to replace the attributive authority of status or position in a more humanizing society. Although I agree that the maximum distribution of power and decision-making is desirable and growth-producing, it is clear that some structured authority is also essential in all social systems. Such authority need not be oppressive provided there are strong checks on its exercise, built into the system.

From a feminist therapy perspective, Fromm, like most therapists, lacks a full appreciation of the centrality of sexism as a fundamental form of human oppression. From the viewpoint of radical therapies he does not emphasize the ways in which empowerment and involvement in changing institutions can be profoundly healing and growth-enabling for oppressed persons. His therapeutic theory is essentially individualistic in spite of his brilliant insights into the societal roots of pathology.

Resources in the Therapy of Karen Horney

Karen Horney was born in Hamburg, Germany, in 1885. Her father was a stern Norwegian sea captain; her mother was Dutch and much more open in her thinking and attitudes than was her father. Horney's medical education was received at the University of Berlin and her psychotherapeutic training at the Berlin Psychoanalytic Institute, where she subsequently became a lecturer. She was analyzed by two of the best-known training analysts in Europe—Karl Abraham and Hans Sachs. At the invitation of Franz Alexander she came to the United States in 1932 and became associate director of the Chicago Institute of Psychoanalysis. She moved to New York in 1934 and taught at the New York Psychoanalytic Institute. Becoming increasingly dissatisfied with orthodox psychoanalysis, she joined with persons of similar views in founding the American Institute of Psychoanalysis. She was the dean of this institute until her death in 1952.

In spite of her orthodox Freudian training, Horney became remarkably growth-oriented in her understanding of human beings and of therapy. Horney's writings influenced my thinking significantly during my years of training as a counselor-therapist. I agree with this evaluation of her contemporary relevance: "Her ideas and understanding of the human person are as alive and fresh today as they were when she first shared them through her writings."[9] Paul Tillich (for whom Horney was a therapist) described the dynamic quality of her personhood in a moving statement at her funeral: "Few people whom one encountered were so strong in the affirmation of their being, so full of the joy of living, so able to rest in themselves, and to create without cessation beyond themselves."[10]

Horney's search for deeper understanding of the distortions and possibilities of human personality was linked with the willingness to challenge many of Freud's ideas. In April, 1941, she walked out of the New York Psychoanalytic Society singing "Go Down, Moses," having been told that her views were utterly out of keeping with psychoanalytic theory. There is something winsome about a person who had the courage to defy the rigidities of the psychoanalytic establishment in this way.

Karen Horney's writings include a wealth of insights of value to growth-oriented counselors, therapists, and teachers. Along with Erich Fromm (with whom she was associated at the Berlin Psychoanalytic Institute and later in New York City) and with Adler, Rank, and Sullivan, she rejected Freud's compartmentalized conflict-centered, biologically reductionistic model of human personality in favor of an emphasis on the functioning of the self as whole in its relational context. She saw that the concept of a unifying, active center of personality is essential to the view that persons possess some freedom to respond intentionally to their situation. Both Horney and Fromm understood personal growth as being centered in the interaction of persons with their particular familial and cultural context. Both therapists shared an interest in understanding how sociological factors create growth-blocking or growth-enabling environments. Both saw their systems as falling within the general framework of psychoanalytic thought, but both rejected Freud's fundamental assumption that the essence of human development is the working out of biological drives and impulses.

Horney saw human beings as possessing the essential resources for wholeness:

> You need not, and in fact cannot, teach an acorn to grow into an oak tree, but when given a chance, its intrinsic potentialities will develop. Similarly, the human individual, given a chance, tends to develop his particular human potentialities. He will develop then the unique alive forces of his real self: the clarity and depth of his own feelings, thoughts, wishes, interests; the ability to tap his own resources, the strength of his will power; the special capacities or gifts he may have; the faculty to express himself and to relate himself to others with his spontaneous feelings. All this will in time enable him to find his set of values and his aims in life. In short, he will grow substantially undiverted, toward self-realization.[11]

Therapy, according to Horney, aims at enhancing self-awareness and self-knowledge. Thus, insight is not an end in itself but "a means of liberating the forces of spontaneous growth"[12] toward one's full potential. Healthy persons are spontaneous in their feelings, actively assume responsibility for their own lives, accept mutual obligations in interdependent relationships, are without emotional pretense, and are able to put themselves wholeheartedly into the work, beliefs, and relationships that are important to them. She saw that growth toward wholeness occurs in relationships of love and respect and that neurotic character patterns are learned by children when their relationships lack these essential qualities.

Horney uses the term *real self* to mean the potential self—all that one has the capacity to become. In contrast, the *actual self* is the way one is at present. In even sharper contrast, the *idealized self* is the exaggerated self-image by which people seek to maintain feelings of worth. Maintaining this perfectionistic self-picture wastes enormous energy, which could be used for growth toward actualizing the real self. This idealized image functions as a substitute for real self-esteem, creates self-idolatry, demands a pattern of rigid relationships, and makes it necessary to constantly compare oneself with others.

In her understanding of human growth, Horney shared with other analysts an emphasis on the lasting influence of the relationships of the first six years. But she regarded these formative experiences as determinative only in persons who have suffered severe emotional deprivation. A deeply hurt and therefore disturbed child, will turn school experiences as well as later relationships into reenactments of their pathology-fostering family relationships. In contrast, relatively healthy children tend to respond appropriately to the actual quality of the school relationships and of later experiences. Like Adler, Horney emphasizes the importance of growth experiences *after* as well as before age six. A reasonably growthful childhood leaves a person free to respond directly and appropriately to the pressures and possibilities of later life. The primary focus in Horney's therapy is on the situation one is now facing and on the current function of behavior, rather than on the discovery of the infantile roots of the problem. For those of us who lead growth groups and do education and therapy mainly with adults, this is a valuable and useful emphasis.

Horney's insights about how excessive anxiety and low self-esteem stifle growth are relevant when working with painfully blocked growth. She uses the term *"basic anxiety"* to mean the deep feeling that is at the heart of severely truncated growth (neuroses). Basic anxiety is "the feeling a child has of being isolated and helpless in a potentially hostile world."[13] Neurotic patterns of relating are desperate attempts to prevent oneself from being overwhelmed by this most painful of feelings.

Horney identified three major neurotic personality patterns, which both stem from and produce further diminishing of growth. Each of these is a defense against feelings of threat, isolation, and helplessness. I find this simple schema useful in identifying the major ways we human beings block our growth in relationships. The first type of defense is that employed by the *"moving toward"* type persons[14] (comparable to Fromm's receptive type). Such individuals are compliant, dependent, and submissive. They seek to defend themselves against basic anxiety by seeking constant approval from others. Their fear of aggressiveness prevents them from satisfying their need for autonomy and assertiveness. They are pleasant, ingratiating, and easy to get along with as long as their exaggerated need for acceptance and love are met. They become very anxious when these needs are not met. Such persons tend to control others subtly by their "weak" submissiveness. In our sexist society, many women are conditioned to use the moving-toward defense.

The *"moving against"* type persons (comparable to Fromm's exploitative type) attempt to defend against anxiety by being hyper-independent, competitive, and aggressive, and by demanding power and prestige. They use others, including their spouses and children, in status seeking and power games. They deny their underlying dependency needs. Our competitive society conditions many men to adopt this growth-inhibiting defense.

"Moving away" type persons are detached and aloof. They have great fear of intimacy and therefore must deny their need for the warmth of human contact. Such persons are essentially loners, who defend against anxiety by distancing. Often they are very conscientious in their work. Many are intellectualizers who keep distance from feelings—their own and others'—by chronic "head trips."

According to Horney, all three of these relational trends are present in everyone. But the relatively healthy person can move among the three flexibly as appropriate in different situations. In contrast, the severely growth-diminished person is frozen into one type of response in all situations. Most people have one trend that is stronger than the others. For example, when I feel threatened I most often use the moving-against defense (a favorite with many of us white, upward-striving males). But I also find myself using unproductive distancing and ingratiating compliance on other occasions.

Horney describes the dynamics of inner conflicts in a way that illuminates the nature of the growth work that many people need to do in therapy or in growth groups. She believed that in our conflicted society, inner conflicts are inescapable. In severely growth-diminished persons these conflicts paralyze creative living. Such persons are like soldiers under fire in a trench. They can live with some safety and even comfort as long as they stay within their defenses, but this position constricts their mobility and freedom severely. So-called neurotic persons seek to resolve conflicts between two sides of their needs (e.g., dependency and autonomy) by ignoring one side and exaggerating the other. Mary, a thirty-two-year-old secretary, adopted the moving-toward defense particularly in relating to men, denying her need for autonomy and assertiveness. But the exaggerated and unrelenting quality of her constant need for male reassurance and approval actually pushed men away. This deprived her of the approval and love that she was attempting to get. Her growth work in therapy focused on learning to recognize, value, and use her repressed assertiveness and to balance her need for love with greater autonomy.

As a practicing therapist, Horney was intimately acquainted with human destructiveness but rejected Freud's view that human beings are inherently destructive. Narcissism is not an inevitable or instinctual phenomenon but results from disturbed early relationships with authoritarian, rejecting, overambitious, or self-sacrificing parents.

> If we want to injure and kill, we do so because we feel endangered, humiliated, abused; because we feel rejected and treated unjustly; because we are or feel interfered with in wishes which are of vital importance to us. That is, if we wish to destroy, it is in order to defend our safety or our happiness or what appears to us as such. Generally speaking, it is for the sake of life and not for the sake of destruction.[15]

Reflecting on her experiences as a therapist, Horney observed that the most powerful forms of anger and guilt that she had encountered were the anger and guilt of unlived life—i.e., of diminished growth.

Horney criticized Freud for his lack of any clear vision of the constructive forces in human beings, his reduction of creativity and love to sublimated libido, and his misunderstanding of strivings toward self-realization as narcissism. Drawing on Albert Schweitzer's use of the terms "optimistic" and "pessimistic" (to mean "world and life affirmation" and "world and life negation") Horney described her own philosophy as follows: "With all its cognizance of the tragic element in neurosis, [it] is an optimistic one."[16]

In contrast to Freud's model of the therapist as detached and impersonal, Horney sees the therapist as a friendly, active person who shows personal concern and sympathy, liking, and respect for the patient. In this way the therapist helps the individual "retrieve his faith in others"[17] by discovering that his fears and hatreds are inappropriate with at least one person.

During Horney's adolescence, turn-of-the-century feminists were emphasizing education for women as a rallying point. With the support of her mother and several of her women friends, the resistance of Horney's father to her going to the gymnasium and on to medical school was overcome. She went on to become a pioneering foremother of contemporary feminist therapists. Three decades before the current writing by feminist therapists, she was publishing papers challenging the blatantly patriarchal presuppositions of Freud. Using the tools and many of the concepts of Freud, she identified his sexist blind spots and pointed to the need for a new psychology of women, understood from the viewpoint of women. She pointed out that Freud had drawn his theory of penis envy entirely from neurotic women and that he had ignored the fact that many men suffer from womb envy. She saw that women are a disadvantaged group in our society and that this cultural reality contributes significantly to their individual psychological problems. In examining the widespread distrust between the sexes, she showed how the patriarchal religion of the Old Testament provided justification for distrust of women and for male dominance. She rightly saw the distrust between men and women as being rooted in the unequal distribution of power between them: "At any given time, the more powerful side will create an ideology suitable to help maintain its position and to make this position more acceptable to the weaker one. . . . It is the function of such an ideology to deny or conceal the existence of a struggle."[18]

In her discussion of the problems of marriage, she shows that many of the difficulties that make good marriages so rare result from the unresolved conflicts people bring to marriage from the ways they are reared as boys and girls—e.g., the unresolved dependency on mothers by the men and the anxiety and low self-esteem produced in women by being trained to respond as submissive and inferior to men.[19] She points to the actual physiological superiority possessed by women in their ability to carry, birth, and nurture new life, showing how many men are envious of this power.[20]

In my work as a pastoral counselor, I find many of Horney's concepts to be valuable for facilitating spiritual growth. She illuminates the dynamics of pathogenic, growth-stifling, guilt- and fear-enhancing religion—the type of beliefs, values, and religious practices that negate joy, freedom, and spiritual creativity. Many people are attracted to such rigid, authoritarian religious orientations because they seem to offer a defense against basic anxiety. Superego religion, which aims at controlling people (oneself and others) through guilt and fear of punishment, helps to create the paralyzing perfectionism of the ideal image. It helps keep people captive of what Horney calls the "tyranny of the oughts and shoulds."

In her early life Horney reacted against her father's stern, dogmatic religion. But she was a spiritual searcher even at seventeen. At that age she wrote a poem in her diary about her struggles to discover inner freedom, the purpose of her life and knowledge of the All. Her daughter, Marianne Horney Eckardt, also a psychoanalyst, describes the poem in this way:

> The poem begins with a restless longing for freedom, and an image of her digging herself out of an old masonry stronghold that a thousand years had built for her. The masonry gives way and buries her. But then her strength stirred, and as the poem continues, "an all-powerful longing . . . drove me forth to wander in order to see, to enjoy, and to know the All. And I wandered—restlessly driven. . . . Released from the dungeon, I joyfully sing in jubilant tones the old song of life, to freedom, to light. But ever so often a question haunts me: What goal am I striving for? . . . And I believe to hear the answer in the murmer of the woods: Rest exists only in the prison's walls. . . . Watchful searching, without complaining; restless striving, but no weary resignation: That is life. Dare to accept."[21]

This same free spirit characterized Horney throughout her life. Paul Tillich shared something of her spiritual journey in this last tribute to her:

> Karen Horney became more and more aware that you cannot listen intensively to people who speak to you, that you cannot even listen to yourself if you do not listen to the voices through which the eternal speaks to us. It was not the voice of traditional religion to which she listened, it was the voices of people, the inner experiences, of nature, of poetry. And in the last year it was the voice from the eastern religion which grasped her heart and made her feel that the limits of an earthly existence are not the limits of our being, that we belong to two orders, although we can only see one of them with our senses. And it was an expression of her indomitable affirmation of life that she chose "reincarnation" as her symbol for the invisible order. More distinctly than in the earlier parts of her life, she heard the sound of the eternal in these last years. But the power of the eternal was always working in her. For the manifestation of the eternal light and love worked in her and through her in all periods of her life.
>
> She knew the darkness of the human soul . . . but she believed that the soul can become a bearer of light. . . . She believed in the light and she had the power to give light to innumerable people. . . . Eternity works in time only if it works in love. And eternity worked love in her. . . . You can heal through insight only if

> insight is united with love. Therefore, many people who felt the light which radiated from her, from her insights and from her love, were healed in soul and body.[22]

Robert Coles, author and child psychiatrist at Harvard, met and had several conversations with Karen Horney when he was a medical student and she was hospitalized in New York City, a few days before her death. Horney knew she was dying. She asked how many women were in his medical school class, and he replied that there were only three out of a hundred students. She asked why that was the case, and they talked about the problems of combining marriage, motherhood, and training in medicine (which she had experienced personally), the resentment of women that many doctors have, and the irony that a profession dedicated to caring for people was so overwhelmingly composed of men. As he left her the last time, she was cordial and hopeful, thanking him for their talk. She spoke of the future: "You are young, and maybe when you reach my age the world will be quite different."[23]

Horney contributed in major ways to making psychoanalytic thought more growth-oriented. Yet, from the growth perspective, there are several limitations in her approach. Although she was keenly aware of the relational and societal roots of individual pathology and health, her therapeutic focus seemed to have remained intrapsychic and individualistic. She explored the *intrapsychic* factors that contribute to problems in marriages but did not emphasize equally crucial *interpersonal* dynamics that reinforce and perpetuate the intrapsychic patterns. As far as I know, she did not work directly with interpersonal systems (such as marriages or families) as such. Her awareness of the societal factors in personal problems apparently did not lead her to emphasize the importance of social and political action to change the pathogenic institutional context in which personal and relational problems proliferate. Although as an analyst she was radical for her times in her feminist views, she lacked the explicit emphasis of radical feminist therapists today on the therapeutic necessity of empowering people in therapy to change the social-political causes of their personal problems. Finally, although the spiritual awareness of her thought increased, particularly in her latter years, the centrality of spiritual-value issues in all human growth was not emphasized explicitly in her therapeutic system.

Resources in the Therapy of Harry Stack Sullivan

Harry Stack Sullivan, founder of the interpersonal school of psychiatry, was born in upstate New York in 1892. During his lonely childhood on his parents' farm, his mother told him tales of their Irish past. One that fascinated him was that one of his ancestors was the West Wind, depicted as a horse running toward the sunrise to meet the future.[24] Sullivan received his M.D. from Chicago Medical College in 1917. He received his psychiatric training with Adolf Meyer at Johns Hopkins and with William Alanson White at Saint Elizabeth's Hospital in Washington, D.C. When Horney and Fromm immigrated to New York, Sullivan discovered that his thought had much in common with theirs. They all shared a strong interest in how cultures affect personal development. The three joined forces for several years. Eventually each developed a distinctive approach while retaining many similarities. Sullivan worked closely with anthropologists Ruth Benedict and Margaret Mead, and with Fromm and Horney as they together challenged classical psychoanalytic theory because of its inadequate instinctual and biological presuppositions. In 1923 Sullivan began teaching and doing research at the University of Maryland Medical School. In 1936 he became a founder of the Washington School of Psychiatry, out of which the William Alanson White Institute of Psychiatry in New York City grew. One of his passionate interests was the application of psychotherapeutic insights to the resolution of social problems. He was active in the formation of the World Federation of Mental Health. He died in 1949 while he was in Paris on a UNESCO project exploring the psychological roots of international conflict.

Sullivan was a kind of remote grandfather figure at the White Institute of Psychiatry when I trained there in the late forties. He still lectured occasionally, and my teachers there reflected the influence of his thought. As a result, his ideas had a considerable impact on the direction of my developing understanding of persons and of therapy. Sullivan was regarded as brilliant and eccentric. (He had five dogs that were in and out of his office most of the time.) Throughout his life he struggled with emotional difficulties and problems in relationships. Awareness of his own problems apparently increased his insight, empathy, and almost maternal compassion for deeply troubled persons. He was known for his remarkable effectiveness in treating young schizophrenics. It is indicative of the esteem in which Sullivan was held that his colleagues assembled his lectures and saw that they were published after his death.

As a therapeutic system-builder, Sullivan is second only to Freud. He was essentially a clinician who wrote for other therapists to communicate what he had learned about his primary concern—how to help deeply troubled people. As I recall from his lectures, his language was very technical and his thought compressed and complicated. It was only when he was describing his work with particular patients that his communication style was dynamic and moving. Since the publication of his lectures (1953–56), appreciation of his contributions has increased. He is now recognized as having made significant contributions to field theory, sociology, and social psychology, as well as to the practice of psychotherapy.[25] His theories seek to show how particular cultures create the warp and woof of personality within them. As a pioneer theoretician he was a foreparent of what eventually became relational and systems approaches to psychotherapy. His understanding of persons offered a fresh, innovative perspective when he introduced it. His primary focus was on blocked growth (pathology) in people he described as "inferior caricatures of what they might have been." But, from his clinical experience, he developed a theory of personality that provides resources which are useful for facilitating growth in people all along the continuum of wholeness.

The central motif of Sullivan's thought is his *interpersonalism*—the conviction that personality is essentially and inescapably interpersonal. All human experiences, even those which seem most solitary, are actually interpersonal in their essence. A man fishing alone in a boat, when he catches a big one, thinks immediately of whom he will tell or he fantasizes the response of persons to his success as a fisherman. Sullivan saw that what goes on *within* people is always intertwined with what goes on *between* them and others. Except on the most abstract level, the within and the between are inseparable. In Sullivan's view it is unproductive to try to define the psychological attributes of individuals (drives, impulses, and such) as though they existed in isolation. To do so simply reflects the inadequacies of our individualistic thought patterns and language. What we refer to as the psychology of individuals is actually a description of persons' patterns of interactions with others—past, present, and future (in fantasy). The most effective way to understand or help people change is to approach them as *selves-in-relationships.* Constructive changes can best be facilitated in individuals by perceiving them in this interpersonal way.

When individuals come for counseling or therapy, it often is illuminating to see them through the interpersonal perspective. This perspective reminds one that persons are the organizing center of their interpersonal network; that who they are is an expression of the quality of their most significant relationships, past and present; that they still carry within them hurts from past relationships; that their present relational system sustains and reinforces their diminished growth; that their hurt will be healed only if they can establish more growthful relationships as they move into the future. As systems therapies emphasize more than did Sullivan, intrapsychic growth is best sustained by constructive interpersonal change.

As was true of Adler, Horney, Fromm, and Assagioli, Sullivan saw the self as having a central role in the organization of all behavior. The "self system," as Sullivan called it, develops out of the child's experiences of the reflected appraisals of need-fulfilling or need-depriving adults in early life. The self system plays a powerful role in enabling persons to meet the two sets of basic human needs—the need for *bodily satisfaction* (food, sleep, sex, closeness to people) and *interpersonal security* (esteem, belongingness, acceptance, the power to meet one's needs). Self-esteem is derived both from the internalized appraisals of significant others in early life and from developing the power to satisfy one's basic needs. In working with persons suffering from damaged self-esteem, Sullivan's insights are particularly useful. Such persons still bear the burden of negative appraisals by adults in their early lives. Their feelings of self-worth will be enhanced both by experiencing and internalizing esteem from significant others (e.g., the therapist or growth group members) and from increasing their competence and power to meet their basic needs.

Sullivan, like Horney, uses anxiety as a key working concept. Anxiety is always an interpersonal phenomenon. Its essence is fear of disapproval. An infant absorbs parental values automatically and empathetically in order to reduce this painful fear. Anxiety is the force by which, for better or worse, the personality's basic contours are molded in early childhood. Children feel anxiety when they go against the culturally approved values as these are embodied in the values of their parents. Children learn to organize their behavior to meet their needs according to culture's values and thereby feel the security of a deeply felt sense of well-being and belonging.

Sullivan's insights about anxiety, cultural values, and self-esteem are particularly useful in parent training and growth experiences. Most parents would like to rear children with constructive values and sturdy self-respect. It often helps them implement this desire to see how their children's esteem is deeply influenced by the evaluations they as parents communicate continually to them and how their children's values are determined, to a considerable degree, by the real values of themselves as parents.

Sullivan understood disordered behavior such as schizophrenia as a pattern of inappropriate and ineffective responses that aim at coping with an overload of anxiety. This is caused by confused and inconsistent relationships in which children cannot learn to avoid overwhelming anxiety. Ineffectively coping with this overload of anxiety produces severely distorted perceiving, thinking, feeling, and relating.

Three patterns of self-referent responses ("personifications" of oneself) develop in children out of their relationships during infancy. *Good-me* feelings are learned in relationships where behavior produces satisfactions and security. *Bad-me* feelings are learned in anxiety-producing situations. The "good me" and "bad me" personifications belong to the self-system. Which one predominates most of the time depends on the need-satisfying quality of early relationships. *Not-me* feelings result from experiences of "primitive anxiety," horror, and loathing, which is beyond verbal description. Not-me feelings appear in images in nightmares and in schizophrenic episodes. (Sullivan saw "bad dreams" as constructive in that they discharge impulses that otherwise might be overwhelming.) Most of us have experienced the polarity of the good-me, bad-me feelings.

Sullivan's view of wholeness, like Freud's, was essentially developmental. His schema of the sequence of life stages defines them, however, by significant change in relationships rather than in terms of internal instinctual development. His six-stage approach complements and corrects the intrapsychic focus of Freud's developmental schema. Stage 1: *Infancy* extends from birth to the development of speech (a learning that alters interpersonal relationships profoundly). During this first period one absorbs good-me and bad-me feelings empathically. Stage 2: *Childhood* extends to maturation of the need and capacity for peer playmates. Stage 3: *Juvenile era* extends to the maturation of the need and capacity for intimate relationships with one's age peers. The child goes to school and must learn to compete and cooperate with peers and to relate to authorities outside the family. Sullivan believed, as did Adler, Horney, and Fromm, that personality is not fixed in early childhood unless the self-system is so crippled by anxiety as to be largely out of touch with reality. Stage 4: *Preadolescence* is the same-sex chum period, which extends to maturation of genital sexuality. Stage 5: *Adolescence:* Early adolescence focuses on the initial patterning of behavior to satisfy sexual intimacy and security needs. Late adolescence extends to the establishment of an intimate love relationship in which the other person is nearly as important as oneself. Stage 6: *Adulthood:* This is the goal of the developmental process by which one becomes, in this stage, a participant in the adult culture. Sullivan describes the healthy adult who has successfully finished the growth stages through adolescence in almost euphoric terms:

> The person comes forth with self-respect adequate to almost any situation, with the respect for others that this competent self-respect entails, with the dignity that benefits the high achievement of competent personality, and with the freedom of personal initiative that represents a comfortable adaptation of one's personal situation to the circumstances that characterize the social order of which one is a part.[26]

Sullivan's descriptions of growth from the interpersonal perspective can provide valuable insights for anyone interested in facilitating optimal development in children and youth.[27]

A serious deficiency in Sullivan's developmental schema is his lack of awareness of the possibilities of continuing to develop throughout the adult stages of life. Like Freud, Sullivan made the fallacious assumption that the die is cast at the end of adolescence and that only intense psychotherapy can effect significant changes.

There was a winsome humanity about Sullivan that emphasized the essential humanness of all persons, including the most disturbed. In discussing the mentally ill, he wrote, "We are all much more human than anything else."[28] His view of the therapist is that of a "participant observer." To facilitate growth one must *be there,* participating as a full human being in the therapeutic relationship. But one must also be an observer who can see what ordinarily is missed and thus help bring clearer understanding of what is occurring in the person and in the relationship. The therapist must function and communicate on these two levels simultaneously.

Sullivan's trust in the healing-growth *elan* is clear in this comment about therapy: "If we clear away the obstacles (to effective relationships) everything else will take care of itself. I have never found myself called upon to 'cure' anyone."[29] Apparently Sullivan's awareness of his own inner problems served to prevent him from taking a condescending attitude toward patients. His basic therapeutic attitude seemed to be: "Despite my inescapable emotional difficulties and personality warps, I will work with troubled people to help them achieve better relationships and more inner strength. Hopefully both of us will learn and grow in the process."[30]

Sullivan's commitment to using psychological and psychiatric understanding to help resolve social problems is one of his significant contributions to a growth-oriented "persons-in-relationships-in-society" approach. He lived only a few years into the atomic age, but he had a vivid concern about our new fearsome capacity to end all human history. He worked with a kind of missionary zeal to rally the mental health community behind the work of UNESCO and the World Health Organization. His essay entitled "Remobilizing for Enduring Peace and Social Progress"[31] communicates his sense of the urgency of the task and his conviction that the social sciences and psychotherapy offer important resources that may help us survive and develop a new age for humankind. Sullivan saw persons in the psychological and psychotherapeutic professions as among the builders of the future.

There are several limitations in Sullivan's thought when viewed from the growth perspective. Although he was aware of the positive potentials that are wasted in disturbed people, he did not have a thoroughgoing, explicit growth orientation in his understanding of therapy. His theories, derived mainly from severely disturbed people, have "the odor of the clinic." Although his theory of personality was profoundly interpersonal, he apparently did not move beyond focusing on one individual at a time in therapy. He had a dawning vision that eventually led other therapists who shared it to treat interpersonal systems directly. But he did not take this giant therapeutic step himself. Sullivan tended to overgeneralize on some of his theories, reducing complex human responses to oversimplified explanation. For example, he sees anxiety as derived entirely from the fear of disapproval. Though this *is* a major source of anxiety, it is only one of several sources. To my knowledge, Sullivan had no interest in facilitating positive spiritual growth. In spite of these weaknesses, Sullivan's system provides valuable insights on which growth-centered counselors and therapists can build. To his credit he was a therapist who sought to be a builder of the future.

For Further Exploration of Growth Resources in Fromm's Therapy

Fromm, Erich. *Escape from Freedom.* New York: Rinehart and Co., 1941. Explores the reasons that freedom is so threatening, and the escapes into conformity and authoritarianism.

———. *Man for Himself: An Inquiry into the Psychology of Ethics.* New York: Rinehart and Co., 1947. A discussion of the possibilities and problems of a psychoanalytically based humanistic ethic.

———. *Psychoanalysis and Religion.* New Haven: Yale University Press, 1950. He sets forth his views on the universal human need for religion, Freud's and Jung's views of religion, and the psychoanalyst as physician of the soul.

———. *The Sane Society.* New York: Rinehart and Co., 1955. Examines the pathology of normalcy in our society and the creation of a society in which human needs will be fulfilled.

———. *The Art of Loving.* New York: Harper, 1956. A popular discussion of the nature and practice of life in a society in which love has disintegrated.

———. *The Anatomy of Human Destructiveness.* New York: Holt, Rinehart and Winston, 1973. A depth exploration of the major theories of human destructiveness and a presentation of Fromm's conceptions of the various types of aggression.

For Further Exploration of Growth Resources in the Therapy of Karen Horney

Horney, Karen. *Our Inner Conflicts, A Constructive Theory of Neurosis.* New York: W. W. Norton, 1945. An exposition of her major theories, including the three defensive ways of relating and the idealized image.

———. *Neurosis and Human Growth.* New York: W. W. Norton, 1950. A restatement and refinement of her earlier works, emphasizing the motif of human growth.

———. *Feminine Psychology.* New York: W. W. Norton, 1967. A collection of Horney's pioneering papers on the psychology of women and our sexist society.

Kelman, Harold. *Helping People: Karen Horney's Psychoanalytic Approach.* New York: Science House, 1971. A systematic presentation of Horney's therapeutic concepts and methods; begins with two biographical chapters.

For Further Exploration of Growth Resources from Sullivan's Therapy

Chapman, A. H. *Harry Stack Sullivan, His Life and His Work.* New York: Putnam's, 1976. Includes a biography and chapters on Sullivan's views on personality development and psychotherapy, and the relevance of Sullivan to current social dilemmas.

Mullahy, Patrick, ed. *The Contributions of Harry Stack Sullivan.* New York: Science House, 1967. A symposium on interpersonal theory in social science and psychiatry, including papers by Clara Thompson and Gardner Murphy.

Sullivan, Harry Stack. *Collected Works,* 2 vols. New York: W. W. Norton, 1965.

———. *The Interpersonal Theory of Psychiatry.* New York: W. W. Norton, 1953. Sullivan's description of the developmental epochs.

———. *The Psychiatric Interview.* New York: W. W. Norton, 1954. Describes the structuring and process of psychiatric interviews.

———. *Schizophrenia as a Human Process.* New York: W. W. Norton, 1965. Sullivan's insightful exploration of schizophrenia.

Chapter 4

Growth Resources in Traditional Psychotherapies

Carl Jung, the Existentialists, Carl Rogers

Growth Resources from Carl G. Jung

Carl Gustav Jung was born in Kesswil on Lake Constance in Switzerland in 1875. His father was a clergyman. Carl was very precocious, reading Latin books at age six. To escape his loneliness and the marital conflicts of his parents, he often played for hours alone in the attic with a wooden figure he had carved for himself. Feeling isolated from the external world, he turned to the inner world of his own dreams, fantasies, and thoughts.[1] When he entered the University of Basel he chose to study medicine and later psychiatry because those disciplines seemed to combine both of his major interests—science and the humanities.

At twenty-five Jung became an intern at one of the most progressive psychiatric centers in Europe, the Burghölzli Mental Hospital in Zurich. From then on, Zurich was his home. By age thirty, he was chief of the clinic and a lecturer in psychiatry at the University of Zurich. He wrote a book reporting his research on schizophrenia, developed the word-association test, and introduced the terms "intravert" and "extravert." Jung married Emma Rauchenbach. They had five children. His wife trained as a psychologist and lectured at the Jung Institute, which was established in 1948.

When Jung became convinced of the validity of many of Freud's ideas, he wrote to him, sending a copy of his book on schizophrenia. Freud invited him to Vienna. When they first met, the two men talked almost non-stop for thirteen hours. A close friendship developed between them. For a time, Freud considered Jung his logical successor. But Jung could not accept Freud's reductionism and his insistance that the roots of all psychopathology are sexual. Freud was troubled by Jung's interest in and views on religion. The break between them finally came when Jung published a book in 1912 developing the view that libido is basically generalized life energy rather than always being sexual. The rupture of their relationship was painful to both men. Jung experienced three years of depression during which he felt that he was going insane. On the surface he was a respected psychiatrist with a thriving private practice, a university lectureship, and a large family. But underneath, Jung felt he was losing contact with reality and that life had lost all meaning. He wrote little and resigned his lectureship because he felt he could not teach. His efforts to treat his problem by attempting to understand it intellectually were to no avail. In desperation, he decided to surrender to the impulses of his unconscious. These led him to build a model village out of small rocks, reliving a time in his childhood when he loved to play with blocks. This play therapy was the turning point of his crisis. He discovered that "the small boy is still around."[2] Playing with the village of stones opened him to a prolonged exploration into his unconscious during the next two years, following his inner images, fantasies, and dreams. What he discovered in his unconscious was like "a stream of lava, and the heat of its fires reshaped his life."[3] From this traumatic mid-years crisis Jung developed a new center and meaning for his life, and a new understanding of personality which he called "analytic psychology." He came to focus increasingly on the resources of the unconscious as revealed in myths, symbols, art, folk tales, dreams, and fantasies. He traveled to Africa and India to study non-Western folklore and symbols. He also came to New Mexico to study the symbols and myths of the Pueblo Indians.

During his recovery from a near-fatal heart attack at sixty-nine, Jung had a series of visions. These precipitated a highly productive period during which he wrote some of his most original and creative books. Of this experience of illumination he later wrote: "I might formulate it as an affirmation of things as they are: an unconditional 'yes' to that which is, without subjective protests—acceptance of the conditions of existence as I see them and understand them, acceptance of my own nature, as I happen to be."[4] After a remarkably productive lifetime of research, writing, and psychotherapeutic practice, Jung died in 1961 at the age of eighty-six.

Some of Jung's insights anticipated similar thrusts in therapies such as gestalt and psychosynthesis. The resources I will now highlight are those which I have found useful in facilitating growth work.

Jung insisted (as did Rank) that creativity is at the center of every person's potential. But he was keenly aware of the ways it is wasted in most people: "The art of life is the most distinguished and rarest of all arts. . . . For so many people all too much unlived life remains over . . . and so they approach the threshold of old age with unsatisfied claims which inevitably turn their glances backward."[5] Jung's essential growth-centeredness comes through clearly in this criticism of Freud's pathology-orientation: "I prefer to look at man *[sic]* in the light of what in him is healthy and sound, and to free the sick man from that point of view which colors every page Freud has written. Freud's teaching is definitely one-sided in that it generalizes from facts that are relevant only to neurotic states of mind; its validity is really confined to those states. . . . Freud's is not a psychology of the healthy mind."[6] He saw psychopathology as rooted in undeveloped resources in persons: "Hidden in the neurosis is a bit of still undeveloped personality, a precious fragment of the psyche lacking which a man is condemned to resignation, bitterness, and everything else that is hostile to life. A psychology of neurosis that sees only the negative elements empties out the baby with the bath-water."[7] He saw that there is a natural process and drive toward wholeness in all persons, on which therapy must depend: "The driving force . . . seems to be in essence only an urge toward self-realization."[8] Therapy is simply a way of facilitating and accelerating this natural developmental process.

Jung called the process of moving toward wholeness "individuation." He wrote: "Individuation means becoming a single, homogeneous being and, in so far as 'individuality' embraces our innermost . . . and incomparable uniqueness, it also implies becoming one's own self. We could therefore translate individuation as 'coming to selfhood' or 'self realization.' "[9]

Jung distinguishes between the *ego*—the center of consciousness—and the *self,* which potentially is the integrating center of the whole personality. The process of wholeness involves the harmonious integration of all aspects of the personality, and the movement of one's center from the conscious ego to the self, which integrates both the conscious and the unconscious personality resources. Wholeness involves the union of opposites. Whole persons have their four psychic functions—thinking, feeling, sensing, and intuition—in balance and available for use when appropriate, even though one function is usually dominant.

Although each person's individuation journey is unique, there are four general dimensions of the process. The first is the unveiling of the *persona,* the mask of social roles by which we relate and express ourselves to the world. The *persona* has both constructive and destructive possibilities. Those who are overidentified with their social roles and overinvested in the impression they are making on the outside world need therapeutic assistance to reduce the rigidity and weight of their *persona* so that it will not exhaust their creative energy. Yet, a healthy *persona* is necessary to protect us from the full impact of social attitudes and forces.

The second stage of individuation involves confronting our *shadow,* the rejected aspects of our personalities which we consider inferior and in conflict with our *persona,* standards, and ideals, and therefore have repressed into our personal unconscious. Jung held that repressed memories and desires become organized around the shadow, forming a hidden, negative self, which is the shadow of our ego. As long as the shadow is repressed and unrecognized it tends to be projected onto others (as in scapegoating) and to dominate us without our being aware of it. Although in dreams the shadow often appears as a dark, primitive, or repellent figure, it is a potential source of spontaneity, instinctual energy, and creativity. As the shadow becomes conscious in therapy, the rejected parts of ourselves are reclaimed, causing it to lose much of its dangerous quality and its ability to dominate the inner life.

The third growth stage of individuation is to confront one's "soul image," the *anima* or the *animus*. Jung held that in the unconscious of women there is an *animus* and in a man an *anima*. These are contrasexual psychic structures around which focus all those tendencies and experiences that do not fit one's self-definition as a woman or a man. This part of the unconscious appears in dreams as a person of the other sex. As long as this structure is unconscious, persons tend to project it onto persons of the other sex, and to love it or reject it there. In marriage counseling it is often helpful if couples can develop some awareness of how much of their unproductive conflict results from their projection of unaccepted aspects of themselves onto the other person, where these attributes are related to with deep ambivalence. For example, a "macho" man and very "feminine" woman each fears, represses, and projects onto the other those feelings and tendencies in themselves that don't fit the rigid sex-role stereotypes of their culture. If the man can reclaim his rejected *anima* and the woman her *animus,* they will be more whole, androgynous people. If such a man can reclaim his soft, vulnerable, feelingful side, and the woman her rational, assertive, analytic side, they will no longer need to either worship or fight these sides of themselves in each other.

The fourth stage of individuation involves developing one's true self as the integrating nucleus of the whole personality, conscious and unconscious. In the self, the opposites can be reconciled in complementary union. The ego is still the center of consciousness, but the self becomes the center of the whole personality. The self is the divine spark, the image of God within each person. Jung wrote: "I thank God every day that I have been permitted to experience the *imago Dei* in me."[10] The self is often symbolized in dreams as a mandala, a circle, or by some symbol of divinity. Jung's concept of the self is very similar to Assagioli's "higher Self," and to the idea of the soul in the Christian tradition. Each refers to the same vital truth—that there is a dimension of transcendence in us human beings and that we are whole only when this dimension becomes the center of our personhood.

Jung believed that the unconscious (which is 90 percent of the psyche) provides the major resources necessary for moving toward wholeness. The unconscious expresses itself mainly in symbols. In contrast to Freud's view, he understood the unconscious as "a great repository of creativeness" which can be used for good or for ill. Prior to the process of individuation, the shadow, the anima, and the self are all unconscious. As they are brought into consciousness, as one's self-awareness grows, they enrich that dimension of personality tremendously.

The deepest level of personality, the *collective unconscious,* represents our psychological heritage from the long story of evolution. It is also our connection with all that now is. The archetypal images of the collective unconscious can be understood as universal symbols of our common human experiences. They appear in many parts of the world in folk tales, legends, and myths, as well as in the dreams and fantasies of individuals.

Even if one does not take all Jung's views about the collective unconscious literally, it seems evident that there is within us a deep level where we are not alone but instead are somehow related to the whole of humankind, history, and nature. The imperfect but meaningful image that expresses a part of what I understand Jung to mean by the collective unconscious is that of a fruit orchard. Each tree has its individual life, unique identity, and space. Yet all the trees are grounded in the same soil, experience the flow of common streams of water and nutrients through the soil, and interact with the same energizing air and sunlight. Each tree interacts with the environment in unique ways that express its own nature and potential—e.g., apple trees produce apples, plum trees produce plums. So it is with us human beings. Each of us is unique and autonomous; yet at the deepest level of our beings, we all are interrelated in a great interdependent network of living things within which we are called to live with sensitivity and caring. Opening ourselves to this transpersonal dimension of ourselves can enhance the sense of meaningful relatedness to the whole ecosystem. This can provide the basis for the ecological consciousness and caring on which our collective survival on spaceship earth may well depend.

Dreams, as the major form of communication from the unconscious, play a decisive role in Jungian as they do in Freudian therapy. But Jung understood dreams very differently from Freud. He saw them as messages from the unconscious, luring us toward greater wholeness. Learning to understand the messages of one's dreams by "befriending"[11] them (rather than analyzing them) is vitally important in removing the blocks and claiming the resources of growth in the unconscious. Frightening dreams reveal those aspects of ourselves which we have rejected and which return as self-created "demons" to stymie our potentializing. When these aspects of ourselves are befriended and reintegrated, they become resources rather than blocks to our growth. The unconscious is the source from which religious experience flows. This conception led one Jungian pastoral counselor, John A. Sanford, to speak of dreams as "God's forgotten language." This view is very similar to the understanding of dreams in the Bible.

There is in Jung a sense of the relational nature of wholeness that has deep affinities with the interpersonalism of Martin Buber. Jung wrote:

> The unrelated human being lacks wholeness, for he can achieve wholeness only through the soul, and the soul cannot exist without its other side, which is always found in a "You."
>
> Individuation has two principal aspects: in the first place it is an internal and subjective process of integration, and in the second it is an equally indispensable process of objective relationship. Neither can exist without the other, although sometimes the one and sometimes the other predominates.[12]

> The living mystery of life is always hidden between Two, and it is the true mystery which cannot be betrayed by words and depleted by arguments.[13]

Jung was much more hopeful and optimisitic than Freud about human beings and their potentializing. Yet, he had a keen awareness of the powerful obstacles and resistances to growth. He wrote, "People will do anything, no matter how absurd, in order to avoid facing their own souls."[14] Each stage of individuation has its dangers and difficulties. In his discussion of marriage as a psychological relationship, he observed, "There is no birth of consciousness without pain."[15]

Jung had a continuing interest in understanding human destructiveness and evil. In reflecting on our world he warned: "Today as never before it is important that human beings should not overlook the danger of the evil lurking within them. . . . Psychology must insist on the reality of evil and must reject any definition that regards it as insignificant or actually nonexistent."[16] Persons become destructive when the opposites within them—conscious-unconscious, introvert-extrovert, *persona*-shadow, and so on—are alienated from each other. The unconscious becomes destructive only when it is cut off from consciousness by repression. As an individual gradually claims and develops the neglected dimensions of the unconscious and integrates these balancing aspects with consciousness, the destructiveness of the reclaimed dimensions is transformed so that they feed the creativity of the person's inner life.

Jung had a strong sense of the many ways in which cultures block individuation. He criticized modern Western societies for having lost touch with the individual, with the mythical and the symbolic, and for having overemphasized the development of the rational, analytical, and mechanical aspects of life. Because of the widespread alienation of people from the resources of their unconscious, modern society breeds psychological problems as a swamp breeds mosquitos.

Jung believed that spiritual growth is a central, indispensable dimension of all movement toward wholeness. He saw the religious need of humankind as so universal and powerful that he regarded it as an innate instinct in all human beings: "However far-fetched it may sound, experience shows that many neuroses are caused by the fact that people blind themselves to their own religious promptings. . . . The psychologist of today ought to realize once and for all that we are no longer dealing with questions of dogma and creed. A religious attitude is an element in psychic life whose importance can hardly be overrated."[17] Jung believed that the discovery of adequate meaning is essential for human growth and health. "It is only meaning that liberates."[18] Much of the suffering and many of the problems of people today are derived directly from the lack of meaning in their lives. "Man *[sic]* needs general ideas and convictions that will give a meaning to his life and enable him to find a place for himself in the universe. He can stand the almost incredible hardships when he is convinced that they make sense; he is crushed when on top of all his misfortunes, he has to admit that he is taking part in a 'tale told by an idiot.' It is the role of religious symbols to give a meaning to the life of man."[19]

Jung had a deep appreciation for the spiritual riches of the great Eastern and esoteric traditions, which he saw as balancing and complementing the Western religious traditions. It is the nonrational, mythical, symbolic, and mystical aspects of religions that are healing and growth producing, according to him. Completely demythologized religions lose their power to be channels through which we can appropriate the riches of the unconscious. Religion, in its mythical and mystical aspects, is needed today to save us from our culture's mass-mindedness. Scientific rationalism, which makes "objective," quantifiable knowledge the only real spiritual authority, feeds mass-mindedness. It causes us to forget that "the distinctive thing about real facts . . . is their individuality."[20] Inner experiences of transcendence are our best defense against losing our sense of individuality in the mass. Religion, according to Jung, can help us balance the overpowering influence of objective "reason" and external reality by keeping us in touch with the rich, nonrational side of reality, and giving us a point of reference that transcends society and all the statistical generalizations on which scientific rationalism focuses. Freud saw and reacted against the old arrogance of religion. Jung saw and reacted to the new arrogance of science.[21]

Jung's approach to growth offers particularly rich resources for the growth tasks of the second half of life. He believed that the approaches of Freud and Adler could help people master the growth tasks of the years before thirty-five, which focus mainly on coping constructively with the external world. But the goals of growth and therapy change radically in the second half. As Jung put it: "We must distinguish between a psychology of the morning of life and a psychology of its afternoon."[22] Jung described the mid-years crisis in this way: "No wonder that many bad neuroses appear at the onset of life's afternoon. It is a sort of second puberty, another 'storm and stress' period, not infrequently accompanied by tempests of passion—the 'dangerous age.' But the problems that crop up at this age are no longer to be solved by the old recipes. The hands of this clock cannot be put back."[23]

Growth work in the second half of life must be inner-directed. The meanings that were found in the outer world in the first half, must now be found within oneself. The mid-years crisis is, at its heart, a spiritual crisis. The values, meanings, and spiritual experiences of one's earlier life must be revised and deepened if one is to cope with the problems and develop the potentials of the second half. Jung wrote: "Among all my patients in the second half of life . . . there has not been one whose problem in the last resort was not that of finding a religious outlook on life. It is safe to say that every one of them fell ill because he had lost that which the living religions of every age have given to their followers, and none of them has been really healed who did not regain his religious outlook."[24]

For many people, growth work in life's second half involves claiming the neglected resources in their "other side," their *anima* or *animus,* and developing whichever of their four psychic functions have been neglected earlier. A man (myself, for example) whose assertive, rational, out-directed side was overdeveloped in his earlier years, needs in the mid-years to balance this by developing his soft, intuitive, relational, feelingful side. Similarly, a woman who overinvested herself in her feelingful, caring, and relating side during her family-nurturing years, needs to develop her neglected rational and assertive side (expressed perhaps in a job outside the home). It is, of course, better for men and women to develop balanced personalities early in life.

One thing I find useful in facilitating the growth of work addicts is Jung's affirmation of the pleasure principle. To the degree that we are whole, we can enjoy the psychological, interpersonal, and spiritual pleasures of our rich, many-leveled psyches. Whereas Freud put his trust ultimately in reason and the control of the pleasure principle by the ego (guided by the reality principle), Jung trusted the nonrational, mystical, artistic side of human experience. He saw the glorification of the rational, divorced from this other side, as destructive to individuals and to society. There is something playful about Jung's style that feels liberating and energizing to me. His use of "active imagination" and art in therapy, and his view of the value of fantasies, are expressions of this spirit:

> Truth to tell, I have a very high opinion of fantasy. To me, it is actually the maternally creative side of the masculine spirit. . . . All the works of man *[sic]* have their origin in creative fantasy. . . . The creative activity of the imagination frees man from his bondage to the "nothing but" and liberates in him *the spirit of play*. As Schiller says, man is completely human only when he is playing.[25]

It seems clear that Jung's robust emphasis on the use of intuitive and playful modalities in therapy is one reason for the effectiveness of this approach. Such activities probably produce change by energizing the resources of the right hemisphere of the brain, in both client and therapist. Such an emphasis is needed to complement and balance the rational, analytical (left-brain) modalities, which have dominated most traditional therapies.

Jung's understanding of growth-enabling therapists emphasized *their* own continuing growth. Analyst and analysand work together on a shared inner journey in which the analyst must also be open to change. In spite of his fascination with theory, Jung observed: "It is a remarkable thing about psychotherapy: you . . . can cure only from one central point; and that consists in understanding the patient as a psychological whole and approaching him as a human being, leaving aside all theory and listening attentively to whatever he has to say."[26] As I reflect on the ups and downs in my counseling relationships through the years, I can resonate to Jung's observation that one can recognize effective therapy by the fact that both the therapist and the client change and grow.

Jung believed that effective therapists must be involved in the life of the world and open to learning from it:

> The critical state of things [socially and politically] has such a tremendous influence on the psychic life of the individual that the doctor must follow its effects with more than usual attention. . . . He cannot afford to withdraw to the peaceful island of undisturbed scientific work, but must constantly descend into the arena of world events, in order to join in the battle of conflicting passions and opinions. Were he to remain aloof from the tumult, the calamity of his time would reach him only from afar, and his patient's suffering would find neither ear nor understanding. He would be at a loss to know how to . . . help him out of his isolation.[27]
>
> Therefore anyone who wants to know the human psyche would be better advised to bid farewell to his study and wander with human heart through the world. There, in the horrors of prisons, lunatic asylums and hospitals, in drab suburban pubs, in brothels and gambling-halls, in the salons of the elegant, the Stock Exchanges, Socialist meetings, churches, revivalist gatherings and ecstatic sects, through love and hate, through the experiences of passion in every form in his body, he would reap richer stores of knowledge than textbooks a foot thick could give him, and he will know how to doctor the sick with real knowledge of the human soul.[28]

Although Jung's seminal thought offers invaluable growth resources, there are limitations to his system as a total growth therapy. The "mystic" side of me is drawn to some of his esoteric theories. But the danger in this side of Jung's thought is that it lends itself to those who need to make of a therapy a kind of esoteric religion. Jung says some very wise and growthful things, but he sometimes says them in an unnecessarily complicated and speculative way. The highly speculative theories, on which his obviously wise thoughts are allegedly based, often seem superfluous. Many of his ideas stand on their own as valid and useful, independent of the theories.

The central thrust of Jung's system is more growth enabling for outer-directed, extraverted people, in my experience, than for those who are inner-directed. Many of us (in our society, which so values extraversion) *do* neglect the riches of our inner worlds—the riches that the artists and mystics of all cultures have explored. For those of us whose inner world is impoverished, Jung's invitation to explore this vast terrain can help us move toward a more balanced awareness of the inner and outer worlds. But some people who are already too inward-turning become even more so as Jungians, investing enormous energy in a seemingly endless exploration of inner reality. The resources in Jung's system, to be used most constructively, need to be balanced by a strong reality-therapy thrust in the therapist. Such a dual thrust is more likely to produce a balance between the inner and the outer reality (which was what Jung meant by wholeness).

From the perspective of feminist psychologists and therapists, Jung is both good and bad news. He recognized and valued the so-called "feminine side" of the psyche (and also of God), which Freud had misunderstood and denigrated. He also showed how wholeness, in both men and women, must involve an integration of both the so-called masculine and feminine sides of their personalities. But in two ways, Jung reflected and reinforced rather than challenged the sexism of his (and our) culture. By labeling the two sides of the psyche "masculine" and "feminine," he unwittingly helped reinforce cultural stereotypes. The soft, nurturing, feelingful side and the assertive, rational, analytical side are *human* capacities in persons of both sexes. In his writings on women it is clear that he misunderstood their traditional home-centered roles, seeing them as normative expressions of inherent biological necessity. Naomi Goldenberg, a psychologist trained in Jungian therapy, declares: "The anima/animus model and its goal of unification works better for men than for women. The model supports stereotyped notions of what masculine and feminine are by adding mystification to guard against change in the social sphere, where women are at a huge disadvantage."[29]

Jung's therapy, like most traditional and contemporary therapies, was essentially apolitical in that he did not see the therapeutic value and, in the case of obviously oppressed people, the *necessity* of helping to empower and motivate those in therapy to work to change growth-oppressive social systems. His brilliant critique of modern society did not prevent his therapy from being weakened by its hyperindividualism.

Growth Resources from the Existential Therapists

A young woman who knew she had been born out of wedlock, unwanted, the result of an accident, struggled in therapy with her haunting sense of rejection and anxiety. She lamented: "I feel I have no right to be!" The issues that she was confronting are those which existential therapists regard as crucial in all therapy—the existential anxiety that stems from the awareness that one might not have been; one's basic sense of identity; and the deep need to be affirmed in one's very essence or being. When such fundamental human issues are ignored by therapists, the growth-enabling effects of their therapy are reduced. The uniqueness of the existential therapies lies not in their methods but in their underlying philosophical assumptions. A variety of therapeutic approaches —from Ludwig Binswanger's psychoanalytic approach to Viktor Frankl's neo-Adlerian methodology—have been associated with the existentialist position in philosophy.[30] The existential therapists hold that therapists' basic philosophical assumptions about the human situation have a profound influence on everything they do in the practice of their art—how they perceive and relate to the client, how they understand the causes of human problems, how they use particular techniques, and how they understand the growth possibilities inherent in crises situations.

I now can reaffirm with even greater conviction (having experienced the existential confrontations of the mid-years) what I wrote earlier:

> The clergyman-counselor's *[sic]* effectiveness will be increased if he immerses himself in the existentialist perspective in psychotherapy. Its emphasis on values, awareness, creativity, freedom (choice and responsibility), authenticity, existential anxiety (and also existential guilt and joy), being, actualization, encounter, confirmation, dialogue, and meaning are all consistent with a religious view of human beings.[31]

The basic philosophy of the existential therapies and its understanding of the nature of human growth is also an invaluable resource for growth-oriented secular counselors and therapists.

My own thinking and practice of counseling and therapy have been challenged and enriched through the years by the existentialist views of the human situation. I was first influenced by the impact of Paul Tillich's theology and its underlying existentialist philosophy in his classes at Union Theological Seminary and through my discussions with him as he advised me on my Ph.D. dissertation. My occasional contacts with Rollo May (at the White Institute of Psychiatry and in the Columbia Seminar on Religion and Health) awakened my awareness of the psychotherapeutic relevance of the existential perspective. In more recent years, therapeutic theories of Viktor Frankl and James Bugental have added further existential input to my thinking. I now see that the underlying philosophy on which Growth Counseling is based as a variation on the existential theme. In this section I will discuss some working concepts from the existential therapies that are useful in helping people increase the depth and effectiveness of their growth work. It will be evident, as I explore these themes, that there are prominent existentialist thrusts in several other therapies, including those of Jung, Perls, Assagioli, and Rogers.

The guiding motif in the existentialist therapies is an emphasis on the uniquely human qualities in all people—e.g., freedom, choice, valuing, awareness, creativity—and on the distinctiveness of each individual. Therapy aims at helping people develop their own authentic being-in-the-world. The working concepts of these therapies are all variations on this underlying theme.

The problems that bring people to therapy are essentially unconstructive ways of attempting to deal with existential anxiety.

> Anxiety in general is the response of the human organism to anything that is perceived as a threat to what one regards as essential to one's welfare or safety. Pathological (neurotic) anxiety arises when contradictory impulses, desires or needs clamor simultaneously for expression or satisfaction. It is the result of inner conflict. It serves the function of keeping material that is acceptable to the self-image repressed. In contrast, existential anxiety is nonpathological or normal anxiety. It arises from the very nature of human existence.[32]

We human beings are the animals who know we will die. We are trapped by our roots in nature with its aging, sickness, tragedy, and eventual death. This existential reality is made profoundly painful by the fact that we are aware on some level (usually not conscious) that we are living-dying creatures. We know that today we are one day closer to death than we were yesterday. This awareness of our mortality is like the background music that plays constantly in many settings, but to which ordinarily we do not consciously listen. Even though we try in countless ways to ignore or blot out the awareness of our finitude, it colors everything we feel, think, and do. Our eventual death and the many forms of living death (e.g., meaninglessness) affect the quality of our consciousness, our relationships, our creativity, and every other aspect of our living.

Psychopathology and the neurotic anxiety that fuels it are abortive attempts to cope with existential anxiety. To paraphrase Tillich's insight, neuroses are ineffective attempts to escape nonbeing by not allowing ourselves to be. Or, as Horney put it, neurotic problems are very costly efforts to avoid the fear of death by not allowing ourselves to feel really alive. To illustrate, when I "depress myself" (as a gestalt therapist would say) and make myself feel only slightly alive, death loses much of its terror because I have so little to lose. But such an avoidance response to existential anxiety is a catch-22 solution because it cuts one off from the only way to constructively cope with this anxiety—saying yes to life by living creatively.

There are no psychological or psychotherapeutic solutions to existential anxiety. There is no way to make it go away. It is "existential" in the sense that it is inherent in our human experience as self-aware creatures. Our frantic attempts to deny it and run from it make its impact on us more destructive (even "demonic"), waste potentially creative energy, and diminish our awareness and aliveness. But existential anxiety can either cripple our growth or be the deepest source of empowerment of the growth *elan*. Existential therapies seek to help people learn to confront and cope constructively with existential anxiety, using it as a source of motivation and energy for creativity and growth. As Rollo May states: "The goal of therapy is not to free the patient from anxiety. It is rather, to help free him from neurotic anxiety in order that he may meet the normal anxiety constructively. Indeed, *the only way he can achieve the former is to do the latter*. Normal anxiety . . . is an inseparable part of growth and creativity."[33]

Existential anxiety can be transformed into a "school,"[34] as the foreparent of contemporary existentialists, Søren Kierkegaard put it. In the context of trust and meaning, it becomes our "teacher" who challenges us to face ourselves, our trivial values, our meaning-starved life-styles. Thus, existential anxiety can become the "mother of the need to know"[35] and a wellspring of energy for developing our potential for full, authentic humanness. Any therapy that focuses only on neurotic anxiety, ignoring the existential anxiety behind it, cuts people off from the basic way of resolving neurotic anxiety—by confronting and transforming existential anxiety into the energy of becoming!

Neurotic and existential anxiety are intertwined in the problems that bring people to therapy. The woman whose discovery of her accidental, unwanted conception triggered a cold wave of existential anxiety, found, as she explored this anxiety in depth, that it was entangled with her guilt-laden neurotic conflicts about sex and anger, pleasure and assertiveness. The intense fear of death, which had been a prominent presenting problem when she came for help, was a blend of her neurotic fears of dying (based on her feeling she deserved to die because of her rage and her "dirty" sexual fantasies) and her existential anxiety. Neurotic and existential anxiety tend to reinforce each other. As Tillich observed, "Those who are empty of meaning are easy victims of neurotic anxiety," and a high degree of neurotic anxiety makes one vulnerable to self-destructive ways of responding to one's existential anxiety.[36] In a therapy relationship, the therapist's awareness of the presence of existential anxiety is crucial to helping the client untangle it from neurotic anxiety and then gradually transform it so that it will not feed the neurotic anxiety.

Existential therapies regard a viable philosophy of life and value system as essential to the transformation of existential anxiety. Viktor Frankl points to the collective "value vacuum" in our society that breeds an epidemic of existential neuroses. The inner emptiness in many people is fed by their distorted values, priorities, and beliefs. Rollo May asks:

> May not the patient's distorted view of the world sometimes constitute his ultimate problems? May not the effective motive of his life lie wholly in the distorted outlook? . . . More and more we

> are coming to ascribe motivational force to cognitive conditions. Instead of the patient's phenomenological view offering us only the first page, perhaps it constitutes the whole problem; it is ultimate as well as preliminary.[37]

> There is an inverse relation between the soundness of an individual's value system and his anxiety. That is, the firmer and more flexible your values, the more you will be able to meet (existential) anxiety constructively. . . . Arriving at sound values is, in the long run, an integral part of the therapeutic process.[38]

To be most healing and growth-enabling, one's values need to have a firm foundation in a personally meaningful philosophy of life or theology. From his death-camp learnings, Frankl concludes: "Belief in an overmeaning—whether as a metaphysical concept or in the religious sense of providence—is of the foremost therapeutic and psychogenic importance. As a genuine faith springs from inner strength, such a belief adds immeasurably to human vitality."[39] Vital, authentic religion (which satisfies what Frankl calls the will-to-meaning) is a powerful resource for growth toward wholeness. "The power of the divine," as Tillich describes it, can enable us to both confront and transform our awareness of finitude.

As I have struggled to handle my own existential anxiety and guilt (the guilt of unlived life) in more life-enhancing ways through the years, I have become aware at times of the power of *existential acceptance*. This experience, I believe, is available to all persons. When we open ourselves to it, we sense our deep at-homeness in the universe, derived from our acceptance by the loving Spirit who is the source and wellspring of life. Feelings of quiet self-affirmation—the serenity and enjoyment of simply being oneself—flow from such an experience. Existential acceptance is a crucial resource for coping constructively with existential anxiety and guilt.

As the existential therapists make clear, therapists should be willing to deal with the spiritual and value issues *explicitly* in the process of therapy. Because spiritual growth is the key to the total growth of persons toward wholeness, all counselors and therapists need to have the skills to be effective *spiritual* growth enablers. Unfortunately, pastoral counselors are the only therapeutic professionals who routinely receive academic and clinical training in how to deal effectively with spiritual growth issues.

Existential therapists emphasize the complexity of the interrelation of existential anxiety and growth. The courage to be is really the courage to *become.* Only as we continue to come alive (which means continuing to develop our unlived potentials) will we be able to transform existential anxiety and guilt. In May's words:

> "Being" is the potentiality by which the acorn becomes the oak or each of us becomes what he truly is. . . . We can understand another human being only as we see what he is moving toward, what he is becoming; and we can know ourselves only as we "project our potential in action." The significant tense for human beings is thus the future—that is to say, the critical question is what I am pointing toward, becoming.[40]

Yet, to become takes courage because the new possibilities, as they emerge, increase existential anxiety.

> Anxiety occurs at the point where some emerging potentiality or possibility faces the individual, some possibility of fulfilling his existence; but this very possibility involves the destroying of present security, which therefore gives rise to the tendency to deny the new potentiality. . . . If there were not some . . . potentiality crying to be "born," we would not experience [existential] anxiety.[41]

The process of moving to transform existential anxiety by coming alive more fully is itself fraught with existential anxiety. Yet it is only as one takes the leap of trust into one's emerging potentials, letting go of old securities, that growth is possible.

The existentialist emphasis on the potential power of one's future is closely linked with the awareness that hope has tremendous energy for motivating human change. Awakening a sense of realistic hope for a new future is an essential dynamic in facilitating growth.[42] The pull forward of our *living future*—the hopeful future that lives in our imagination—is a powerful resource for creative change. Affirming goals that effect persons' authentic potentialities is one step toward creating their own futures. But working toward their goals is often ineffective unless persons are encouraged to keep picturing the futures toward which they desire to move. As both Jung and Assagioli make clear, imaging yourself as you'd like to be tends to energize the effort it will require to move toward that potentiality.

Another prominent theme in existential therapies is *freedom,* with its correlates *choice* and *responsibility.* Therapists in the existentialist tradition reject all forms of determinism (including those of Freud and Skinner). Such views are seen as invalid ways of understanding human beings which can be used to escape from the freedom and responsibility that are essential for growth. As James Bugental puts it, the main task of existential therapy is to correct clients' distorted perceptions of themselves and others, which arose in an attempt to block awareness of existential anxiety, and thereby help them "accept the responsibilities and opportunities of authentic being in the world."[43] Growth is understood as involving a continuing series of choices. May writes: "Actually in real life it is a matter of long, uphill growth, to new levels of integration—growth meaning not automatic progress but re-education, finding new insights, making self-conscious decisions, and throughout being willing to face occasional or frequent struggles."[44] The aim of existential therapy is to encourage people to *choose life*—i.e., to choose to really live, fully and authentically. The urgency and importance of making pro-life choices usually doesn't dawn on people until they get in touch with the excessive costs of choosing not to choose (drifting) and of choosing not to live as authentically and fully as they can. *Commitment* to change and growth is seen by existential therapists as a prerequisite for both depth insight and creative change: "The patient cannot permit himself to get transforming insight or knowledge until he is ready to decide, takes a decisive orientation to life, and has made the preliminary decisions along the way."[45]

The existential perspective, in my experience, is particularly valuable in crisis counseling. Every significant crisis is a potential spiritual growth opportunity. Experiences of sickness, loss, and bereavement crack the fragile shell of pseudo-omnipotence that most of us wear, confronting us with the brevity and vulnerability of our lives. The existential anxiety from such a crisis can motivate a much-needed reformulation of our life investment plans. Looking death in the face (as one does during medical crises and in bereavement) can enhance life. I remember well an experience of confronting my own vulnerability and fear of death, during an unexpected hospitalization, several years ago. As I gradually emerged from this existential crisis, I recall how precious life felt. The sky looked bluer, the grass greener, people more vivid—because I felt so much more alive than I had felt for years. Rollo May describes what one experiences in such crises: "With the confrontation of non-being, existence takes on a vitality and immediacy, and the individual experiences a heightened consciousness of himself, his world, and others around him."[46]

What is the process by which the existential therapies enable growth? James Bugental reports that there are two dimensions to this process.[47] The analytic phase is the repair, restorative dimension on which most traditional therapies have concentrated. The ontogogic phase (I call this the existential phase) is the future-oriented potentializing, growth-in-meaning dimension. In my experience, these two dimensions do not necessarily follow one after the other in sequence. Rather, the therapist's awareness that there *is* a dimension of active growth and spiritual potentializing, in addition to the dimension of removing the blocks to growth (pathology), allows the process to move back and forth between these complementary therapeutic-growth dimensions. A "celebration of being," as Bugental calls it, is often experienced as one develops more of one's unique potentialities.

Viktor Frankl has shed considerable light on practical ways of helping people develop meanings to live by. In his view, there are three kinds of values in which people can find meaning. In *creative values,* meaning is derived from doing something that one regards as significant: "The conviction that one has a task before him has enormous psychotherapeutic and psychohygenic value. . . . Nothing is more likely to help a person overcome and endure objective difficulties or subjective troubles than the consciousness of having a task in life."[48] In *experiential values* meaning is derived from something beyond oneself—for example, enjoying beauty or being loved. In *attitudinal values* meaning is derived from choosing a life-affirming attitude toward even desperate situations. Frankl recalls: "We who lived in concentration camps can remember the men who walked through the huts comforting others, giving away their last piece of bread. They may have been few in number but they offered sufficient proof that everything can be taken away from a man but one thing: the last of the human freedoms—to choose one's attitude in any circumstances, to choose one's own way."[49] Even in terminal illnesses there is a possibility of actualizing attitudinal values: "Whenever one is confronted with an inescapable, unavoidable situation, whenever one has to face a fate which cannot be changed, e.g. in incurable cancer; just then one is given a last chance to actualize the highest value, to fulfill the deepest meaning, the meaning of suffering. For what matters above all is the attitude we take toward suffering, the attitude in which we take our suffering upon ourselves."[50] According to Frankl's approach, the role of the therapist is to challenge people to find their own meanings that are potentially present in their concrete life situations. These often are meanings that emerge from discovering how they can make some contribution to other persons or to the good of humankind. Frankl believes that there must be self-transcendence in one's framework of meaning. Self-actualization, if sought only for its own sake, is self-defeating. Genuine self-actualization is a by-product of fulfilling meanings that involve self-trancendence.

The existentialists' understanding of the therapist as an

existential partner is one of their most growth-enabling contributions. To be effective in "rediscovering the real living person amid the compartmentalization and dehumanization of modern culture,"[51] therapists must be genuine persons who are really present with their full humanity including their own awareness of their finitude. The concept of "presence" means really *being there* with the other, experiencing vividly that particular person's emerging uniqueness in that moment. Growth tends to be most energized in relationships in which the therapist is most present. To be present, we must set aside all the professional ways by which we distance ourselves from clients and seek to dull our own existential anxiety—e.g., diagnostic labels, psychodynamic theories that we "put" on people, professional roles and status symbols, favorite techniques that we use mechanically. Therapeutic techniques enable healing and growth only when the therapist is really present. Then the techniques flow from the awareness of the unique, changing, growth needs of a particular person. When two persons are really present with each other, there is genuine meeting. They can experience an enlivening I-Thou relationship, to use Martin Buber's familiar term.

The basic philosophical orientation of the existential therapies is an invaluable resource in growth-oriented counseling, therapy, and education. This orientation corrects many of the weaknesses of Freud's reductionistic and deterministic philosophy of being human. The existential perspective restores the awareness that we human beings are formed in the image of the Spirit of the universe! The practical value of this philosophy of personhood and of therapy depends, of course, on how it is implemented in actually doing therapy. (In the case of Viktor Frankl, there seems to be some discontinuity, even contradiction, between the existential philosophy he espouses and the methods he uses.[52]) Because I have discussed methods of counseling on existential problems and facilitating spiritual growth in detail elsewhere,[53] I will not explore the methods of such counseling and therapy further here.

Growth Resources from Carl Rogers' Therapy

Carl Rogers was born in 1902 in Oak Park, Illinois. His parents were strict, fundamentalist Christians. During his sophomore year at the University of Wisconsin, he decided to study for the ministry. The following year, at the age of twenty, he spent six months in China as a delegate to the World Student Christian Federation conference in Peking. This experience opened up his world to people of diverse intellectual, cultural, and religious backgrounds. As he interacted with other student delegates his fundamentalist beliefs gradually weakened. He discovered he could think for himself and trust his own experiences. He describes the psychological transformation that resulted: "From the date of this trip, my goals, values, aims and philosophy have been my own and very divergent from the views which my parents held and which I had held up to this point."[54]

After graduating from Wisconsin, Rogers studied at Union Theological Seminary in New York City, where he encountered persons influenced by the growth theories of John Dewey. His doubts about his religious commitment increased, and he decided to transfer to Teachers College, Columbia University, where he completed a Ph.D. in educational psychology with E. L. Thorndike. During his twelve years at a child guidance center in Rochester, New York, his therapeutic orientation changed from a formal, directive approach toward what became client-centered therapy. He acknowledges the influence of Otto Rank's thought in this transformation. Subsequently, Rogers taught psychology at Ohio State University, the University of Chicago, and the University of Wisconsin. In 1963 he resigned his professorship at Wisconsin and moved to LaJolla, California, where he was one of the founders of the Center for the Studies of the Person, a loose-knit training-research group of persons from various helping professions. He now spends his time writing, lecturing, relating to his family and colleagues, and gardening. Of the latter activity he says: "I garden. Those mornings when I cannot find time . . . I feel cheated. My garden supplies the same intriguing question I have been trying to meet in my professional life: What are the effective conditions of growth? But in my garden, though the frustrations are just as immediate, the results, whether success or failure, are more quickly evident."[55]

Rogers' system was the first American psychotherapy that achieved widespread prominence. His ideas and methods have had a significant influence in America on education, industry, group work, and pastoral psychology, in addition to counseling and therapy. No therapy with the possible exception of Freud's has had as great an impact on the development of pastoral counseling.

My first training in pastoral counseling was Rogerian in its orientation. I had more than two years of valuable therapy with a person whose methods were mainly client-centered. However, in retrospect I now see that my growth could have been furthered much more rapidly if that therapist had been trained in more active and confrontational methods. Rogers' vision of growth, described in almost lyrical prose, helped to awaken my interest in exploring the growth approach further. Although my "revised model" for pastoral counseling[56] was an attempt to overcome certain inadequacies in the Rogerian and Freudian models of therapy, my model was built on many of the contributions of both these therapists.

Four motifs in Rogers' approach to counseling and therapy represent continuing contributions to the psychotherapeutic enterprise—his growth orientation; his emphasis on listening responsively and acceptingly to clients; his awareness that the emotional *quality* of the therapeutic relationship is the key to whether or not it nurtures growth; and his commitment to subjecting the therapeutic process and outcome to careful research. When I read Rogers and when I have heard Rogers speak, I am impressed by the depth and vigor of his growth orientation.

Rogers' thought, particularly about inner, psychological growth, includes a wealth of insights that are valuable for growth-oriented counselors, therapists, and teachers. More than any other therapist, he illuminates the flow and direction of creative change within persons. In his major theory book, *On Becoming a Person,* Rogers declares:

> It [the process of growth] means taking continual steps toward being, in awareness and expression, that which is congruent with one's total organismic reactions. To use Kierkegaard's more aesthetically satisfying terms, it means "to be the self which one truly is." . . . This is not an easy direction to move, nor one which is ever completed. It is a continuing way of life.[57]

The growth goal toward which Rogers' therapy seeks to help people move is the "fully functioning person." This concept has much in common with Maslow's self-actualizing person. Rogers' goal has many facets. Although persons move in ways that express their uniqueness, Rogers identifies what he sees as some universal directions of the process. These include letting go of facades and becoming more real and transparent, acquiring greater awareness of one's total inner experiences, listening to and trusting the guidance of one's organism, rediscovering and accepting those parts of oneself which have been "disowned," learning to live fully in the now.

> In general, the evidence shows that the process moves away from fixity, remoteness from feelings and experiences, rigidity of self-concept, remoteness from people, impersonality of functioning. It moves toward fluidity, changingness, immediacy of feeling and experience, acceptance of feelings and experience, tentativeness of constructs, discovery of a changing self in one's changing experience, realness and closeness of relationships, a unity and integration of functioning.[58]

As people discover themselves more fully, they automatically come to trust and affirm what they discover:

> When a client is open to his experience, he comes to find his organism more trustworthy. . . . There is a gradual growth of trust in, and even affection for the complex, rich, varied assortment of feelings and tendencies which exist in him at the

organic level. Consciousness, instead of being the watchman over a dangerous and unpredictable lot of impulses, of which few can be admitted to see the light of day, becomes the comfortable inhabitant of a society of impulses and feelings and thoughts, which are discovered to be very satisfyingly self-governing when not fearfully guarded.[59]

Rogers' profound trust in the dependability of the growth *elan* is clear:

> Gradually my experience has forced me to conclude that the individual has within himself the capacity and the tendency, latent if not evident, to move toward maturity. . . . A drive toward self-actualization . . . is the mainspring of life, the tendency on which all psychotherapy depends. It is the urge which is evident in all organic and human life—to expand, extend, become autonomous, develop, mature—the tendency to express and activate all the capacities of the organism or the self.[60]

Yet, though spontaneous, the growth process is not easy:

> This process of the good life is not . . . a life for the faint hearted. It involves the stretching and growing of becoming more and more of one's potentialities. It involves the courage to be. It means launching oneself fully into the stream of life. Yet the deeply exciting thing about human beings is that when the individual is inwardly free, he chooses as the good life this process of becoming.[61]

Rogers' underlying theoretical concept, the phenomenological perspective, is one illuminating way of understanding persons. This view holds that each person's unique phenomenal field, the total "world" of that particular person's experiencing, determines her or his behavior. Those parts of this field which one perceives as relatively stable attributes of oneself constitute the self-concept. Only the configuration of perceptions of the self that are admitted to awareness are a part of the self-concept. Rogerian therapy aims at enabling people to change their self-concept in some of the ways described above.

The relationship between *being* and *becoming* in Rogers is almost identical to the paradoxical theory of change later articulated in gestalt therapy: "The curious paradox is that when I accept myself as I am, then I change. I believe that I have learned this from my clients as well as within my own experience—that we cannot change, we cannot move away from what we are, until we thoroughly accept what we are. Then change seems to come almost unnoticed."[62]

Rogers operates out of what might be called a "natural childbirth" understanding of growth in therapy: "I can state my overall hypothesis in one sentence. If I can provide a certain type of relationship, the other person will discover within himself the capacity to use that relationship for growth and change, and personal development will occur."[63] The therapist's only role is to provide such a relationship: "I rejoice at the privilege of being a midwife to a new personality. As I stand in awe at the emergence of a self, a person, I see a birth process in which I had had an important and facilitative part."[64]

There are six psychological conditions that are both necessary and sufficient to facilitate growth:

> A psychological contact (sense of each other's presence) between therapist and client, a state of incongruence in the client, a state of congruence in the therapist, unconditional positive regard for and empathic understanding of the client by the therapist, and the client's perception of the therapist's positive regard for and empathic understanding of him. Diagnosis, professional knowledge, are not considered necessary by Rogers and may, indeed, . . . be obstructive.[65]

The growthful quality of therapeutic relationships is dependent on the degree of authenticity and actualization of the therapist. Rogers observes: "The degree to which I can create relationships which facilitate the growth of others as separate persons is a measure of the growth I have achieved myself. In some respects this is a disturbing thought, but it is also a promising and challenging one."[66]

In his later thought, Rogers has moved beyond the exclusively intrapsychic focus of his earlier books to devote more attention to growthful relationships. In *Becoming Partners: Marriage and Its Alternatives* he concludes that four basic elements make for long-term sustained growth by both persons: (1) mutual commitment to working together on the relationship because that relationship is enriching their love and lives and they wish it to grow; (2) open and full communication of feelings, positive and negative; (3) not accepting the roles and expectations of others; (4) continuing personal growth by both persons toward becoming the unique persons they potentially are. In such relationships each person lives out of this awareness:

> Perhaps I can come to prize myself as the richly varied person I am. Perhaps I can openly be more of this person . . . be free enough to give of love and anger and tenderness as they exist in me. Possibly then I can be a real member of a partnership, because I am on the road to being a real person. And I am hopeful that I can encourage my partner to follow his or her own road to a unique personhood, which I would love to share.[67]

As do the feminist therapists, Rogers affirms the essential equality of any relationship that is mutually growthful.

One of Rogers' valuable contributions is his critique of the way most educators overemphasize intellectual skills and undervalue the intuitive and emotional dimensions of whole-person learning. He is critical of the way they defeat self-learning (the only real learning) and stifle creativity by their built-in coercion and by seeing the student as the passive, dependent recipient of the "knowledge" transmitted by the teacher. Rogers quotes one man's reflections on the deadening effects of his graduate training: "This coercion had such a deterring effect [upon me] that, after I had passed the final examination, I found the consideration of any problem distasteful for me for an entire year."[68] The student Rogers quotes was Albert Einstein!

Rogers' influence, together with my own disillusionment with the results of traditional teaching methods, has encouraged me to seek ways to make my classes more growthful. In the last ten years I have moved increasingly toward experiential teaching (using self-awareness exercises, role playing of counseling methods, live demonstrations of growth groups, and so forth), which involves the students' own feelings, responses, and needs; asking the students to draw up their own "learning contract" based on what *they* want to get from a given course or workshop; expecting students to participate in the teaching by sharing in some systematic way the insights they have discovered to be meaningful; revealing my own struggles, uncertainties, and weaknesses; and asking the students to evaluate anonymously the course, including my teaching.

In spite of Rogers' pioneering growth contributions, his approach has some serious inadequacies. Although he challenges and rejects the pathology model that had dominated most traditional psychotherapies since Freud, Rogers retains the predominant *intrapsychic focus* that has weakened the growth impact of these therapies. This focus has been broadened to some extent in his writings on small groups, on close relationships such as marriage, and on intergroup relationships. But his approach to these relationships is mainly an extrapolation of the principles of one-to-one counselor-client relationships. Rogers underemphasizes the special dynamics within and between social systems (e.g., families, industries, schools, economic-political systems) which must be changed if the whole system is to nurture rather than diminish individual growth within it. Even though he has given much attention to groups, he does not emphasize the fact that every personal problem is rooted in and fed by its social context. Furthermore he does not emphasize the wholesale diminishing of potentializing (for both women and men) caused by institutional-societal sexism or the *therapeutic* necessity of empowering persons to work together to eradicate systemic growth oppression through social-political action. Of the six dimensions of whole-person growth,[69] Rogers concentrates most of his energy on two dimensions (inner psychological and relational growth), underemphasizing the other four.

A closely related deficiency in Rogers' approach is a neglect of the *power* dynamics of growth, which Adler and the radical therapists rightly emphasize as crucial. Most therapists would agree on the importance of the positive qualities in therapeutic relationships that Rogers sees as essential for making them growth-enabling. Research findings reported by Charles Truax and Robert Carkhuff show that the therapeutic triad—empathic understanding, positive regard, and congruence—are highly correlated with constructive change in therapy whatever the conceptual orientation of the therapist.[70] But few therapists would agree that these positive qualities are all that is needed for effective therapy with all types of persons. Rogers' approach is excellent for establishing healing-growthing relationships, but with many people, it is what the therapist does within these relationships, *after* they are established, that determines the outcome! For clients who are crippled by self-rejection and guilt, unconditional (although I doubt if either acceptance or positive regard can ever be totally "unconditional" in us finite human therapists) positive regard and acceptance often are precisely what they need for healing and growth. But Rogers leaves no place for the constructive confrontation that is essential in working growthfully with many other people. To illustrate, among the people who come to our pastoral counseling and growth center for help, many desperately need a counselor who has the caring and courage to "speak the truth in love" to them. Persons with manipulative life-styles can easily manipulate passive therapists, who simply follow their lead. For persons with weak or confused consciences and those who act out their inner pain in ways that are damaging to themselves and others, the most loving and growthful thing a therapist can do is to confront them honestly with the consequences of their behavior! To fail to hold up the reality of their destructive behavior, in a context of genuine caring for them, is to withhold what they *must* have if they are to change. Rogers builds his total approach on only half the growth formula.[71] By making caring and acceptance, without confrontation with reality, the sole basis for therapeutic change, he provides an inadequate foundation for growth.

A related inadequacy in Rogers' understanding of therapy is his lack of awareness of the ingenuity and power of the resistances to growth within us human beings. His faith in the spontaneous flowering of persons in an accepting-caring-honest relationship is naïve and ineffective when one does therapy with those who are locked into self-sabotaging, self-deluding defenses against having to change. The dark, out-of-awareness destructiveness, the tragic trappedness, and the growth-stifling misuse of their limited degree of choicefulness (factors that were so brilliantly illuminated by Freud and other depth therapists) are virtually ignored by Rogers. It seems as if, in freeing himself from moralistic fundamentalism, he dismissed any need for a depth understanding of human pathology, evil, and destructiveness. When one encounters persons in whom the growth *elan* has been frozen for many years in a self-crippling psychosis, the inadequacy of Rogers' understanding of such grotesquely distorted personhood is evident.

The exclusive use of Rogers' midwifery model does not allow therapists to develop the differential methodology that is essential in responding to the needs of persons who require more active, structured, educative approaches. It behooves all therapists and teachers to respect the growth *elan* in people and to know that only as that vital energy is activated will they grow. But it does not follow that it is necessary or constructive to put all the responsibility for the direction, pace, and content of the therapeutic sessions onto them. In my experience, clients who are bright, verbal, and strongly motivated to change (as many of Rogers' clients must have been) often respond growthfully to a client-centered approach. But the majority of hurting people seen by mental health therapists and by ministers for counseling respond more rapidly and growthfully when therapists use more active, confrontational, and reeducative methods as these become appropriate in the flow of each session. In his resistance to behavioral methods (a la Skinner), Rogers seems to dismiss the fact that active, purposive reeducation (cognitive, relational, and behavioral) is precisely what some people must have to cope with life more constructively. Many people need active involvement of the therapist as creative teacher, coach, and guide on their growth journey. Alcoholics, for example, often experience relatively passive therapists as essentially withholding.

Rogers' phenomenological perspective has serious limitations when it is used as the only way of understanding human beings. The dimension of depth and mystery (represented in psychoanalysis by the unconscious) is underemphasized in Rogers' thought. Furthermore, by itself, the phenomenological view leads to a subjective hyper-individualism that weakens Rogers' approach to therapy; Rogers declares:

> The individual increasingly comes to feel that this locus of evaluation lies within himself. Less and less does he look to others for approval or disapproval; for standards to live by; for decisions and choices. He recognizes that it rests within himself to choose; that the only question which matters is, "Am I living in a way which is deeply satisfying to me and which truly expresses me?" This I think is the most important question for the creative individual. . . .
>
> When one actively feels as though it is valuable or worth doing, it is worth doing.[72]

The emphasis on trusting their own feelings and wants can be a growthful corrective for people who have allowed the values, demands, and expectations of others to straitjacket their autonomy. But in the complexity and ambiguity of human relationships, many decisions can be made creatively only by dialogue and negotiation with those whose lives and needs intertwine and often conflict with our own. Furthermore, people who have been reared by permissive parents who did not set firm limits tend to use this emphasis to legitimate their narcissistic "me-ism."

Rogers' approach lacks a place for either explicit value reformulation or for actively facilitating spiritual growth. Apparently he does not regard either of these as essential. In a conversation with Paul Tillich, Rogers made his own lack of any need for a spiritual dimension clear.[73] One can affirm the values that are implicit in his philosophy of therapy—the value of feelings, of inner freedom and autonomy, of self-honesty (congruence), of empathic understanding and of respect for each person's unique growth choices and direction. But in a time when value confusion reinforced by growth-strangling faith systems often is at the center of the problems that bring people for help, it is essential that counselors, therapists, and teachers be competent and free to deal with these issues explicitly whenever appropriate.

For Further Exploration of Growth Resources in Jung's Therapy

Goldenberg, Naomi. *Changing of the Gods, Feminism and the End of Traditional Religions.* Boston: Beacon Press, 1979. Chap. 5 is a superb critique of Jungian psychology as it relates to religion.

Hanna, Charles B. *The Face of the Deep: The Religious Ideas of C. G. Jung.* Philadelphia: Westminster Press, 1967. Deals with Jung's ideas about God and the unconscious, sin and guilt, the psychology of the soul, and the present spiritual crisis.

Hillman, James. *Insearch: Psychology and Religion.* New York: Scribner's, 1967. Based on lectures given to ministers on analytical psychology and pastoral counseling; includes a discussion of the feminine grounding of religion.

Jung, Carl G. *Memories, Dreams and Reflections.* New York: Random House, 1961. Jung's powerful, candid autobiography provides an excellent introduction to his major ideas.

———. *Collected Works of C. G. Jung,* ed. H. Read, M. Fordham, G. Adler. Princeton: Princeton University Press, 1967–; Pantheon Books, 1953–67. Includes almost all of Jung's writings.

———. *Modern Man in Search of a Soul.* New York: Harcourt Brace, 1933. Discusses the nature of spiritual needs and how they are frustrated in the modern world.

Sanford, John A. *Dreams, God's Forgotten Language.* Philadelphia:

Lippincott, 1968. A Jungian pastoral counselor's understanding of dreams.

Singer, June. *Boundaries of the Soul: The Practice of Jung's Psychology*. Garden City, N.Y.: Doubleday, 1972. A clear description of Jungian theory and therapy.

Ulanov, Ann, and Ulanov, Barry. *Religion and the Unconscious*. Philadelphia: Westminster Press, 1975. Discusses the function of religion in the human psyche; mythology and religious experience; suffering and salvation from a Jungian perspective.

For Further Exploration of Growth Resources in the Existential Therapists

Boss, Medard. *Psychoanalysis and Daseinsanalysis,* trans. Ludwig B. Lefebre. New York: Basic Books, 1963. Describes his basic revision of psychoanalytic theory and practice as these were influenced by existentialism.

Bugental, James F. T. *The Search for Authenticity*. New York: Holt, Rinehart and Winston, 1965. Presents an existential-analytic approach to psychotherapy reflecting the influence of Maslow, Tillich, and May.

Clinebell, Howard. "Counseling on Religious-Existential Problems" in *Basic Types of Pastoral Counseling,* chap. 14.

———. "Spiritual Growth—The Key to All Growth," in *Growth Counseling,* chap. 4.

———. "Philosophical-Religious Factors in the Etiology and Treatment of Alcoholism," in *Quarterly Journal of Studies on Alcohol,* September, 1963, pp. 473-88.

Frankl, Viktor E. *Man's Search for Meaning: An Introduction to Logotherapy*. New York: Pocket Books, 1963. A description of his death camp experiences and a brief statement about logotherapy.

———. *The Doctor and the Soul: An Introduction to Logotherapy*. New York: Alfred A. Knopf, 1962. Describes the basic philosophy and methods of this type of existential therapy.

May, Rollo, et al., eds. *Existence, A New Dimension in Psychiatry and Psychology*. New York: Basic Books, 1958. A collection of papers on existential psychotherapy by May, H. F. Ellenberger, Ludwig Binswanger, et al.

May, Rollo, ed. *Existential Psychology*. New York: Random House,

1961. Includes papers by Abraham Maslow, Carl Rogers, and Gordon Allport, in addition to two by May.

May, Rollo. *Man's Search for Himself.* New York: W. W. Norton, 1953. Applies the learnings from existential therapy to help readers understand the human predicament and rediscover their selfhood.

———. *Psychology and the Human Dilemma.* Princeton: Van Nostrand, 1967. Essays on the contemporary situation, anxiety, existential psychotherapy, freedom, and responsibility.

Tillich, Paul. *The Courage to Be.* New Haven: Yale University Press, 1952. Explores the relationship between existential and pathological anxiety, theologically and psychologically.

For Further Exploration of Growth Resources in Carl Rogers' Therapy

Hart, J. T., and Tomlinson, M. E., eds. *New Directions in Client-Centered Therapy.* Boston: Houghton Mifflin, 1970. Major figures in various fields discuss how they have extended Rogers' approach in therapy, education, and research.

Rogers, Carl. *Client-Centered Therapy.* Boston: Houghton Mifflin, 1951. Rogers' first formal statement on theories of personality and of therapy. He now sees the statement as too rigid, but it is still a significant book.

———. *On Becoming a Person: A Therapist's View of Psychotherapy.* Boston: Houghton Mifflin, 1961. Spells out in a personal way his major concepts.

———. *Freedom to Learn.* Columbus: Chas. E. Merrill, 1969. Rogers' clearest challenge to educators; he develops the view that most education discourages real learning.

———. *Carl Rogers on Encounter Groups.* New York: Harper, 1970. Reports his findings on the process of small growth groups.

———. *Becoming Partners: Marriage and Its Alternatives.* New York: Harper, 1972. Explores various approaches to marriage, reporting on factors which make for long-term growthful relationships.

Chapter 5

Growth Resources in Behavior-Action Therapies

The behavior-action therapies are a diverse cluster of therapeutic approaches that share the conviction that all the problems which people bring to therapy are essentially unconstructive behavior resulting from faulty learning. Using many different techniques, these therapies apply the basic principles of learning theory to enable people to unlearn ineffective behavior and learn more constructive behavior in its place. The behavior therapies are also called "action therapies" because of their emphasis on using direct, action-oriented methods to enable clients to learn new behavior. These therapies contrast with all the "insight therapies" derived from Freud, which regard dynamic inner changes in attitudes, feelings, and self-perception as the primary means of therapeutic change including changes in behavior.

The foundations of behavior therapies were constructed by the Russian physiologist Pavlov's experiments in conditioning animals early in this century.[1] Around 1920 behaviorist psychologist John B. Watson and his students discovered that they could produce phobias in children by simple conditioning procedures and cure those who were already phobic by counter-conditioning. In the 1930s, psychologist O. Hobart Mowrer developed a classical conditioning method for treating enuresis that proved effective. He used a pad and a bell that rings when the child wets the bed. Around 1950, Joseph Wolpe (then a South African psychiatrist) developed a counter-conditioning method called "systematic desensitivation," which he found eliminated neurotic anxieties in many of his patients in a relatively brief time. He obtained dramatic results in treating phobias and sexual impotence, both of which were considered relatively intractable in psychoanalytic therapies.[2] Around the middle 1950s some of behavioral psychologist B. F. Skinner's students at Harvard began to apply to human beings his methods of instrumental or operant conditioning,[3] developed during a quarter century of laboratory research mainly with animals. Whereas Wolpe has concentrated on extinguishing old unadaptive behavior, these therapies emphasized shaping new constructive behavior through positive reinforcement. By simply rewarding behavior that was constructive and reality-oriented, in mental hospital wards (using a so-called "token economy") they found that they could increase drastically such "uncrazy" behavior on the part of psychotic patients, many of whom had not responded to traditional therapies.

Since 1960, the floodgates of behavior therapies have opened wide. Learning theory principles have been applied to many types of problems in living. "Some of the most important applications have been to the training of retarded children, to the elimination of sexual disorders, to the large-scale amelioration of adult psychotic behavior, to the training of autistic children, to the re-education of delinquent adolescents . . . to marriage counseling, to weight control and to smoking reduction."[4]

The behavior therapies derived from the research of Skinner focus exclusively on changing overt, measurable behavior. In contrast, the cognitive-behavior approaches broaden the focus to also include changing "covert behavior" such as beliefs, expectations, concepts, and feelings. Aaron Beck's "cognitive therapy"[5] and Albert Ellis' "rational emotive therapy"[6] emphasize the crucial role of thoughts and beliefs in maintaining and changing unadaptive behavior. Albert Bandura's approach employs classical and operant conditioning methods to change behavior but he uses these in a social learning framework that highlights the importance of cognitive processes in facilitating and maintaining desired changes.[7] Unlike Skinner, who sees behavior as entirely the product of conditioning by the external social environment, the cognitive behavior therapists emphasize the human capacity for self-directed behavior change. They focus on helping people increase self-control and mastery over their own lives. The cognitive behavior therapies provide the most useful growth resources currently available among the behavior therapies.

Learning theory principles probably will be applied to an increasing variety of personal, family, and community problems in the years ahead. Behaviorism is the dominant orientation in most academic departments of psychology. There is therefore an enormous pool of knowledge and expertise available there for enriching the therapeutic disciplines. It is salutary, indeed, that the findings of the mainstream of empirical research in psychology are now being applied to resolving a host of severe human problems. The application of the general principles of learning to the growth work of functional people is a natural and potentially productive extension of these behavior-action therapies.

In my experience, many of the working concepts and techniques of behavior-action therapies are effective in helping people change and grow. From a growth perspective, these therapies do not constitute a totally adequate therapeutic approach for everyone. However, they do provide a variety of conceptual and practical tools that can be integrated with resources from other therapies for use in enabling growth. In this chapter, I will highlight some growth resources from the behavior-action therapies which I have found useful. I also will describe some resources from several approaches that, though not usually labeled behavior therapies, all focus primarily on changing overt and/or covert behavior.

Principles and Methods of Behavior Therapies

There are several working assumptions that the diverse behavior therapies hold in common.[8] In the parentheses following each of these assumptions, I will contrast them with the assumptions of traditional, psychoanalytically oriented therapies:

(1) Behavior therapies regard the painful "symptoms" that bring people for help as the real problem to be treated. (Traditional therapies see symptoms as surface manifestations of deeper, usually hidden causes.) (2) Behavior therapies consider and treat life- and growth-disrupting problems as faulty, maladaptive learning. (Most traditional therapies accept the medical model, which understands mental, emotional, and relational problems as "illnesses" that must be healed.) (3) The primary therapeutic focus of behavior therapies is on changing behavior, overt and/or covert. The overall aim is to help people unlearn life-destructive behavior and learn life-enhancing skills. Improved behavior generally produces improved feeling. (The focus of traditional therapies is on changing destructive feelings, attitudes, and self-perceptions through insight, which is assumed to produce behavioral changes.) (4) The behavior therapies see the therapist primarily as a teacher of effective behavior. (The traditional therapies view the therapist as a healer or enabler of inner growth.) (5) Behavior therapies are present-oriented. They see the origins of behavior as largely irrelevant to therapeutic change and growth. (Traditional therapies focus on helping people relive the origins of problems in the past and thereby finishing incomplete growth.) (6) Behavior therapies seek to identify and change the stimuli that trigger problematic behavior and the rewards (positive reinforcements) that cause it to be repeated and earned. (Traditional therapies seek to identify and change hidden "causes" from the past that continue to influence the present from the unconscious mind.) (7) Most behavior therapies emphasize the importance of having limited, specific, and measurable behavioral change goals so that the effectiveness of therapy can be empirically validated. (Traditional therapies tend to define their goals more globally and subjectively so that empirical measurement of their effectiveness is very difficult if not impossible.) (8) Most behavior therapists regard a therapeutic relationship of warmth and trust as important because it facilitates more rapid learning. Skinnerian-based therapists generally view the therapist-client relationship as of

little importance to change in therapy. (Traditional therapies understand the establishment of a therapeutic relationship as essential since the relationship is the primary arena of therapeutic change.) (9) Because the goals are limited and concrete in behavior therapies, and their methods designed to facilitate specific learnings, they tend to be shorter in duration. (Traditional therapies tend to be longer-term.) (10) Behavior therapies have an aura of hope based on the conviction that what has been learned can be unlearned and the belief that everyone has some capacity to learn new, more constructive behavior. (There is a feeling associated with *some* traditional therapies that deeply diminished growth can be unblocked only partially and via a long, expensive process.)

An Illustration of the Behavior Therapy Process

To illuminate the process and some of the methods of cognitive-behavior therapy, here is how Mrs. S., a twenty-nine-year-old, part-time librarian was helped:[9]

> When she came for therapy, she described strong feelings of worthlessness, anxiety, and depression accompanied by tension, headaches, and insomnia. Tranquilizers from her physician had not helped. She sought therapy when her husband accused her of being "mentally disturbed" and threatened to divorce her. The therapist spent the first session listening to her pain and thus establishing a trustful, cooperative relationship. Then he began a behavioral assessment of Mrs. S.'s situation, seeking to identify the particular behavioral excesses (e.g., frequent rages) and behavioral deficits (e.g., underassertiveness) that were producing her distress. The therapist asked her to keep a diary in which she recorded daily events and her reactions to them. This self-monitoring helped both Mrs. S. and the therapist discover the timing and frequency of her distress-causing behavior. After a half-dozen sessions, the assessment pinpointed these behavior difficulties which became the goals of therapy—her unassertiveness; her inability to express her feelings, which the therapist saw as leading to a build-up of anger, resentment, and guilt (about her anger); the fact that she had never

experienced orgasm; and her low opinion of herself, which was reinforced by the covert behavior of self-deprecating thoughts.

During the process of making the behavioral assessment, the therapist decided tentatively on several therapeutic tools that he could use in helping her change her painful behavior and feelings. Since most of her problems focused on her marriage relationship, Mrs. S. agreed to include her husband in the therapy. The therapist began a program of relaxation training to help her learn to relax at will whenever she became aware of rising tensions. This gave her a means of reducing her insomnia, headaches, and anxiety. The therapist simultaneously started assertiveness training, coaching her as she rehearsed more assertive ways of responding in situations in which she had been hyper-submissive. The third facet of therapy was a Masters and Johnson type approach to helping the couple deal with her lack of orgasms. With the support and collaboration of her husband, she began to have orgasms after a few weeks. The quality of their relationship was enhanced by this success and by Mrs. S.'s more outgoing behavior. To help her extinguish her self-deprecating thoughts, the therapist encouraged her to list and repeat to herself several true and constructive statements about herself that were incompatible with her unrealistic feelings of worthlessness. After about four months of therapy, Mrs. S. had achieved a dramatic lessening of her depression, self-rejection, and anxiety. Using her new emotional freedom and self-confidence, she decided to return to school to pursue an advanced degree. This account shows how cognitive-behavioral methods can be used to help persons claim and develop their strengths, enrich their relationships, and expand their vocational horizons.

Behavioral Methods in Marital Counseling

Behavior-action therapies provide a variety of resources for marriage counseling as well as for other relational counseling and therapy. Marital happiness is seen by behavior therapists as produced by particular need-satisfying behavior. All married couples are both students and teachers of each other. They constantly increase or decrease the probability that need-satisfying behavior will occur in the other. David Knox, a behavior marital therapist, states: "Marital behaviors, like all behaviors, are learned, or rather taught—according to their consequences. A reinforcer is a consequence that increases the probability that a specific behavior will recur."[10] Counseling consists of identifying the particular behaviors that are satisfying and those frustrating for a given couple, and then, using learning theory, teaching them to increase the valued behaviors while decreasing need-depriving behaviors.

I find it useful in marriage counseling and therapy to encourage couples to describe their problems in terms of the specific behaviors that each would like decreased, terminated, modified, increased, or developed. This emphasis establishes concrete goals toward which they need to work to make their marriage more satisfying and pleasurable. Since the goals they set involve specific behaviors, both the couple and the counselor can know when they are making progress in moving toward these goals.

Three behavioral methods are particularly useful in marriage and family counseling. *Selective reinforcement* consists of helping couples or family members identify the specific responses that reward desired and undesired behaviors and then teaching them to increase the reinforcement of desired behavior and to terminate reinforcement of undesired behavior. It is often very enlightening for couples to discover the ways they are "sinking their own canoe" by unwittingly rewarding the very behavior they find annoying in each other. Nagging, for example, tends to reinforce negative behavior by rewarding it with attention.

Exchange contracting is another valuable tool in all relationship counseling. After both persons identify the specific behaviors they would like changed, the counselor helps them negotiate a mutually acceptable contract specifying what behaviors each will terminate or increase in exchange for changes in the other. A related behavioral technique called *shaping* is useful in this do-it-yourselves change process.

Shaping consists of breaking down a complex interacting cluster of behaviors (such as a marriage relationship) into small components. By focusing on and reinforcing one or two components at a time, persons in marriage counseling gradually reshape their own relationship. Behavioral methods, like any marriage-counseling tools, can be effective only if both parties value the relationship enough to have some commitment to reconstructing it.

To illustrate how behavioral approaches can be integrated with traditional role-relationship counseling methods, here are the steps that often occur in the process of couple marriage counseling:[11]

> *Step 1*—The counselor establishes rapport with both persons by listening with warmth and empathy as they take turns describing the painful problems that brought them for help. The pattern of their self-other defeating behavior gradually becomes clearer as the counselor listens and asks gently probing questions to clarify how each responds in their negative cycles of interaction. *Step 2*—The counselor describes briefly how behavioral change methods and exchange contracting may help them decrease their pain and increase their satisfactions. After the anger and hurt have been expressed and thus reduced (which frees the couple to hear and think more clearly), the counselor may say:
>
> From what you've shared with me, it's clear that each of you is experiencing tremendous pain and not much satisfaction in your relationship. You're caught in a mutual hurting cycle. Each of you, out of your pain, is responding in ways that bring more hurt. An example of how this vicious cycle operates in your relationship is ——. I'd like to encourage you to learn how to interrupt this self-sabotaging cycle and get more satisfactions for both of you back into the way you relate. This would involve working out at each session an agreement about what each of you is willing to do, during the coming week, to make things better for your spouse in exchange for changes on the other's part to make things better for you.
>
> *Step 3*—If both agree, they are asked to prepare (perhaps as "homework") a list of the specific undesirable behaviors that each

would like the other to change, ranking these from the least to the most undesirable. *Step 4*—Both are also asked to make a list of how they respond to behaviors they find undesirable in each other, to discover how they unwittingly have rewarded such behavior. *Step 5*—Each then prepares a list of satisfying behaviors he or she would like to have increased or added by the other, rank ordering this list also. *Step 6*—In light of these lists, the spouses are then coached as they negotiate a simple, workable "exchange contract" in which each agrees to reduce or eliminate some undesirable behavior and replace it with behavior the other desires. To encourage implementation, positive and negative consequences should be specified for each person, in addition to the positive satisfaction of what the other agrees to do—e.g., a back rub or no back rub; golf or no golf. The counselor serves as communications facilitator and arbitrator, giving them affirmation (positive reinforcement) as they gradually learn the essential skill of negotiating a more fair and workable mutual change contract. The probability of successful implementation of the early change plans is increased if the couple is encouraged to begin with relatively low-priority, low-threat items on both their desired and undesired lists. *Step 7*—The couple is encouraged to implement their change contract between sessions, expressing approval (positive reinforcement) whenever a desired behavior replaces an undesirable one in the mate's behavior. They are asked to avoid reinforcing undesirable behavior by ignoring it when it occurs. Whatever increase they achieve in reciprocal, satisfying behavior tends to be self-reinforcing. In subsequent weeks, the couple is helped to move to higher (and more difficult) priority wants and needs in their exchange re-contracting. *Step 8*—During the process of self-change, the couple is asked to each keep careful records of their own and the other's success in implementing the agreement. These records are brought to counseling sessions, making it possible for clients and therapist to monitor concrete changes in the behavioral aspect of their relationship.

Couples should be encouraged to "shape" new desired behavior patterns in each other by affirming even very small steps toward those goals—e.g., "I really appreciate your hanging up your clothes, dear" (ignoring other messy behavior that hasn't changed). Both individuals are encouraged to use "contingency contracts" with themselves and to reward themselves when they do something that both persons desire—e.g., I agree with myself to watch my favorite television program only if I have spent —— (amount of time) with the children during the preceding week."

Throughout the change process, the counselor tries to model positive reinforcement by expressing affirmation of each of their small successes in learning new, desired behaviors. The counselor may coach the couple by *behavioral rehearsal* during the sessions to help them practice the new mutual-fulfilling behaviors (including more effective communication skills) which they will need to implement their exchange contracts and learn better ways of coping with marital conflict and crises. For example, the counselor may ask: "Will you show me how you plan to communicate so as to prevent the buildup of resentment between you?"

This behavioral exchange process is more complicated in actual practice than it sounds when the steps are summarized. The effectiveness of the techniques can be increased markedly if they are integrated with insights and methods from other therapies. For example, structural analysis from TA can be used to help couples learn to "keep their Adult in the driver's seat" so that they *can* negotiate and implement a more mutually satisfying marriage contract. (See chap. 6.) Behavior therapy methods should be used flexibly and in conjunction with methods from traditional therapies that deal directly with change-blocking feelings and attitudes.

Sex Therapy and Enhancement Using Cognitive Behavioral Methods

The newer therapies for sexual dysfunctions and diminution provide a clear illustration of the therapeutic value of learning theory principles. Traditional psychoanalytic therapists view persistent problems of sexual dysfunction as surface symptoms of underlying conflicts and anxieties related to deeply fixated psychosexual development. Understood in this way, the only hope for recovery is long-term analytic therapy. Unfortunately, the general effectiveness of such therapy in treating sexual problems has not been impressive.[12] In sharp contrast to this approach, the short-term sex therapies pioneered by William H. Masters and Virginia E. Johnson, using cognitive-behavioral approaches, often produce impressive therapeutic results. In these therapies, many problems of sexual dysfunction are understood as being rooted not in deep psychosexual pathology but in faulty learning in two areas—learning sex-negative rather than sex-affirmative feelings and attitudes, and failing to learn the behavioral skills that enable two people to pleasure each other effectively and thus enjoy sex more fully.

Much of the treatment in these approaches is not "therapy" in the traditional sense but simply attitudinal and behavioral reeducation. In these therapies sex-affirmative attitudes and feelings are gradually developed by a couple as they identify with positive understandings and attitudes of the therapist and as they learn, through coaching and practice, new, non-demand pleasuring skills. Performance and fear-of-failure anxieties, which cause much sexual dysfunction and diminution, are gradually extinguished. This is done by focusing on practicing sensate arousal exercises for their own inherent pleasure, with no intention or need to "succeed" by reaching any goal such as orgasm. Non-demand pleasuring exercises also have proved to be useful for couples who do not suffer major sexual problems but simply wish to develop more of their pleasure potentials.

The effectiveness of behavioral sex therapy techniques is increased when they are integrated with psychodynamic insights and therapeutic methods and with resources from marriage therapy. Helen Singer Kaplan's approach utilizes resources for all three of these therapies.[13] Traditional psychotherapy is used when needed to resolve anxieties and inner conflicts that block change-producing use of the behavioral techniques. Marital therapy is used to resolve interpersonal anger and conflicts that diminish full sexual responsiveness and feed a couple's resistance to doing behavior-changing exercises. It should be noted that often there is positive or negative reciprocity between sex and the other forms of communication in a marriage. As the marriage relationship grows stronger, sex tends to improve, and vice versa. Guided imagery techniques can also be a valuable part of sex therapy with persons who fail to respond to initial behavior intervention (due to pleasure or failure anxieties) or who fail to reach the level of sexual arousal that they desire.[14] Behavioral sex therapies, supplemented by psychodynamic therapy and marital therapy when needed, have had a dramatically higher rate of effectiveness in treating sexual dysfunctions than have the traditional therapies.

Growth Resources in Reality Therapy

Reality therapy, developed by psychiatrist William Glasser, is an action-oriented therapy that aims at enabling people to change their behavior so that it will fulfill their basic needs (to give and receive love and to feel worthwhile to themselves and others) in the real world of relationships in ways that do not deprive others of the possibility of fulfilling their needs.[15] (This is what Glasser means by "responsibility.") Although Glasser does not identify his approach with the cognitive behavior therapies, its effectiveness can best be understood in learning theory and behavioral terms.

Glasser rejects the pathology model of traditional psychotherapy, believing that labeling people with psychological and relational problems "sick" robs them of responsibility for changing their behavior and gives them an excuse for continuing as they are. He faults traditional therapies for concentrating on exploring the past and the unconscious, and on attempting to help people change attitudes or achieve insight *before* they change their destructive behavior. He assumes that people have the ability to change their behavior if they choose. Glasser declares, "Waiting for attitudes to change stalls therapy whereas changing behavior leads quickly to change in attitudes, which in turn can lead to fulfilling needs and further better behavior."

In reality therapy, the therapist is essentially a teacher of more need-satisfying living who uses a three-step process of growth:

> First, there is involvement: the therapist must become so involved with the patient that the patient can begin to face reality

> and see how his behavior is unrealistic. Second, the therapist must reject the behavior that is unrealistic [irresponsible] but still accept the patient and maintain his involvement with him. Last, . . . the therapist must teach the patient better ways to fulfill his needs within the confines of reality.[16]

The heart of the second step is continuing confrontation with the destructive consequences of behavior. No "reasons" for the client's irresponsible, need-depriving behavior are sought or accepted by the therapist. The therapist actively works to get clients to face the reality they are avoiding including the self-defeating consequences of their behavior. Questions such as these are asked, "Does what you are doing get you what you really want?" "If not, what will you do differently in order to obtain the consequences you want?" When clients are confronted persistently by a therapist with whom they are involved, they are forced repeatedly to decide whether they will take the responsible path. When they decide that they do not like the negative consequences of their irresponsible behavior, they become more open to learning responsible behavior, which produces more satisfying consequences.

Reality therapists painstakingly help persons to examine their daily activities and relationships to learn more effective ways of behaving and relating which will satisfy their basic needs. The therapist must be a firm reality-respecting guide and model: "The therapist must be a very responsible person—tough, interested, human and sensitive. He must be able to fulfill his own needs and must be willing to discuss some of his own struggles, so that the patient can see that acting responsibly is possible though sometimes difficult."[17] By his attitudes and responses to the client's behavior, the therapist seeks to reinforce reality-based, responsible behavior.

One of the values in Glasser's approach from a holistic growth perspective is his commitment to applying reality therapy's philosophy and principles to institutional-societal systems. His *Schools Without Failure,* for example, applies his approach to increasing the capacity of schools to help develop more effective and responsible children and youth.

Reality therapy, as a therapeutic tool, is uncomplicated in its working concepts and effective in much short-term counseling. It is particularly effective with troubled adolescents and with adults who are acting out their problems in ways destructive to themselves and others; with adults who have a pattern of self-sabotaging, impulsive behavior; with alcoholics; and with persons having underdeveloped or distorted consciences who need firmer and more constructive inner controls to guide their behavior. Reality therapy provides a simple and useful approach for helping almost anyone who is coping ineffectively with crises. Unless it is supplemented by other therapies, it is not adequate with persons who are suffering from distorted or punitive consciences, from severe inner conflicts, or meaning-of-life issues that block constructive behavior changes. But in our society, where so many people act out their hunger for love, esteem, and meaning in destructive, irresponsible ways, Glasser's therapy is a valuable growth resource.

Growth Resources from Crisis Counseling

Crisis intervention methods, as these have developed over the last four decades, offer resources to help oneself and others cope with both developmental and accidental crises growthfully. Research pioneered by Erich Lindemann and Gerald Caplan at Harvard increased the understanding of how people cope with a wide variety of losses and crises. These research findings have provided a solid conceptual foundation for the development of crisis intervention techniques (which have many affinities with reality therapy and the approach of the ego analysts). Let me summarize the working principles of crisis intervention theory.[18] To "get inside" these principles experientially, I recommend that you apply them to a current or recent crisis in your own life:

(1) Crises happen *in* rather than *to* us. The heart of a crisis is our response to a situation that we experience as stressful or emotionally

hazardous. Since a crisis is essentially an inner experience, we have the potential of choosing to respond in ways that mobilize our coping resources. (2) The life situations in which we are vulnerable to inner crises are those in which we experience a loss or the threat of a loss of something important in our lives. A cluster of painful feelings—e.g., grief, anxiety, confusion, powerlessness, depression, anger, disorientation, inner paralysis—constitute the essence of the crisis experience. These feelings result from the ineffectiveness of our old coping skills to meet the psychological needs that are present after the loss. (3) Stresses, changes, losses, and crises occurring in a short time span are cumulative. As Thomas Holmes's research demonstrates, experiencing a series of major changes in a short period of time makes people vulnerable to developing psychological, psychosomatic, or relationship problems.[19] This fact underlines the crucial importance of providing support and caring to persons going through multiple changes and losses. (4) Crises are forks in our growth road. If we learn to cope constructively with a heavy crisis or series of crises, we will develop new personality skills for handling future crises. The human personality is like a muscle. If we use it to cope with difficulties, it grows stronger. If we avoid using it, by various escape mechanisms, it grows weaker. (5) Most of us have a variety of hidden resources that we can mobilize for handling crises. We usually don't discover these inner strengths until stressful circumstances force us to do so. This is why crises are potential growth opportunities. (6) The goals of crisis counseling are to help people do their "grief work" (expressing, working through, and resolving the painful feelings), mobilize their coping potentialities, including learning new coping skills, and thus to grow stronger. (7) Discovering the origins of inadequate responses to crises is usually unnecessary to improve coping. As William Menninger put it, "You don't need to know how a fire started to put it out." The focus of crisis counseling, as of behavioral therapies generally, is learning to act more effectively in the present. (8) Experiencing the energy of hope for change when we are traumatized by crises, provides the power that is essential for mobilizing our inner resources. Hope often is *the* important variable in determining how we cope in difficult life situations. The counselor's function as hope-awakener is therefore crucial in crisis intervention work.[20] Realistic hope is awakened by a variety of means. It is "caught" from the counselor's warm support and affirmation of the person's potential capacities for coping. It grows stronger as the person gradually learns to take constructive action. (9) A key resource for coping with our crises is the strength and quality of our interpersonal support system. Crisis counseling seeks to help people turn to others who care about them, believe in them, and are honest with them. (10) Handling heavy stresses, losses, and handicaps constructively tends to give one instant rapport with other people confronting similar crises. In crisis work it is important to encourage people to reach out with an "insider's" understanding and caring to others in similar deep water. The experience of mutual growthing, which is part of the power of self-help groups like AA, illustrates a dynamic that can be used productively in much crisis counseling.

It *is* possible for us human beings to transform many of the minuses in our lives into at least partial pluses! It is an expression of the wonder of being human when people take miserable circumstances and discover unexpected possibilities for some good, even some growth in them! Asking people, *after* they have coped with a heavy crisis, questions like these—"What have you learned from this painful situation?" or "Has anything positive come out of this miserable situation you've been in?"—helps awaken awareness of ways they have grown, as a result of struggling to handle the crisis.

Growth Resources in Rational-Emotive Therapy

Rational-Emotive Therapy (RET) is a cognitive therapy (rather than a behavior therapy) created by psychologist Albert Ellis. It complements behavior therapies by focusing on the cognitive determinants of ineffective behavior. According to Ellis, the well-being and growth of persons are determined by how they use four essential and interdependent human processes—perceiving, feeling, acting, and thinking. Disturbances in our feelings, perceptions, and action arise, to a considerable degree, from irrational and invalid thoughts and beliefs such as these:[21]

—I must be perfectly adequate, competent, and achieving before I can think of myself as being worthwhile.
—I must be approved or loved by almost everyone I know for virtually everything I do.
—When I am very frustrated, treated unfairly, or rejected, I must view myself and things in general as awful and catastrophic.
—My emotional misery is derived from external pressures, and I therefore have little ability to control or change my feelings.
—I must preoccupy myself and keep myself anxious about things that seem dangerous or fearsome.
—I must blame myself (and others) severely when I (or they) make serious mistakes or do something wrong.
—It is catastrophic if I cannot find perfect solutions to the grim realities in my life.
—It is easier to avoid facing difficulties than to take self-responsibility and develop more rewarding self-discipline.
—All the beliefs held by respected persons or by our society are accurate and should not be questioned.

The process by which we disturb ourselves has three stages according to RET: A. *Activating event*—Someone criticizes us harshly and unfairly. B. *Belief system*—Our perception of this event is colored by the irrational belief that one's worth is dependent on others' approval. C. *Consequent emotion*—As a result, we feel depressed, worthless, and as though a major catastrophe has occurred.

The process of correcting these feelings has two steps: D. *Disputing the irrational belief*—This involves learning to identify the irrational thoughts or beliefs that we are saying to ourselves and then correcting these self-damaging inner statements. E. *Event is transformed*—The activating event is reevaluated in light of a rational and valid idea—"I don't have to be approved by everyone in order to have a sense of my basic worth." Constructive feelings and behavior flow from the rational belief.

RET therapists actively challenge their clients' irrational ideas, expectations, and beliefs. They teach their clients to do the same and then to substitute rational, self-accepting ideas for dealing with the inevitable frustrations, which occur in everyone's life in this very imperfect world. Ellis describes how he works with a client: "I try many maneuvers to try to achieve a consistent goal: to see how quickly I can get him to . . . understand exactly what he is doing to make this thing bothersome, and to discover what he can do to stop bothering himself."[22]

The basic theory of RET is useful in helping people identify and interrupt the disruptive belief-feeling-behavior cycles in which they are caught. Most psychotherapies deemphasize the role of concepts and beliefs in producing emotional distress and distorted behavior. In contrast, this therapy (and others like it) recognizes the critical influence of the cognitive dimension in both our problems and our growth.

The cognitive therapies provide valuable resources for those of us who are concerned with correcting growth-diminishing religious beliefs. The rigid theology of many individuals and families both reflects and reinforces the rigid values and life-style by which they constrict their growth and freedom. Head-on attacks on their defensive, security-giving belief systems (as in the RET's approach) often are ineffective in helping them change to more growthful beliefs. But it is important for pastoral counselors and other therapists to be aware of the ways in which their beliefs feed and exacerbate their negative feelings and behavior. The therapist's gentle but direct efforts to enable them to reevaluate and revise their pathogenic beliefs may help them gradually relax their defensive hold on growth-constricting beliefs. Such "theotherapy" usually takes considerable time, but it can be crucial in liberating the potentials of individuals and family systems to grow spiritually and otherwise.[23]

Some Limitations of Behavior Therapies

The behavior therapies have both strengths and weaknesses when viewed from a whole-person, growth perspective. There is validity in their view that all persons function (to at least some degree) like computers programmed by past experience. (In persons whose growth is severely blocked, e.g., psychotics, the automaton-like aspects of their personalities dominate much of their behavior.) As behavior therapists claim, the principles of learning on which their therapies are explicitly based also describe the ways in which the change produced by other therapies takes place. Certainly the techniques for self-reprogramming of faulty learning—e.g., those developed by the sex therapies—can be valuable to persons all along the mental health continuum.

But the underlying philosophy of personality in classical behaviorism is partial and therefore, by itself, an incomplete understanding of human beings. Radical behaviorists like B. F. Skinner understand all human behavior reductionistically, as controlled entirely by the external environment. Skinner declares: "As we learn more about the effects of the environment we have less reason to attribute any part of human behavior to an autonomous controlling agent."[24] Such a view ignores the fact that there is a self-determining, inner dimension to persons, a dimension that is most evident in relatively whole or "healthy" persons. This view eliminates human freedom, choice, and intentionality. By attending only to external, observable behavior, the radical behaviorists make therapeutic change measurable, but they achieve this by ignoring all the rich, inner choiceful dimensions, all the complexity and mystery of human beings. Such a view also ignores the dimension of Spirit, the transcendent Self.

Fortunately, most behavior therapists do not operate out of a rigid S-R (stimulus-response) Skinnerian model of personality. Rather they work from an S-O-R (stimulus-organism-response) model, which recognizes that most people have some ability to choose among their options. The cognitive-behavior therapists have corrected the Skinnerian view of persons to a considerable degree by focusing on changing inner, covert behavior such as beliefs and feelings as well as overt behavior.

The analytic emphasis on the deeper dynamics of human behavior and the behaviorist emphasis on regarding behavioral "symptoms" as real problems both have therapeutic validity. As the behavioral therapies hold, many maladaptive learned behaviors do require therapeutic attention. Alcoholism is a vivid example of a "runaway symptom." The excessive drinking, which leads eventually to alcoholism, initially may have been motivated by anxiety and conflicts from deeper levels of the personality. But the use of alcohol as a self-prescribed pain-deadener creates a runaway symptom of increasing drinking in a vain attempt to overcome the psychological and physiological pain resulting from previous excessive drinking. What began as a surface symptom becomes a problem demanding treatment in itself. As AA has shown, unless the vicious cycle of this addictive process can be interrupted (by avoiding the first drink), sobriety will not be achieved and any underlying psychological problems will remain inaccessible to therapy. But some alcoholics feel worse, not better, when they stop drinking. Their intrapsychic sources of conflict, guilt, and anxiety must be treated by psychotherapy if their sobriety is to be permanent. This same principle applies to many non-alcoholics. It is possible to change some destructive feelings by learning to behave more constructively. But some hidden, conflictual feelings must be resolved therapeutically if behavioral changes are to be permanent. A whole-person approach focuses simultaneously in therapy on changing both overt behavior and underlying feelings, values, attitudes, concepts, and beliefs (covert behavior). This often involves the use of behavioral methods in conjunction with complementary methods from depth therapists.

Psychologist Perry London, who has contributed to the development of the behavior-action therapies, observes:

> Not all the problems that people bring to psychotherapy can be, with equal ease, identified as limited problems of function, and even when they can, it is not always possible to restore functioning without radical changes in the patient's system of meaning. Phobias are good examples of clear-cut symptoms where function is lost and may be directly restored, and we may likewise grant that many other psychic problems rest in learned anxieties. . . . But one cannot speak so glibly of dysfunction of husbands who are

> unhappy with their wives and seek counsel, or of young people who, fearing an insecure and shadowed future, fear to cast themselves into it in love and work . . . , or the aging whose fear of what is ahead co-mingles with regret at what is left behind, and seek both solace and repair.[25]

In the contemporary world it is impossible to ignore the epidemic of meaninglessness, which produces many of the psychological, psychosomatic, behavioral, and relational problems of those who come seeking help. Behavioral methods are most effective with clear behavioral dysfunction. They become progressively less helpful for problems in which meaning-emptiness plays a larger and larger role.

Behavior therapies have been labeled by some of their critics in the humanist tradition as forms of "mind manipulation" and even "therapeutic brainwashing." There is evidence that learning theory techniques have been misused in manipulative ways in some institutional settings without the informed consent of those being changed. It is probably true that behavioral approaches lend themselves to this type of manipulative, covert misuse. But it is invalid to dismiss all the helpful behavioral approaches because they are vulnerable to misuse. As in all sound therapy, persons who come for help should be free to choose the goals of change. The choice ordinarily is made in collaboration with the therapist, but the directions of change desired by the persons receiving therapy usually should be ultimately respected. Behavioral methods should be used openly and their probable effects explained to the clients. With persons not able to make the decision for themselves—e.g., very small children and mentally ill persons who are out of touch with reality—it may be necessary for others to choose the directions of change without their consent. But such exceptions to the basic principle of self-determination should be made with great caution, using built-in safeguards, and only with persons who are really incapable of choosing. The ultimate goal of the behavioral methods, when they are used growthfully, is to *teach troubled persons self-help tools* for enabling them to increase their own self-determination and effectiveness in living. This is the way in which many of the cognitive behavior therapies are now being used.

It is important to use behavior therapies in the context of systems-oriented approaches (described in chapters 9 and 10). Otherwise behavior therapies, like any individualistic approaches, can be misused to adjust people to pathogenic relationships, institutions, or cultures. To do this is to inhibit, in the long run, full human growth.

Finally, it is important to use behavioral methods with a light touch and a nonmechanistic style. This anecdote illustrates the importance of this approach:

> A famous rat psychologist has been trying for years to conduct experiments which would show him how to raise the I.Q. of rats. . . . [He] persevered and set up laboratory situation after laboratory situation and educational environment after educational environment and the rats never seemed to get any smarter. Finally, quite recently, he issued a statement that the only thing he could discover in ten years which made rats any smarter was to allow them to roam at random in a spacious and variegated environment.[26]

What is true of rats seems to be even more true of human beings!

For Further Exploration of Growth Resources in Behavior-Action Therapies

Beck, Aaron T. *Cognitive Therapy and Emotional Disorders.* New York: International Universities Press, 1976. Integrates cognitive and behavior approaches.

Clinebell, Howard. *Growth Counseling: Coping Constructively with Crises.* Nashville: Abingdon Press, 1974. A series of eight crisis-counseling training courses on cassettes with a users' guide.

Dustin, Richard, and George, Rickey. *Action Counseling for Behavior Change.* Cranston, R.I.: Carroll Press, 1977. Discusses learning theory, action counseling techniques with individuals and groups.

Ellis, Albert, and Harper, Robert A. *A Guide to Rational Living.*

Englewood Cliffs, N.J.: Prentice Hall, 1961. Applies the rational-emotive therapy approach to problems in living.

Foreyt, John P., and Rathjen, Dianna P., eds. *Cognitive Behavior Therapy, Research and Application.* New York: Plenum Press, 1978. A collection of papers on the use of cognitive behavior methods with a variety of types of problems.

Glasser, William. *Reality Therapy: A New Approach to Psychiatry.* New York: Harper, 1965. An introduction to the theory and practice of reality therapy.

———. *Schools Without Failure.* New York: Harper, 1969. Applies reality therapy principles to improving education.

Kaplan, Helen Singer. *The Illustrated Manual of Sex Therapy.* New York: The New York Times Book Co., 1975. A manual on sex therapy illustrated with drawings of couples.

———. *The New Sex Therapy: Active Treatment of Sexual Dysfunction.* New York: Brunner/Mazel, 1974. A book on the theory and practice of Kaplan's sex therapy, integrating methods from learning theory, dynamic psychotherapy, and marital therapy.

Knox, David. *Dr. Knox's Marital Exercise Book.* New York: David McKay, 1975. A do-it-yourself guide for couples using behavior methods to resolve problems in such areas as communication, sex, alcohol, friends, parents, children, and money.

———. *Marriage Happiness, A Behavioral Approach to Counseling.* Champaign, Ill.: Research Press, 1971. A valuable application of behavioral techniques to marriage counseling and therapy.

Levis, Donald J., ed. *Learning Approaches to Therapeutic Behavior Change.* Chicago: Aldine, 1970. A series of papers exploring the history, principles, and theory of behavioral therapy.

London, Perry. *The Modes and Morals of Psychotherapy.* New York: Holt, Rinehart and Winston, 1964. Contrasts insight and action types of therapy, and describes the approaches of some of the major behavioral therapies.

Mash, Eric J.; Handy, Lee C.; and Hamerlynck, Leo A. *Behavior Modification Approaches to Parenting.* New York: Brunner/Mazel, 1976. The uses of behavioral methods in training parents.

Stone, Howard. *Crisis Counseling.* Philadelphia: Fortress Press, 1976. A succinct introduction to crisis intervention methods.

———. *Using Behavioral Methods in Pastoral Counseling.* Philadelphia: Fortress Press, 1979. A practical guide to the use of behavioral approaches.

Stuart, Richard B., and Davis, Barbara. *Slim Chance in a Fat World.* Champaign, Ill.: Research Press, 1972. A behavioral approach to overcoming obesity.

Switzer, David K. *The Minister as Crisis Counselor.* Nashville: Abingdon Press, 1974. Describes crisis intervention theory and its use by pastoral counselors, with chapters on grief, family crises, and divorce.

Wolpe, Joseph; Salter, Andrew; and Reyna, L. J. *The Conditioning Therapies.* New York: Holt, Rinehart and Winston, 1964. Describes the challenge of various conditioning therapies to psychoanalysis.

Yates, Aubrey J. *Behavior Therapy.* New York: Wiley, 1970. Describes the application of behavioral methods to a wide variety of human problems.

Chapter 6

Growth Resources in Transactional Analysis

Transactional Analysis (TA for short) was developed by psychiatrist Eric Berne, who was born in Montreal, Canada, in 1910. He received his medical degree at McGill University and his psychiatric training at York Psychiatric Clinic. After extensive training at the New York City and San Francisco Psychoanalytic Institutes, his application for membership as a psychoanalyst was rejected. Apparently this spurred him to develop his own understanding of personality, relationships, and therapy.[1] TA did not receive widespread attention until *Games People Play* was published in 1964. (It sold over three million copies.) Berne lived in Carmel, California, dividing his practice between that city, where he did his writing, and San Francisco, where he also led a TA training group. He was a shy person who kept considerable distance from others, including those who cared about him. He loved and admired the fun-loving Child in other people and always arranged to have a party after training seminars. He died of a coronary in 1970.

In my two brief contacts with Eric Berne,[2] I was struck by the freshness of much that he was saying and the relevance of many of his ideas to my work. In my experience, TA is one of the four most fruitful sources of tools for use in growth-oriented counseling, therapy, and teaching—the other three being gestalt therapy, psychosynthesis, and feminist therapy. I make use of TA's conceptual tools regularly in teaching and growth groups, in counseling and therapy. TA's concepts are easily taught. Its language is non-threatening, even playful. Many people can use its concepts and methods as self-help tools. In marriage counseling and enrichment, the relational orientation of TA makes it particularly valuable. The system lends itself to integration with other, complementary approaches such as gestalt therapy.

TA's Understanding of Growth

TA offers an easily understood conceptual picture of the nature and goals of growth. Its theory of growth is based on a tripartite understanding of personality. All persons have three dimensions, or "ego states," in their personalities—Parent, Adult, Child (PAC). Our Parent ego state consists of the internalized attitudes, feelings, and behavior patterns of our parents (and other authority figures—e.g., teachers) as we experienced them in the early years of our lives. The inner Parent has two parts—the *nurturing Parent,* which is caring and loving, and the *prejudicial Parent,* who is full of demands, "oughts," and "shoulds." The Child ego state consists of the feelings, attitudes, and behavior patterns of the little girl or boy we once were. This ego state also has two parts—the *natural Child,* who is spontaneous, playful, and creative; and the *adapted Child,* who is dominated or "spoiled" by the inner Parent. The Parent and Child, though formed in early life, continue to function actively in current behavior and relationships. The Adult ego state is the present-oriented, coping-with-reality part of the personality. Each of the ego states is essential for a full life. The Child brings creativity, intuition, spontaneity, and enjoyment to one's life. The Parent side enables one to be a good parent to one's children. Because of its accumulated experience, it frees the Adult from having to make innumerable decisions daily (such as looking both ways before crossing a street). The Adult is essential for coping constructively with reality.

A healthy, growing person, in TA's understanding, is one in whom there is "a happy mixture of Parent, Child and Adult with the Adult in the driver's seat."[3] In such persons, the free, effective Adult takes information from the Child, the Parent, and from external reality, and then makes a decision to act in a way that will result in movement toward constructive goals. Persons can function intentionally only to the degree that their Adult is emancipated from control by their Parent and Child sides. The liberated Adult can then choose when it is appropriate to be guided by the inner Parent and when to let the fun-loving, natural Child frolic freely. The ultimate goal of TA therapy is "autonomy," which is manifested in the recovery of three capacities—awareness, spontaneity, and intimacy. Awareness allows one to enjoy being alive in the present. Spontaneity means freedom to choose and liberation from the compulsion to play manipulative games. Intimacy is the game-free openness of the aware person.

TA is essentially a growth- and hope-centered approach. Based on his therapeutic work in mental hospitals with "regressed" patients who had failed to respond to other therapies, Berne came to a startling conclusion. He became convinced that everyone, even "deteriorated" schizophrenics, has a complete Adult which can be mobilized! The potential for growth is still there, even in persons labeled "hopeless" by conventional psychiatric diagnosis. The crucial issue in therapy is how to activate the long-neglected Adult. As Eric Berne put it, "There is always a radio, the problem is how to get it plugged in."[4] So-called "immature" people are those in whom the Child side takes over inappropriately and unproductively.

Berne was keenly aware of what came to be called the "Pygmalion effect" in therapy. He saw the importance of relating to persons in terms of their strengths and potentialities rather than their weaknesses and "pathology": "If a patient is treated as though he had a 'weak ego,' he is likely to respond accordingly. If he is treated as though he had a perfectly good ego which only needs to be activated . . . he will become more rational and objective toward the outside world and toward himself."[5]

Berne's growth orientation was saved from superficial optimism by a realistic view of the power of games and scripts, which make the achievement of game-free spontaneity, awareness, and intimacy exceedingly difficult. "Games" are stereotyped, repetitive, mutually manipulative interactions between two people. Berne wrote, "A game is an ongoing series of complementary ulterior transactions progressing to a well-defined, predictable outcome."[6] Games are also defenses by which we seek to protect ourselves from not-okay feelings. Every game has a pay-off for both persons, but the price is high. Games are the opposite of open, authentic, loving, and growing relationships.

By observing their parents' games, young children learn the one or more games that will dominate interaction among their ego states and in their relationships through their lives. In addition, children adopt an unconscious life plan or "script," which they expect to fulfill. This expectation causes them to behave (without their being aware of it) so as to make their script come true. To the degree that a person's games and scripts are functioning outside their awareness, they are locked into feelings and behavior programmed by their old Parent and Child tapes. Under these circumstances, their feelings of autonomy and freedom are largely illusory.[7] Their growth potentials are frozen.

In spite of this deep programming, the Adult does have the power to change. TA therapy aims at helping people empower their inner Adult to change from programmed responses to more spontaneous, appropriate, and constructive responses in each situation. Berne declared, "While every human being faces the world initially as the captive of his script, the great hope and value of the human race is that the Adult can be dissatisfied with such strivings when they are unworthy."[8] As people become aware of their games and scripts, and the destructive consequences of being under their control, the motivation to change increases. The momentum of change accelerates as they discover that, in fact, they *can* change, to some degree! Although Berne held considerable hope for fortunate individuals (who have TA therapy) to break out of the trap of their programming, he was pessimistic concerning the possibilities of people generally doing so.

TA concepts are useful growth tools all along the wholeness

continuum, from relatively dysfunctional to highly functional persons. When they seem appropriate, I present the basic PAC tool during an early session and then coach clients on how to use it. Some people, of course, do not find the TA approach useful. However, relatively functional people often begin to use TA concepts quickly to understand and mobilize their inner responses and change their relationships. The fact that TA helps some people acquire freeing insights quickly (often within the first session) is one of its assets. With less functional people, a series of sessions of "coaching" in using TA tools is usually required before they begin to have the skill to use them on their own.

Structural Analysis in Growth-oriented Counseling

There are four phases of the process of TA therapy, each representing a significant dimension of personal growth work. The first three are useful in short-term crisis counseling, in growth groups, and in marriage enrichment and counseling. All four phases are useful in longer-term therapy. The first phase, *structural analysis,* seeks to help people learn to recognize when particular ego states are in the driver's seat of their inner lives. The aim is to free the Adult to guide behavior and to choose when to let the Parent and Child sides be activated.

I usually introduce the PAC approach in counseling or growth group sessions by diagramming it on a sheet of paper and giving an illustration or two of the times I let my own Parent and Child take over unconstructively. I then ask if what I have described throws any light on feelings and problems that we have been discussing. Some clients respond immediately, giving examples of how they let their Child or Parent sides take over. I explain that they may find it helpful in changing the responses they don't like, to practice being aware of when these takeovers occur. By attending to our inner Parent-Child responses we exercise and thus strengthen our Adult. If, during a counseling session or growth group, I sense that a person's Child or Parent is turned on, I may inquire, "Which part of you is in the driver's seat now?"

The question often activates the person's Adult awareness, which gives him or her power to choose other responses.[9]

In a key passage Berne declared:

> Actionism is an essential feature of structural analysis. The Adult is regarded in much the same light as a muscle which increases its strength with exercise. Once the preliminary phase of decontamination and clarification [of the Adult] are well under way, the patient is expected to practice Adult control. He must learn to keep the Adult running the show for relatively long periods. . . . It is he, and not the Child, who decides more and more effectively when the Child shall take over.[10]

Structural analysis is particularly useful in crisis counseling to help persons interrupt the vicious cycles of panic and paralysis (their frightened Child), which produce inappropriate behavior, which in turn increases the feelings of panic and helplessness. The crisis counselor's task is to make her or his nurturing Parent available to the person by showing genuine caring and warm empathy. This nurturing tends to quiet the frightened Child in the person and to free energy (which was going into the Child ego state) for use by the person's coping Adult. But, all during this nurturing support, the counselor should raise reality questions, which often help to activate the person's Adult. I use four types of questions to help persons mobilize their Adult: What are the important things in this crisis with which you must deal? With which part of your crisis situation will you deal *now* in order to begin improving things? What concrete plans will you make for this constructive action? What resources within yourself and your relationship (including your spiritual resources), can you use in implementing this action plan? Berne was convinced that feelings will change if behavior changes. As people in crises use their Adult to improve their situation in small but significant ways, their self-confidence, hope, and cope-ability gradually increase.

Structural analysis can be useful to us "workaholics" to help us understand and diminish our addiction to excessive working. The repetitive will-of-the-wisp message from one's demanding

Parent to one's adapted Child is clear: "Keep working! Keep achieving! *If* you ever accomplish enough, I *may* accept you." Liberation of one's playful Child from the domination of the demanding Parent can occur as one's Adult learns to enjoy this fun-loving, creative, spontaneous part of oneself.

Transactional Analysis in Growth-oriented Counseling

The second phase of TA growth work, *transactional analysis,* aims at helping persons learn to recognize and control the Parent-Child ego states, which are dominating their transactions with other people. For example, many of the mutually frustrating, circular fights that bring couples to marriage counseling are Parent-Child transactions. To illustrate, a husband, arriving late, responds defensively to his wife's Adult questions about his lateness by coming on with his critical Parent (evident in his accusing, condescending tone of voice and verbal attack): "If you weren't such a nagging bitch, maybe I'd want to get home faster! Did you ever think of that?" Wife (whiny, angry Child voice): "I've got a right to complain when you're so damn selfish and don't care about me!" Such circular P-C arguments produce escalating mutual hurt and distancing, never a resolution of the basic issues between two people. P-C fights can be interrupted only if one party activates her or his Adult and hooks the other's Adult. When such an unproductive argument occurs during a counseling session or marriage group, the counselor may ask, "Are you aware of what's going on between you?" In some cases, this question activates their Adult sides so that they become aware of their futile P-C cycle. Then through Adult-to-Adult negotiations, they may work at resolving their conflicting needs by constructive compromises that enable some of each person's needs to be met.

One of the unique assets of TA is that it provides conceptual tools for discovering the interrelationships between what occurs *within* an individual and what occurs *between* that person and others. This linking between intrapsychic and interpersonal dynamics makes TA particularly useful in relationship counseling and enrichment work. Back-and-forth movement in counseling, from structural analysis, focusing on interaction among the three ego states within each individual, to transactional analysis, focusing on what is going on between the persons, often illuminates the correlation of these two dimensions of our lives.

In marriage enrichment workshops, it is helpful to teach structural and transactional analysis to couples as a tool for interrupting their own negative spirals of conflict. The exercise at the end of this chapter can be used to teach this experientially, or a couple can be asked to reenact a recent unproductive argument in front of the group. Such a reenactment usually results in a demonstration of Parent-Child interaction. In using this approach, it is essential to debrief the feelings stirred up in the participants thoroughly and then to ask them to suggest and try (in role playing) alternative ways of communicating that will avoid the mutual-frustrating P-C interaction. In this way one coaches couples in Adult-to-Adult communication, thus enabling them to experience effective ways of resolving conflicts.

It is important in work with couples to help them learn to activate their nurturing Parent sides to give each other more positive "strokes," the warm expressions of appreciation and affirmation that all of us need. Negative cycles of mutual deprivation happen less frequently when couples learn to give and receive more affirming strokes and thus to initiate cycles of mutual nurture.

Structural analysis and transactional analysis are useful tools in youth counseling and teen growth groups. The key growth task with which many adolescents struggle is how to keep their Adult in the driver's seat, to avoid slipping back into unproductive behavior domination by their inner Child, and yet to allow their playful Child to enjoy life. Many teen-agers understand TA concepts quickly and enjoy the playful experience of "catching" their own and one another's games. By exercising their Adult sides in this way, they strengthen their ability to keep them in the driver's seat of their lives.

The third phase of the TA process, *game analysis,* consists of helping persons learn to identify and interrupt the repetitive self-defeating game or games they are programmed to use in relating. It is difficult, but many people *can* learn to recognize and interrupt old repetitive games. They can learn to avoid having their adapted Child hooked when someone comes on as prejudicial Parent. To the extent that their Adults can interrupt their manipulative games, their potential for authenticity and intimacy will be increased. Most married couples have one or two games which dominate their interaction. Some favorite marital games are: "If It Weren't for You . . ." (the projection of blame); and "Uproar" (having a fight to avoid anxiety-producing sexual intimacy); "Why Don't You—Yes But" (futile P-C advice-giving); "I'm Only Trying to Help You" (rationalizing manipulative behavior); "Kick Me" (played by a submissive person); and "Look How Hard I've Tried" (to convince the counselor one is the "helpful" and "righteous," wronged partner). Game analysis helps people discover the payoff of their games, the rewards they must be willing to give up in order to stop the games. The payoffs are often defenses against fears and "not-okay" feelings. In spite of the payoffs, nobody really wins interpersonal games, for the price of playing such a game is to sacrifice an open, loving, intimate relationship. An important reward of interrupting one's marital games is that one can thus avoid teaching them to one's children.

The fourth phase of TA is *script analysis*. This aims at helping people identify their unconscious life plan, which they expect and are living out. Some people are "programmed" with tragic scripts, which cause them to live as losers with overwhelming feelings of powerlessness and joylessness. An example of a tragic script is that of a woman whose father was an alcoholic. Her unconscious script called for her to keep trying to prove that she could do a better job with an alcoholic than her mother did with her father. Consequently, by the time she came for counseling, she had married and divorced a series of three alcoholics. The goal of script analysis is to help people free themselves from the control of their scripts by becoming aware of them and then mobilizing their Adult to choose a more potentializing life plan.

TA can be a tool in liberating ourselves from the growth-restricting sex-role programming most of us internalized as small girls and boys in our culture. Hogie Wyckoff observes:

> As women and men we were socialized to develop certain parts of our personalities while suppressing the development of other parts. . . . Sex role scripts invade every fiber of our day-to-day lives. . . . A man is "supposed to be" rational, productive, hardworking, but he is "*not* supposed to be" emotional, in touch with his feelings, or overly loving. On the other hand, a woman is not supposed to think rationally, be able to balance the checkbook, or be powerful.
>
> A particularly unhealthy result of male-female sex role training is that gaps have been created in people which limit their potential to become *whole* human beings. Often what happens with men and women is that they feel incomplete when they lack a partner of the opposite sex, so that they continually look for fulfillment in another.[11]

In our culture men are pressured to conform to a script that impoverishes their lives and relationships by preventing the full development of their nurturing Parent and their free playful Child. They are pressured by culturally defined male scripts to always stay Adult—rational, strong, in control. Typical life-distorting scripts for men include "Big Daddy," "Playboy," and "Jock." Women are impoverished by being culturally scripted to overdevelop their nurturing Parent (and thus to exist for the purpose of taking care of and pleasing "their man" and their children) and to feel powerless because they have not developed their potential Adult competencies. Scripts which trap the potential of many women include "Mother Hubbard" (who takes care of everyone but herself), "Poor Little Me," "Nurse," and "Queen Bee."[12] In their guide to the use of TA by women for self-liberation, Dorothy Jongeward and Dru Scott declare:

> When a woman becomes aware of the negative or destructive elements in the messages she has been programmed to follow, she realizes that she has options. . . . She no longer limits her growth to bend to the boundaries set by collective pressures. Just as a little girl can make early decisions that affect the blueprint of her life [her script], a woman can make a redecision to change her life's direction in a positive way. She can help the little girl inside choose to be a winner.[13]

When men and women reclaim their full selves by breaking out of their culture's conditioning, they can relate to each other as equals in a satisfing variety of ways: Adult-to-Adult (in solving a reality problem together); playful Child-to-playful Child (in good sex, for example); nurturing Parent-to-Child (as one cares for the other during sickness or a crisis in that person's life); and nurturing Parent-to-nurturing Parent (when they are engaged in mutual affirmation and caring).

As a growth-oriented therapy, TA is essentially a self-help approach. The role of the therapist is that of enabler, teacher, and coach, whose task is helping people's Adults learn to interrupt their own growth-diminishing games and scripts. TA therapists aim at relating to their clients Adult-to-Adult, thus activating or "hooking" their Adult. They often tell clients openly what they are doing in therapy and why. TA counselors seek to work themselves out of a job as quickly as possible by teaching clients the basic tools they need to activate their own Adults.

TA offers resources to growth-oriented counselors who are committed to changing the wider systems beyond intimate relationships. A crucial need of our times is to develop institutions that encourage and support Adult behavior. Authority-centered, Big Parent institutions and governments try to keep people's submissive Child sides in control of their inner lives. Such institutions diminish the growth of millions of people.[14]

Churches are particularly prone to being Big Parent institutions. When they are, they stifle the very thing they exist to facilitate—spiritually centered growth toward wholeness. In *Born to Love* Muriel James shows how to use TA to enhance the life of a church. She discusses how TA's concepts can be used in discussing theological concepts; in understanding the dynamics of a committee; in holding a staff or a congregational meeting; in choosing music for the choir; in preaching and in teaching as well as in personal growth and counseling groups.

TA Resources for Spiritual Growth

Although Eric Berne had little to say about religion, Thomas Harris, Muriel James, and Tom Oden have applied TA to religious and ethical growth in illuminating ways. Harris observes: "The Parent-Child nature of most western religions is remarkable when one considers that the revolutionary impact of most revered religious leaders was directly the result of their courage to examine Parent institutions and proceed, with the Adult, in search of truth. It takes only one generation . . . for an inference about experience to become a dogma."[15] Clergypersons have often retained control over their people by fostering in them "Not-Okay Child" feelings of fear and guilt, which constrict their spiritual growth. Without a free, energized inner Adult, the prejudicial Parent and the over-needy Child will distort one's beliefs, values, and experiences of God. Parental religion is a projection of infantile wishes onto the way one perceives spiritual reality, thereby blocking authentic spiritual experiencing. TA is a useful tool for helping people "put away childish things" spiritually by de-Parentifying their religious attitudes and beliefs. This process frees them to develop their own Adult beliefs based on their own spiritual searching and discoveries. By letting go of their projection of prejudicial Parent attitudes onto God, they free themselves to experience the nurturing, loving Parent and reality-affirming Adult aspects of God's Spirit.

TA can help facilitate growth in the areas of ethics and values. To the extent that people's behavior is controlled by old programming (P-C games and scripts) no free choices are possible. Therefore, no genuine ethical behavior can occur. In spiritual growth work, people can evaluate their old ethical programming (internalized in their childhood conscience) and claim as their own those values which ring true in their Adult experiences. As long as people are living out of the secondhand values that they internalized from their parents, they will always be ethically ambivalent and self-sabotaging in their behavior. As people develop their own Adult values they can commit their life-styles to them more wholeheartedly.

Muriel James and Louis Savary have added an important dimension to TA in their discussion of the "spiritual self." They see this as the deepest core of our being, which unites and enlivens the three ego states. They describe religious experience "as awareness of the Power Within penetrating the Inner Core, flowing through the Parent, Adult, and Child, and expressing itself in relation to God."[16] The "Power within us" is the renewing experience of the Spirit of love. When the Power Within flows through one's Child, one's relationships with God and with people become more trusting and loving. When it flows through one's Parent, one is empowered to respond to one's own needs *and* the needs of others! When it flows through one's Adult, a person will be enlivened in the area of responsible decisions based on accurate perceptions of reality.

TA's Limitations from a Growth Counseling Perspective

From the Growth Counseling perspective, TA has much to offer. It also has some weaknesses and limitations. Because TA is essentially a rational therapy, it requires supplementation by more in-depth, feeling-level methods. Certain gestalt therapy methods, for example, complement TA, by providing effective means of changing growth-blocking Parent and Child tapes. Muriel James' and Dorothy Jongeward's *Born to Win* and L. Richard Lessor's *Love and Marriage and Trading Stamps* are books that integrate TA and gestalt approaches.

Another limitation of TA is the oversimplified way in which the PAC ego states are often described. Clinical experience has made it clear to me that there are several different Child sides from different stages of our early lives.[17] There is not just one Parent but several, representing our mothers and fathers and other authority figures as we experienced them at various stages of our early lives. These inner Parents often are in conflict among themselves. There is also an inner Adolescent, who tends to become activated when we relate to teen-agers.[18] Our Adolescent's inner Parents are different from those of our Child simply because our parents responded differently to us as teen-agers than they did to us as children. The persons we once were, at each life stage, are still there influencing our present lives. Our inner relationships from the past are much richer and more complex than the simplistic PAC schema suggests. It's important in our growth work for our Adult to get acquainted with all these inner "persons" from our past. Getting to know and like our inner Adolescent, for example, can enable us to relate more constructively to teen-agers.

Tom Oden points out that Eric Berne tends to champion the natural Child and castigate the Parent as the primary culprit in diminishing a full life.[19] There is no doubt that the spontaneity and creativity of many people *is* diminished by rigid, controlling inner Parent messages. Many of us *do* need to be liberated from such oppressive Parent influences within ourselves. But many younger people today have not internalized heavy-handed Parent ego states. Their parents were emotionally absent or ethically confused and afraid to set dependable limits. Such people need to re-Parent themselves by developing constructive inner guidelines to enable them to have responsible, mutually caring relationships. Because of Berne's valuing of the natural Child, TA has tended toward hyperindividualism that underestimates the need for healthy self-other commitments for covenants of *mutual* growth. When using TA in growth work it is important to utilize the contributions of people like Muriel James and Tom Oden, who have gone far beyond Berne in emphasizing a sense of interpersonal and societal responsibility as a part of TA.

In *Game Free* Oden has developed a "theology of interpersonal communion," which increases the usefulness of TA as a spiritual growth resource by strengthening its theological foundation. There is an awareness in Christianity that ultimate Reality itself undergirds and affirms our "Okay-ness." This awareness can help people move from self-rejection to self-acceptance. As Oden puts it: "God lets us know through historical events that we are, despite our sins, okay, affirmed, accepted, embraced with infinitely forgiving love."[20]

Experiencing Your Parent-Adult-Child-Adolescent

The purpose of this exercise is to let you experience several of the many valuable dimensions of your personality. The exercise can be used in a variety of counseling and growth-group situations. (In the instructions that follow, stop at each slash mark, giving yourself time to do what has been suggested. In a growth group, have someone read the instructions, giving ample time at each slash mark to complete the task.)

> Find a comfortable place to sit where you won't be disturbed for at least twenty to thirty minutes./ Wiggle and stretch your body, letting it hang loose./ Take several deep breaths, letting any tensions you feel flow out as you exhale. Close your eyes as you do this./ Now, in your mind create a motion picture of the house or apartment where you live now. Make it as vivid as possible, being aware of the colors, sounds, smells, and anything else that's important to you in your home./ See yourself alone in your house. What are you doing? How do you feel?/ Now bring any other people who live with you into the picture. Be sensitive to changes in your feelings./ Now go back in your memory and create a clear picture of the first house you lived in as a small child, adding colors, sounds, smells, and so on, which are associated with that house in your memory./ Be yourself as a small child alone in your favorite room of that house./ What are you doing? How do you feel about living in that house? Try letting yourself *be* that child for a while./ Bring one of your parents into the room with you./ What is going on between you? How does each of you feel about the other?/ Bring your other parent into the room. What is happening among the three of you?/ What are the feelings of each of you?/ If you lived with only one parent, be aware of how the last instruction made you feel./ Recall a time when your parents punished or criticized you severely. Relive that experience fully in your mind./ Recall a time when your parents behaved affirmingly and lovingly. Relive that experience./ Bring others who lived in

that home (siblings, other relatives, pets) into the room, one at a time, being sensitive to what happens between you and in your feelings./ Go out of your home, now. Be aware of how you feel about your relationship in the neighborhood/ at school/ in your church/ with other relatives./ Now recall the happiest day of your childhood. Relive that day, savoring the good feelings you still have about it./ Recall the most unhappy day of your childhood—the time you felt most miserable, hopeless, or rejected. Relive that day, re-experiencing the painful feelings you still have about it./ Be aware of the part of you that has been *in* your childhood situation and the other part which has been watching from your present adult perspective./ Let this Adult part of you express your warmth, esteem, and caring for your inner Child. Comfort and caress the hurting Child within you./ Say to your Child, "I love you" (using your name)./ How does the Child respond to your love and nurture?/ Now, form a picture of the house or apartment in which you lived as an adolescent./ See yourself as a teen-ager in that house./ Be that teen-ager for a while. How do you feel about yourself? About life?/ Repeat the experience of bringing your parents and other significant persons into the room, one at a time./ How do your feelings compare with those you experienced in your childhood home?/ Relive an experience of criticism or punishment by your parents when you were an adolescent./ Relive an experience of being praised, loved, appreciated./ Go out of your house now and join your teen-age friends./ What are you doing with them? Have your feelings changed?/ What are your feelings about sex? About masturbation?/ About religion?/ Right and wrong?/ The church?/ Growing up?/ Relive leaving home. Say good-bye to your family. What are your feelings and theirs?/ Be aware of the Adult part of you that has been observing yourself as a teen-ager. Try to let yourself as an Adult do something to express your love and esteem to the teen-ager within you./ Before opening your eyes, think about how you experienced your inner Child and Teen-ager./ How do these inner parts of yourself influence your present feelings and relationship?/ When you are ready, open your eyes./ Discuss your learnings with a trusted friend./

In this exercise, I hope that you got in touch with your inner Child and your inner Adolescent, as well as the Parents you carry within you. Your Adult was the part of you that watched what was happening, from your present perspective. The experience of letting your Adult express warm love and respect to your inner Child and your Teen-ager is a form of "self re-parenting."[21] This is a valuable way to care for yourself, to be a good nurturing Parent to yourself. By using the strength and warmth of your Adult, you can forgive your parents for their inadequacies (which all parents have) and reprogram your inner Parent to be more caring. (I found it helpful when my parents died to comfort "Junior," the Child within me, by holding and rocking him in my fantasy.)

If this exercise was helpful, I suggest that you use the same approach to revisit other periods of your life (in childhood, youth, young adulthood, and so on) to do the unfinished growth work from each of those stages. Do this with a trusted friend or in a small growth-support group. If you encountered an accumulation of powerful and painful feelings at any life stage, you may need the help of a skilled therapist to work that through. Working through old, unfinished pain and blocked growth can reduce the power of one's past and release vital energy for living with more creativity and zest in the present!

Further Exploration of Transactional Analysis

Berne, Eric. *Games People Play.* New York: Grove Press, 1964. A compendium of many types of games; includes an initial chapter summarizing the overall TA system.

———. *Principles of Group Treatment.* New York: Oxford University Press, 1966. Describes how to use TA in growth and therapy groups.

———. *Transactional Analysis in Psychotherapy.* New York: Grove Press, 1961. The most comprehensive and technical discussion of TA's principles.

———. *The Structure and Dynamics of Organizations and Groups.* Philadelphia: Lippincott, 1963. TA's approach to group dynamics.

———. *What Do You Say After You Say Hello?* New York: Grove, 1972. A detailed discussion of scripts.

Campos, Leonard, and McCormick, Paul. *Introduce Yourself to TA.* Stockton: San Joaquin T.A. Institute, 1974. A valuable pamphlet giving a summary and overview of TA in simple language.

Harris, Thomas A. *I'm OK—You're OK*. New York: Harper, 1969. A popularization of TA, which includes application of its principles to ethics, religion, and organizations.

James, Muriel. *Born to Love: TA in the Church.* Reading, Mass.: Addison-Wesley, 1973. A discussion of using TA principles in the church including their relevance to theology.

———, et al. *Techniques in Transactional Analysis for Psychotherapists and Counselors.* Reading, Mass.: Addison-Wesley, 1977. Forty-three papers on the philosophy, principles, methods, and applications of TA, and the relation of TA to other therapies.

James, Muriel, and Jongeward, Dorothy. *Born to Win: TA with Gestalt Experiments.* Reading, Mass.: Addison-Wesley, 1971. An integration of TA framework and gestalt therapy methods.

James, Muriel, and Savary, Louis M. *A New Self.* Reading, Mass.: Addison-Wesley, 1977. A valuable self-help book using TA.

———. *The Power at the Bottom of the Well: TA and Religious Experience.* New York: Harper, 1974. Explores the spiritual self seen as the power and the integrative center of the three ego states.

Jongeward, Dorothy. *Everybody Wins: TA Applied to Organizations.* Reading, Mass.: Addison-Wesley, 1976. Relates TA to understanding and changing organizations and institutions.

———, and Scott, Dru. *Women as Winners: TA for Personal Growth.* Reading, Mass.: Addison-Wesley, 1971. Uses TA and gestalt methods to help women create a new, positive identity.

Lessor, Richard, and Acton, Clare C. *Love, Marriage and Trading Stamps: A TA and Gestalt Approach to Marriage.* Chicago: Argus Communications, 1971. TA and gestalt therapy methods for use by couples to improve their marriages.

Oden, Thomas C. *Game Free: The Meaning of Intimacy.* New York: Harper, 1974. A theological discussion and critique of TA.

Reuter, Alan. *Who Says I'm OK? A Christian Use of TA.* St. Louis: Concordia, 1974. A theological-biblical discussion and critique of TA.

Steiner, Claude. *Games Alcoholics Play: An Analysis of Life Scripts.* New York: Grove Press, 1972. A discussion of the dynamics of the games alcoholics and those around them play.

———. *Scripts People Live.* New York: Bantam Books, 1974. A discussion of life scripts and how to change them.

Chapter 7

Growth Resources in Gestalt Therapy

The founder of gestalt therapy was psychiatrist Fredrick Perls. Born in Berlin, in 1893, he trained as a psychoanalyst before going to scrve for a timc in the South African medical corps. Perls gradually began to question and reject psychoanalysis. In 1947, he published a revision of Freud's basic theories and methods.[1] Perls came to the United States in 1952, settling in New York, where he began an institute for gestalt therapy. He moved to California in the early 1960s. By 1966 the Esalen Institute had become his primary community, his "place of being." There the charisma of his personality and his skills as a therapist impressed many persons in the human potentials movement, including many younger therapists. Perls died in 1970 while attempting to establish a gestalt-oriented therapeutic community on Vancouver Island.[2]

Throughout his life, Perls was a searcher who experienced and drew on a wide variety of philosophical and therapeutic approaches in creating gestalt therapy—psychoanalysis, gestalt psychology, bioenergetics (he was analyzed by Wilhelm Reich), psychodrama, existential philosophy, Taoism, Zen Buddhism, and the thought of Kurt Goldstein.[3] The rapid increase in the influence of his approach since his death is evident in the development of several gestalt therapy training institutes and the burgeoning writings of creative therapists who continue to modify, amplify, and enrich his original formulation.

Gestalt therapy is one of the most innovative therapies now available. It provides significant resources for growth-oriented counselors, therapists, teachers, and group facilitators. Its underlying philosophy is existentialist, holistic, and growth-centered. The word "gestalt" is used to mean "figure formation," a holistic configuration that determines all its parts. Gestalt therapy is particularly useful in helping functional people enhance their awareness and deepen their relationships, and it can be integrated in a complementary way with other growth-oriented therapies, particularly TA and psychosynthesis. This therapy has been an important resource in my own growth struggles in recent years.[4]

Insights About the Nature of Growth

The growth-orientation is robust and wholehearted in gestalt therapy. It identifies the key problem of people in our times as inner deadness; its goal is to increase psychological aliveness by facilitating growth toward wholeness. At a training workshop for therapists, Perls stated, "We are here to promote the growth process and develop the human potential."[5] He spoke of the increasing disillusionment of therapists, including himself, with the medical model. He described neurosis in Maslowian terms as a "growth disorder," which, he observed, shifts it from the medical to the educational or reeducational field.[6] To grow is to fulfill one's deep need to create. As one gestalt therapist puts it: "The act of creation is as basic as breathing or making love. We are driven to create."[7]

There is a radical holism in Perls' understanding of persons. The focus of therapy is on the organism-as-a-whole, on enabling persons to actualize the essential unity that transcends the sum of their parts. Perls rejected the split in much philosophy, psychology, and psychotherapy between the mind and the body, the human organism and the wider interpersonal environment. There is an organic unity in whole or healthy persons both within themselves and in their ongoing interaction with their environment. In healthy persons the ever-changing "contact boundary" between their organism and their environment is permeable and flexible. These qualities enable them to establish need-fulfilling contact with others, but also to withdraw from contact when privacy is needed. When the boundary between the organism and the interpersonal environment becomes rigid and nonpermeable, behavior becomes inflexible and stereotyped and people lose the ability to draw essential psychological nourishment from their ever-changing relationships. Awareness arises at the contact boundary with the interpersonal environment. Healthy contact is the lifeblood of growth, the means of relating to others with awareness, therefore nourishingly and growthfully. Therapy aims at increasing the quality of one's contactfulness.

Perls declared, "Every individual, every plant, every animal has only one inborn goal—to actualize itself as it is."[8] There is a deep trust in gestalt therapy in "the wisdom of the organism." Human beings possess an inborn capacity to meet their needs and thereby to grow. The task of therapy is to "fill in the holes in personality (created by the disowned or rejected aspects of oneself), to make the person whole again."[9] By enabling persons to relive and finish the incomplete experiences that they carry from the past, the configurations or gestalts of these experiences are completed. In this way the energy that has been locked up in unfinished gestalts becomes available for use in self-awareness and relationships. This process enables persons to move from being supported and controlled by others toward increased self-support and freedom to choose to relate to others in need-satisfying ways.

There are two interdependent poles of growth—increasing awareness of and contact with one's total mind-body organism, and increasing awareness of and contact with other people and the world (one's environment). Increased contact with others depends on increased self-awareness and self-support. My relationship with others can be only as deep and authentic as is my relationship with my own inner center. Awareness of the many polarities within oneself—kindness-cruelty, top dog-underdog, for example—allows a person to discover the unity of these seemingly antithetical sides of oneself.

There are three zones or dimensions of awareness: inner awareness of one's organism and its needs; awareness of the outer world as experienced by the senses; and a middle zone (Perls called this the DMZ) composed of our fantasies, imagination, memories, beliefs, interpretations, prejudices, and our total social programming by our culture. Perls criticized Freud for concentrating so much on understanding the middle zone that he virtually ignored the other two zones. In contrast to Freud's trust in learning by the exercise of reason (producing insight), Perls emphasized learning by moving from direct experiences of the environment and of one's organism to understanding.

The middle zone *can* function in a healthy, constructive way—e.g., in creative activities. But often it distorts perceptions and diminishes awareness of both the organism and the world outside the organism. To illustrate, a person sees a spider, adds old memories and fallacious beliefs (that all spiders are dangerous) from the middle zone to this experience, thus becoming inappropriately frightened, without checking to discover that it is a harmless, even beneficent garden spider. Therapy seeks to increase accurate awareness of both one's organism and the world by clarifying the middle zone, e.g., by helping the person discover the inaccurate belief about all spiders that prevents distinguishing beneficent from dangerous spiders.

The major blocks to growth in gestalt therapy all involve diminished awareness of what one is experiencing in the here-and-now. Reduced awareness prevents one from perceiving accurately, feeling alive, coping freely and responsibly with one's ever-changing situation. Perls held that there are four basic psychological mechanisms in the DMZ that reduce awareness and contact with oneself and others, and thereby constrict growth: *Introjection* is the "swallowing whole," in undigested form, of the attitudes, beliefs, values, oughts and shoulds, usually from parents or other authority figures. These internalized messages (Parent tapes in TA) prevent people from distinguishing what their organism really feels, needs and wants, from what others want them to feel and do. *Projection* involves disowning one's feelings and fantasies, impulses, and desires by putting these outside oneself and seeing them in other people. Projection distorts perception of others, deprives the individual of the power and potential resources of the rejected aspects of the self. *Retroflection* consists of turning inward on oneself what one would like to express to others. To illustrate, a woman feels frustrated and angry at her husband because of his disregard of her needs. But, in response to a middle zone belief—"a good woman doesn't express anger"—a belief produced by her sexist programming, she turns the anger on herself and gets a sick headache. Depression and many psychosomatic problems are the result of retroflexed anger. Behind every projection and retroflection is an introjection—an internalized message that prevents one from expressing feelings and from using a potentially valuable part of oneself (such as the assertiveness in one's anger). The fourth growth-blocking mechanism, *confluence,* is the lack of a clear sense of the boundary between one's organism and the environment. This diffused sense of identity makes impossible the healthy rhythms of flexible contact with and withdrawal from others. By these four psychological mechanisms people reduce their awareness of themselves and others, and deprive themselves of potential strengths that would enable them to stand on their own feet and function effectively.

When children do not get the acceptance, support, and nurture they need from others and cannot yet provide adequate self-support and nurture from within themselves, they learn to manipulate others to try to get their needs met. They do this by pretending to be stupid, helpless, submissive, or weak; by pleasing and flattering, and by other phony games. They also learn to manipulate themselves to conform to other's expectations by self-improvement games (called "should-isms"). All these manipulative maneuvers reduce their awareness of and contact with themselves and their strengths. Therapy seeks to interrupt such growth-blocking, self-other manipulation.

From her therapeutic work with women, Miriam Polster describes the ways in which our sexist society alienates many women from their strengths, teaching them to retroflect their real feelings and manipulate men to try to get their needs met: "Growing up a woman in our society leaves a psychological residue that cripples and deforms all but the most exceptional woman. . . . Our society reinforces in women dependent, exploitative and defensive behaviors aimed at procuring conventional and stereotyped rewards. . . . No wonder many women give up the fight."[10]

The goals of growth in gestalt therapy are really *directions* of continuing change. Artist-therapist Joseph Zinker summarizes these growth directions when he states that he hopes a person in therapy

> moves toward greater awareness of himself—his body, his feelings, his environment; learns to take ownership of his experiences, rather than projecting them on others; learns to be aware of his needs and to develop skills to satisfy himself without violating others; moves toward a fuller contact with his sensations, learning to smell, taste, touch, hear and see—to savor all aspects of himself; moves toward the experience of his power and the ability to support himself, rather than relying on whining, blaming or guilt-making in order to mobilize support from the environment; becomes sensitive to his surroundings, yet at the same time wears a coat of armour for situations which are potentially destructive or poisonous; learns to take responsibility for his actions and their consequences; feels comfortable with the awareness of his fantasy life and its expressions.[11]

The Process of Growth

Perls saw choicefulness as the wellspring of all growth. There can be no creative change until persons begin to get a sense of their own power and responsibility—that is, the *ability to choose to respond* to their organism's real needs by taking action to meet them. Persons are responsible for creating their own lives by the choices they make moment by moment. By helping people become more aware, therapy makes them more choiceful, more free to grow in a self-chosen direction.

The "paradoxical theory of change"[12] in gestalt therapy holds that when one really becomes aware in the "now," change unfolds in its own way. By being fully *in* the present, the growthful direction in which one needs to move becomes clear. The only place from which one can take a step is where one actually is. Thus, living in the future or the past prevents one from taking intentional growth steps. Miriam and Erving Polster put it well: "When a person gets a clear sense of what is happening inside him, his own directionalism will propel him into whatever experience is next for him."[13]

Increasing awareness is both the goal and the means of growth. Awareness restores self-support by enabling one to "take back one's power, mobilizing one's 'center.' "[14] Because one's contact with others depends on inner contact (awareness) with oneself, increased self-awareness is a prerequisite to more need-satisfying relations with others. Increased awareness also empowers the growth that results from experimenting with new behavior which in turn facilitates further growth in awareness.

The methods of gestalt therapy are nonanalytic and integrative. Interpretation, the key method of analytical therapies, is rejected as a counterproductive mind-game by which therapist and client both avoid experiencing the "now" fully. The therapeutic focus is on "the what and how in the here and now." Perls rejected as an irrelevant waste of time the search (which is central in all insight-oriented therapies) for the *why* of behavior. All behavior has many causes, and each of these causes has many causes. Attempts to unearth past causes do nothing to stimulate growth. Such efforts lead away from full awareness in the now, the only time that growth can possibly occur.

Growth-blocked ("neurotic") people are unable to live in the present. Their energy is wasted by guilt from unfinished, past happenings and by anxiety from fantasies about catastrophic future dangers, which they strive to ward off by frantic planning and rehearsing. Such persons consequently lack energy and awareness to enjoy living in the present moment, the only time anyone *can* be alive and aware. As the Polsters declare: "The major problem of good living is to keep up to date with the possibilities which exist rather than being stamped on the ass for all time by experiences which were only temporary."[15] As persons in therapy try to attend to the flow of here-and-now experiencing, unfinished experiences from the past keep interrupting their awareness. By paying attention to *what* is experienced now from the past, and *how* they are blocking present awareness, past experiences can be worked through and completed and that energy made available for living now. Instead of seeking to remove resistances to growth, the therapist encourages people to enter into their resistances, exaggerate and "lean into" them and thus to get in touch with the power-for-growth that is there in their resistances.

According to Perls there are five layers through which people must move as they grow from deadness to aliveness, from trappedness to freedom: (1) The *cliche layer* is composed of superficial contacts with oneself and others—e.g., "Nice day, isn't it?" Relating mainly on this level is a kind of token existence. (2) The phony, *role-playing layer* consists of the games by which we manipulate one another in vain attempts to get our needs met. (3) The *impasse or phobic layer* is the level at which one experiences the fear of emptiness or nothingness which lies behind the manipulation. This occurs in therapy when the therapist frustrates the person's manipulative games (e.g., defensive intellectualizing) by refusing to play them. (4) If persons resist the urge to flee and instead stay with the fear, they reach the *implosive or death layer.* The experience of losing the manipulative games by which one has survived brings the awareness of deadness and terror (called "hitting bottom" in AA), the experience of being paralyzed (imploded) by opposing inner forces. (5) By staying in touch with their deadness, persons then move to the *explosive layer,* in which they experience rebirth as one or more of four types of creative energy is released—repressed anger, unfinished grief, orgasm (in sexually blocked people), and the explosion into joy and laughter which Perls called *joie de vivre.* On this layer of growth a more authentic person emerges, capable of experiencing tragedy and joy, pain and laughter, more able to create her or his own future. It is clear that the process of therapy involves struggle and pain and ecstasy, death and rebirth. As Perls puts it in an oft-quoted line: "To suffer one's death and to be reborn is not easy."[16]

My personal growth in a gestalt workshop group I attended several years ago followed the basic flow of this process.[17] I was confronted there with a situation where I had to relate as myself, without the protective wall of a professional title or the status of a leader or teacher. In that setting my games became painfully evident, first to the therapists and to perceptive group members and gradually to me. I became aware of the deadness of my voice and my body much of the time; the ways my "nice guy" front and my intellectualizing games both feed and sugarcoat my anger; the way I tend to lock up my energy by not breathing fully; the way I give my power away to others, seeking by manipulation to get validation from them; the way I spend energy rehearsing in my mind what I will say to get approval from others; the ways I cut myself off from my laughing, playful, don't-give-a-damn side and thus burden myself and others as a "heavy"; the way I often stay distant from my center and therefore out of deep contact with others; the way I tend to live "five miles ahead on the road" worrying and planning; the ways I postpone living and savoring the real experiences of this moment. My anxious attempts to be a "successful" gestalt therapy patient (another game) naturally led to increased frustration and eventually despair. The impasse that followed was, indeed, deathlike. I experienced an explosion of energy, and the joy of being alive (expressed as a dancing mountain stream) when I finally gave up the frantic search for "the answer" and spontaneously began to laugh at myself and my futile attempts to manipulate myself and others.

The role of the gestalt therapist in the growth process is not that of "changer," teacher, or helper. It is to provide a relationship that will be an environment of growth, within which one can confront one's deadness and experience rebirth to one's own strengths, responsibility, pain, and joy. The therapist seeks to balance contact (supportive awareness and acceptance of the here-and-now person) and "skillful frustration" of the person's aliveness-avoiding manipulations. Perls saw the therapeutic relationships as an authentic encounter between two human beings, not a variation on the doctor-patient relationship. The therapist seeks to be present as a real person interacting in a fluid, active way with the other. There can be a playful, joyous dimension for the therapist in this encounter. In describing the therapist as an artist involved in a creative, loving encounter, Joseph Zinker identified a parallel with the experience of Artur Rubinstein, who said that "playing the piano is like making love, it fills me completely with joy."[18]

Spiritual Growth Resources in Gestalt Therapy

Many of gestalt therapy's insights and methods can be used to help persons move from growth-blocking to growth-nurturing religious experience. The authoritarianism, moralism, and legalism of much traditional religion diminishes spiritual awareness by encouraging people to *project* their own spiritual powers onto deity (thus impoverishing their inner lives), *introject* self-punishing beliefs that diminish self-other esteem and distort relationships, and *retroflex* vital assertive and sexual energies, thus blunting their aliveness. Gestalt therapy challenges the "aboutism" of endless intellectualizing (in theology and philosophy) concerning the "ultimate meaning of life" which so often becomes a substitute for the direct, enlivening experiencing of spiritual reality.

Although Perls was a nontheist who rejected his Jewish heritage, there are significant affinities between the best in the Judeo-Christian tradition and gestalt therapy. Its holistic orientation is reminiscent of the whole-person understanding of human beings in the Old Testament tradition.[19] Perls' emphasis on authentic living, on encountering the "fertile void," on death and rebirth, on awakening to one's potential and powers—all have affinities with the salugenic (wholeness-nurturing) dimension of the Judeo-Christian heritage. The influence of Eastern philosophies in Perls' thought is reflected in gestalt therapy, for example, in his Taoist-like admonition, "Don't push the river, it flows by itself,"[20] and in the paradoxical theory of change.

Several spiritually oriented gestalt therapists have sought to develop the spiritual growth potentials inherent in this approach. Claudio Naranjo has explored the many affinities between both Eastern and Western religious traditions and gestalt therapy.[21] Joseph Zinker describes creative therapy as a relational religious experience:

> Being fully present for each other in a given hour . . . is like worshipping together. . . . It is an interesting paradox that we discover our most important inner ecstasies in the process of moving beyond ourselves into other lives. It is only after such an intimate transaction . . . that we can enter into more ascending, religious transactions. To speak with God one must first give up one's narcissism, and to give up one's narcissism one must enter into an authentic dialogue with fellow human beings: To speak with God one must speak with humankind.[22]

Weaknesses of Gestalt Therapy

From the Growth Counseling perspective, gestalt therapy has several significant weaknesses. It is impoverished by the reductionistic elements in Perls' thought. In reacting against growth-blocking moralism, he reduced all values to "shouldisms" and dismissed them without seeing that authentic values are essential in human wholeness. In reacting against sterile intellectualizing he seemed to reduce all intellectual activities to mind games. Reacting against the paralysis of endless analysis in therapy, he failed to see that cognitive understanding and self-insight *can* help mobilize one's resources for creative change. In his appropriate rejection of authoritarian religions, Perls failed to see the essential role of salugenic spirituality in human growth. There was no awareness in his thought of a transcending dimension, a higher Self in human beings. He dismissed the concept of the self, in fact, as "a relic from the time when we had a soul."[23] This deficiency points to the need for integrating a spiritually oriented approach like psychosynthesis with gestalt in developing ways to maximize whole-person growth.

In his fight against symbiotic dependencies, Perls fell into the other extreme, hyperindividualism, expressed in his much quoted "gestalt prayer": "I do my thing and you do your thing. I am not in this world to live up to your expectations and you are not in this world to live up to mine. You are you and I am I, and if, by chance, we find each other, it's beautiful. If not, it can't be helped."[24]

This prayer, in Perls' mind, may have been only a teaching device and not a statement of a basic philosophical principle. But as a perceptive gestalt therapist observes, the emphasis on doing one's own thing can, with only minor distortions, be used to justify destructive, psychopathic behavior.[25]

The hyperindividualism in gestalt therapy seems to be particularly offset by Perls' view that a group is a microcosmic world in which people can expand their awareness and try out new behavior. However, when he worked in a group setting, he kept the entire therapeutic process centered on himself. Consequently he missed the unique power of therapy or growth groups—the developing, through group-centered interaction, of a group climate that frees everyone in that group to grow and to become mutual growth facilitators.

A weakness in gestalt is an underemphasis on the responsibility of truly liberated persons to strive to change the oppressive structures of society. Perls was keenly aware of the social sources of diminished growth. It is from the collective psychosis of our culture that we learn our phony, deadening games. But in response to this awareness he offered only the image of the autonomous, self-directed individual standing against the insanities of society. There is little or no awareness of the extent to which the capacity to take full responsibility for one's life presupposes a degree of freedom from social, economic, and political oppression that is not available to two-thirds of the world's peoples. There is no sense of the interdependency of individual and societal wholeness and no call for using one's therapy-developed strengths to help overcome growth-crippling institutional injustice and oppression.

It is not surprising, then, that the growth-stifling impact of institutional sexism has received little attention in gestalt therapy literature. The multiple ways in which our society cripples the full becoming of women and, in different ways, of men, is almost ignored. A refreshing exception to this near silence is an insightful statement by Miriam Polster on "Women in Therapy: A Gestalt Therapist's View." Gestalt therapy can help women repair the damage of sexism in their lives by enabling them to stop giving their power away to men and to sexist institutional practices. But even valuable self-powering and self-responsibility techniques can be used against women to excuse our male-dominated social systems. The authors of *Feminism as Therapy* report:

> Too often women friends of mine have told me of incidents in Gestalt groups where they have made connections between their problems and the social system and been told to quit blaming outsiders for their problems.
>
> Everything is not my projection, and there are many things over which I have little control no matter how clear and sane and together and responsible I become. . . . Women have been taking personal responsibility too long for difficulties in their lives whose roots are social. It is time we put some of the responsibility where it belongs, on the oppressive political-economic system.[26]

The near vacuum of social responsibility in gestalt therapy's philosophy is highlighted by this version of the gestalt prayer in a radical therapy journal: "I do my thing, and you do your thing. I am not in this world to live up to your expectations and you are not in this world to live up to mine. You are you and I am I, and if by chance we find our brothers and sisters enslaved, and the world under fascist rule, because we are doing our thing—it can't be helped."[27]

Perls' hyperindividualism and lack of systemic awareness was counterbalanced, to some degree, by developments of his thought in his later life and by others since his death. Just before his death, he declared that therapy could only be done fully in a community that supported growth. His collaboration in establishing a kind of gestalt commune or kibbutz on Vancouver Island (which disintegrated after his death) is an example of his growing sense of need for community. The relational awareness of Joseph Zinker and the Polsters, who write of going beyond cure and growth to the development of a new communal climate,[28] is an example of more systems-oriented gestalt therapists. They show that gestalt has the potential of becoming a more systemic and political therapy.

Growth Methods from Gestalt Therapy

Gestalt therapy offers a rich variety of methods for growth work. All gestalt methods are ways of enhancing awareness. In what follows, I'll describe a few gestalt approaches that I have found useful, presenting them so that you can try them yourself before you attempt to use them with others. Before proceeding, it's important to emphasize a danger that gestalt shares with some other therapies—its vulnerability to the abuse of its powerful techniques by inadequately trained therapists. At its heart, gestalt therapy is an orientation, a philosophy of how persons change and grow. It is not a set of therapeutic gimmicks. Particular techniques emerge from the therapist's flowing awareness of the growth needs of a particular person. The choice of techniques results from the therapist's understanding of the gestalt philosophy and principles. To be aware of the person's unfolding needs, the therapist's mind must be clear of pre-selected techniques.

Attending to the Whole Person (Beginning with Yourself): Because of our organic oneness, everything we do reflects our here-and-now being. Our awareness of body messages in ourselves and others—posture and movement, voice quality, breathing, muscular tension, and so forth—often reveals more than words about growth blocks. To experience this, close your eyes and be aware of any part of your body that feels up tight right now./ Carry on a dialogue with that part of you, speaking out loud for the part and then for "yourself." Let your words flow, and see what emerges./ Close your eyes again and be aware of some motion you feel like making with your body./ Now, do it, repeating the motion several times, exaggerating it more each time./ Let sounds that express how you feel come out as you do this./ Be aware of the message to yourself in what you have been expressing with your body./

A man is sitting in a growth group with crossed legs making small repetitive kicking motions with one foot. When it seems appropriate, I ask if he is aware of what his foot is saying to him. Or I may invite him to "be your foot and carry on a dialogue with the rest of yourself." What emerges into his awareness is the frustration, anger, and aggressive feelings that he has been retroflexing and expressing covertly through body language.

From the Here-and-Now to the Then-and-There: To increase your awareness of the here-and-now, try this experiment. Become aware of how you are experiencing yourself in your present situation with its surroundings, relationships, happenings, smells, temperature./ Now, if you're feeling tired or bored, think of another situation that you've enjoyed in the past, a setting where you'd prefer to be right now./ Go there in your imagination./ How have your feelings and your energy level changed?/ In your mind, go back and forth several times between your present situation and the other one, savoring the differences in the two./ Now, see if you can bring some of the energy and feelings from the other situation into the present one to enliven your experience now./ Go back and forth until you feel more comfortable and "present" in the here-and-now.[29]

Increasing Awareness by Enactment: This approach uses dramatization of some aspect of a person's life, within a counseling session or growth group. Here is how the Polsters use the method:

"It may start from a statement he makes, or from a gesture. For example, if he makes a small gesture, we may ask him to extend this movement to a fuller dimension. Suppose when he does he finds that the movement feels like a lion sitting on its haunches. We ask how that feels. He says it makes him want to growl. Go ahead and growl. So he does; with this he begins to move around the room, pawing at people. By the time he is done he has frightened some people, amused others, beguiled others and discovered his own held-in excitement. This excitement shows him a new side of himself—the power side, the animal side, the side that moves vigorously into contact—and he begins to realize something of what he has been missing in life. Well timed, and recurring at appropriate moments, such characterizations tap into the individual's action system, opening up new directions."[30]

This method can be used in a variety of forms—e.g., to enact and work through an unfinished, energy-wasting experience from the past or to enact a polarity in one's life—being devilish or angelic—to help one "own" and integrate both sides.

To get inside this approach, close your eyes and image some animal that you would like to be./ Now, open your eyes and *be* that animal for several minutes. Let yourself go, making the appropriate sounds and movements. Do this until it feels finished./ What feelings did you experience? Did you discover any new aspects of yourself?/ Share your experience with a friend./

Take Back Your Power and Response-ability: Gestalt therapy uses a variety of methods to help people become aware of and interrupt the process of giving their power away to other people and to circumstances. For example, the next time you're anxious about something you have to do in the future, try completing the sentence as many times as possible, "Right now I'm frightening *myself* with the fantasy that . . ." You'll probably discover catastrophic fantasies and expectations to which you are giving your power (to do your best) away. By separating your fantasies from whatever is real in your fears, you can use your energy to prepare to handle the reality situation effectively./ Make a series of statements beginning with the words, "I'd like to do the following, but I can't . . ."/ Repeat the statements changing all the "can'ts" to "won'ts."/ Be aware of how you feel when you make the change./

Here is another power-responsibility reclaiming approach. Close your eyes and imagine that you are a client in therapy wrestling with a difficult personal problem. The therapist says to you: "I'd like to use you as a consultant. What advice would be helpful to you in this situation?"[31] Be aware of your feelings as the therapist affirms your potential wisdom and gives responsibility for your therapy back to you./

The Empty Chair Dialogue: This approach has a wide variety of uses in counseling and growth groups. The method is invaluable in helping those experiencing painful losses to do their "grief work" by bringing into the open and perhaps finishing the energy-depleting inner dialogue (usually of guilt and anger) with the lost person. The individual, in fantasy, puts the person with whom he or she has unfinished feelings, in an empty chair and then alternately speaks to and for that person, moving back and forth from one chair to the other in the process. It is important to encourage the person to continue this dialogue until some resolution has occurred, as shown by the person's experience of inner quiet and increased energy. Many of us are carrying around "ghosts" of powerful unfinished feelings about long-past relationships. The increased flow of creative energy, when these feelings are worked through, often is dramatic.

It is possible to use the dialogue method as a self-help technique. After my father's death, I went alone to the cemetery and carried on an extended dialogue with the dad I carry in my memory, expressing some of the unfinished feelings of sadness and anger, guilt and love and gratitude about our relationship. The empty chair method can also help in working through feelings about people who are still alive but with whom direct confrontation is either impossible or probably unproductive—e.g., a rigid boss on a job you still want to keep, an aged parent with whom an open confrontation would be destructive, or an ex-spouse toward whom one has energy-wasting resentments.

Empty chair work can help people re-own rejected, "alien" parts of themselves. It can also help resolve conflicts between aspects of one's personality. We waste enormous quantities of life and energy in the civil wars among potentially complementary parts of ourselves. Here is an awareness exercise to let you experiment with such a dialogue: Close your eyes and picture a chair in your imagination./ Put the part of yourself that feels weak, inadequate, and one-down in the chair./ Be aware of how that person in the chair feels./ Now, picture another part of yourself—the part that feels strong, effective, competent—standing so as to look down on the person in the chair./ Be the standing person now, and give the sitting one a lecture to get that person to shape up. Put your feelings into what you're saying!/ How does the one in the chair feel and respond?/ Carry on a dialogue between the two for a while, first being one and then the other./ Be aware of the feelings stirred up in each person by the dialogue, the power in each position, the energy consumed by the conflict, the increasing polarization that occurs./ Now, see if you can change the dialogue so that it leads to reconciliation between these two sides of yourself (which Perls calls the "underdog" and the "top dog")./

Dream Work: According to gestalt theory, dreams are messages about the holes in one's personality gestalt. Each person or thing in a dream is a disowned part of the dreamer. The person is invited to tell the dream or act it out, not as a story from the past, but in the present tense, and then finish the dream in fantasy. Here is how Fritz Perls described the use of dreams in one's own growth work:

"In Gestalt Therapy we don't interpret dreams. We do something more interesting with them. Instead of analyzing and further cutting up the dream, we want to bring it back to life . . . to re-live the dream as if it were happening now.

You can do a tremendous lot for yourself on your own. Just take any old dream or dream fragment, it doesn't matter. As long as a dream is remembered, it is still alive and available, and it still contains an unfinished, unassimilated situation.

So, if you want to work on your own, I suggest you write the dream down and make a list of *all* the details in the dream. Get every person, every thing, every mood, and then work on these to become each of them. Ham it up. . . . Really *become* that thing. . . . Turn into that ugly frog or whatever is there—the dead thing, the live thing, the demon—and stop thinking. Lose your mind and come to your senses. Every little bit is a piece of the jigsaw puzzle which together will make up a much larger whole—a much stronger, happier, more complete *real* personality."

Then the person has the different parts of the dream dialogue with one another. "As the process of encounter goes on, there is mutual learning until we come to a oneness and integration. . . . Then the civil war is finished, and your energies are ready for your struggles with the world."[32]

For Further Exploration of Growth Resources in Gestalt Therapy

Fagan, Joen, and Shepherd, Irma, eds. *Gestalt Therapy Now: Theory, Techniques, Applications.* Palo Alto, Calif.: Science and Behavior

Books, 1970. Twenty-five papers by gestalt therapists including Fritz and Laura Perls. Dedicated to "Fritz . . . a profound and disturbing teacher."

Hatcher, Chris, and Himelstein, Philip, eds. *The Handbook of Gestalt Therapy*. New York: Jason Aronson, 1976. Twenty-five chapters on various techniques, and a section on the relation of gestalt therapy to other therapies—TA, bioenergetics, biofeedback, and art therapy.

Perls, Frederick S. *Ego, Hunger and Aggression*. New York: Random House, 1947. Explains the theory of gestalt therapy as it developed from psychoanalysis and gestalt psychology.

———. *The Gestalt Approach: Eyewitness to Therapy*. Ben Lomond, Calif.: Science and Behavior Books, 1973. The manuscript on which Perls was working when he died. A theoretical exposition of gestalt therapy and a transcript of a series of filmed therapy sessions with Perls as therapist.

———. *Gestalt Therapy Verbatim*. Lafayette, Calif.: Real People Press, 1969. A discussion of the principles of GT, including transcripts of several sessions.

———. *In and Out the Garbage Pail*. Lafayette, Calif.: Real People Press, 1969. Perls' candid, humorous, anecdotal autobiography. Communicates the flavor of his colorful personality. Describes the beginnings and development of GT.

Polster, Erving, and Polster, Miriam. *Gestalt Therapy Integrated: Contours of Theory and Practice*. New York: Brunner/Mazel, 1973. An exploration of key concepts of GT.

Schiffman, Muriel. *Gestalt Self-Therapy*. Menlo Park, Calif.: Self Therapy Press, 1971. Techniques for self-growth using GT.

Smith, Edward W. L., ed. *The Growing Edge of Gestalt Therapy*. New York: Brunner/Mazel, 1976. Explores the relation of GT to other therapies—Jungian, Existentialism, Zen, TM, and Taoism.

Stevens, John O. *Awareness: Exploring, Experimenting, Experiencing*. Lafayette, Calif.: Real People Press, 1971. Awareness and communication exercises focusing on inner communication, fantasy journeys, pair communication, art, and movement.

Zinker, Joseph. *Creative Process in Gestalt Therapy*. New York: Brunner/Mazel, 1977. Shows how the therapist is really an artist.

Also see the books combining TA and GT by Lessor and James/Jongeward in bibliography at end of TA chapter.

Chapter 8

Growth Resources in Holistic Health, Biofeedback, and Body Therapies

If counseling and therapy are to enable whole-person growth they must use methods that raise the level of physical vitality as well as those which enliven the psychological dimensions of people's lives. Most traditional psychotherapies have been just that—therapies for the psyche. By virtually ignoring the human body, they have exacerbated the dualistic mind-body split, which diminishes the vitality of both. Sam Keen observes:

> The *psycho*-therapeutic method that evolved from Freud's vision has been antisomatic and antierotic. It has been so concerned with producing a strong, realistic ego that it has more frequently enabled men *[sic]* to work than it has liberated them to love. The body has been considered the special province of the medical profession. This has been perpetuated by the division of labor made by the healing professions.[1]

In contrast to the professional compartmentalization in which psychotherapists traditionally have participated, wholeness-oriented counselors and therapists must seek to facilitate healing and growth in all dimensions of people's lives, including the physical dimension.

This chapter highlights body enlivening resources from three interrelated thrusts in the contemporary health-therapy field—the holistic health movement, biofeedback, and the body therapies. Each thrust offers insights and methods that can help strengthen the physiological foundation of whole-person growth.

Growth Resources from Holistic Health

The holistic health movement is having an increasing impact among health professionals, including counselors and psychotherapists. The movement includes an increasing number of persons from the medical professions who are not satisfied with either the philosophy or the results of main-line, highly specialized medical practice. The movement has also attracted many persons who are interested in nonorthodox healing methods. The whole-person philosophy of the movement makes closer peer collaboration among the various health-care professionals essential. Growth-oriented counselors and therapists should see themselves and be seen by other health professionals as an essential part of any whole-person health team.

The guiding principles of holistic health reflect emphases that are weak or missing in both the philosophy and practice of orthodox medicine. These principles coincide with some of the basic concerns of growth-oriented counseling and therapy:[2]

—Health is much more than the absence of sickness. It is the *presence* of high-level wellness. There are many degrees of wellness just as there are many degrees of sickness. Health professionals, including counselors and psychotherapists, should be committed to nurturing high-level wellness rather than simply waiting until people develop illnesses that require treatment. The technology of modern medicine, oriented to treating gross pathology and trauma by surgery, powerful drugs, and space-age technology, has little to do with either the degree of wellness of individuals or the general level of wellness in society.

—High-level wellness involves balanced and integrated interaction among all the interdependent dimensions of people's lives. Holistic health is concerned with increasing people's wellness levels in the physical, mental, emotional, spiritual, interpersonal, and environmental[3] areas; but its primary focus is the whole person, who is more than simply the sum of these various aspects.

—The keys to achieving and maintaining wellness are wellness-awareness and self-responsibility. Wellness-increasing behavior in one area of a person's life tends to encourage wellness behavior in other areas. Persons who respect, enjoy, and care for their bodies by general wellness practices are less inclined to engage in self-hurting behavior such as smoking, chronic overeating, or overdrinking of alcohol.

—Two major determinants of levels of wellness (or sickness) are one's *life-style* and the level of *chronic stress* in one's life. Changing to a wellness life-style and reducing stress can simultaneously help to increase the satisfactions in one's life and reduce the risk of illness. Here is how Donald B. Ardell describes the potential rewards of a wellness life-style: "There is excitement, adventure, enjoyment, fulfillment for us on earth. A wellness lifestyle will not guarantee . . . that you experience these states but it can certainly bend the odds your way. At a minimum, you can expect that a healthy body, emotional equilibrium, and an alive mind will give you one hell of a good start. . . . Be well, drink deep, go for it."[4]

Here are seven interrelated strategies that counselors and therapists can use to help clients raise their levels of wellness:[5]

(1) *A wholeness-oriented counselor-therapist should encourage increased self-responsibility by clients for their total health and for their life-styles.*

It's important for wellness-enablers to communicate, by their general attitudes if not in words: "You are in charge of your own life. Others [including health care professionals and counselors] have influence, can make things easier or more difficult, but in the end you must make your own choices and accept responsibility for what . . . health or disease occur in your life."[6] This emphasis on self-responsibility seeks to counteract a major cause of unwellness in Western societies—the "medical model" in which people view themselves as passive "patients" and view physicians as having primary responsibility for their health and healing. Self-responsibility is the key to increased wellness in all areas of our lives. Even when factors beyond a person's control play a role in causing illnesses, the responsibility for responding in the most constructive way possible still is with the individual. The awakening of self-responsibility is absolutely essential in any counseling or therapy that is to be growth-enabling. Self-responsibility for one's wellness has many practical ramifications, including the six strategies described below.

(2) *A wholeness-oriented counselor-therapist should encourage clients to increase their nutritional awareness and practice sound nutrition as the foundation of high-level wellness.* A vicious cycle operates in many people's lives between their emotional problems and their eating, drinking, and smoking patterns. Many people use overeating (including eating enormous quantities of junk foods), smoking, and excessive drinking of alcohol as forms of self-medication in a vain attempt to treat their stress, depression, and low self-esteem. Unfortunately the use of junk food, alcohol, and nicotine as temporary, self-prescribed pain-reducers tends to produce even more pain in the long run. Many psychological and emotional problems apparently are exacerbated by poor nutrition. Furthermore, the level of zest and positive satisfactions in living are lowered in many people by poor nutrition and/or the overconsumption of food and alcohol. Most psychotherapists have focused their healing efforts on only the first side of the two-way interaction between how we feel and what we eat and drink. In contrast, whole-person approaches must direct their healing efforts to both sides, since both are causes as well as effects of levels of unwellness. Many people could raise their general level of wellness at the same time they enhance their appearance and self-image, by doing two things—drastically reducing or eliminating the intake of junk food, refined sugar, and other carbohydrates, saturated fats, alcohol, and nicotine; and adding more healthful foods to their diets including vegetable proteins, whole-grain cereals and bread, raw vegetables and fruits, and high fiber foods.[7]

(3) *A wholeness-oriented counselor-therapist should challenge clients to keep physically fit by exercising vigorously several times a week.* The human body is designed, by evolutionary survival needs through the millennia, for vigorous

physical activity. A Rutgers anthropologist declares: "When we run, we are . . . reviving the work of yesteryear, hunting-gathering work. The muscles, bones, cartilage, lungs, heart and mind of the primate best adapted to running *want* to be used. When we use them (within reason, and with appropriate concern for slowly increasing strength, stamina, etc., and correcting for age) we feel better. When we don't run or do some similar exercise, we feel worse."[8] Unfortunately, inactivity is a way of life and a serious health hazard for many people (45 percent of Americans say they never exercise). Chronic inactivity contributes to a wide variety of medical problems, including premature aging, obesity, heart disease, chronic fatigue, and hypertension. Apart from reducing the likelihood of illness, the benefits of keeping fit through exercise are impressive. Studies have shown that many people find jogging an effective way of lifting depression, releasing stress, and increasing feelings of self-esteem. Fast walking is one of the most healthful exercises. Finding a form of vigorous exercise that one enjoys is the secret of getting a double (health and pleasure) benefit from the activity.

Like many males I was turned off in my youth by the glorification of super-competitive sports in which I did not excel and by unimaginative physical education classes. During most of my young-adult years I did not exercise vigorously (except for foolish binges of overexertion on rare occasions such as mountain climbing, backpacking vacations). But during the last fifteen years I have discovered that jogging several times a week helps to energize my mind, reduce my depression, and tone up my body. Within the last two years I have found that a twenty-minute session of hatha (physical) yoga exercises, in the morning or evening, is remarkably enlivening.[9] The stretching and breathing exercises have enabled me to gradually recover body flexibility and awareness that I had lost through years of sedentary living. I feel generally more alive and energized now in the later mid-years than I did in my twenties and thirties!

(4) *A wholeness-oriented counselor-therapist should teach clients one or more of a variety of relaxation techniques for*

reducing stresses regularly. Chronic stress contributes to many types of physical, emotional, interpersonal, and psychosomatic problems. When the normal fight-or-flight response to stress (with its elevated heart rate, blood pressure, and body tension) becomes a continuing pattern of living, the body pays a high price. Protracted unrelieved stress depletes the body's remarkable self-defense and self-repair resources. Learning to reduce unnecessary stress and cope better with unavoidable stress is an essential ingredient in a wellness life-style.

There are many self-quieting techniques that counselors and therapists can teach to clients as well as practice themselves. One of the most popular of these, meditation, has been shown to produce significant physiological benefits including lowered blood pressure and heart rate, and the increased flow of oxygen to the brain.[10] Other ways of entering one's "serenity zone" include tensing and releasing all one's muscles; breathing deeply for a few minutes; listening to tranquil music; soaking in a hot bubble bath; experiencing the rhythms and energies of nature; and reliving in one's imagination a peaceful experience. A misconception that often serves as an excuse for not using stress-reducing techniques is the belief that they require large blocks of time and a quiet place. I know a young minister who reports that he can enter a serene inner space while waiting for a traffic light to change. This obviously isn't the most ideal place to meditate, but his experience shows that a person who has learned methods of inner quieting can use them almost anywhere. I find that simply asking myself occasionally, "In what part of my body am I stressing myself?" increases my awareness of the need to release tensions regularly.

(5) *A wholeness-oriented counselor-therapist should encourage clients to live in an ecologically sound, environmentally aware way.* High-level wellness life-styles should include a concern for other people and for the whole interdependent biosphere. To live in an environmentally aware manner means living in ways that respect and protect the biosphere so that it can become more wellness-sustaining for all living things. One can help, in small ways, by "living lightly on the earth"—e.g.,

by eating lower on the food chain, recycling reusable materials, conserving fossil fuel energy (and other nonrenewable resources), composting organic materials to enrich the soil, using solar energy, and taking part in environmental educational and political action organizations. As Donald Ardell points out: "Living ecologically is a 'no-lose' proposition. Even if you personally do not change the world, you will find that doing well with less helps to make you feel better by giving the satisfaction that comes from doing your part."[11] It is also healthful to shape one's personal living space so that it nurtures wellness. For example, an abundance of plants has added a nurturing dimension to our home.

(6) *A wholeness-oriented counselor-therapist should encourage clients to evaluate as well as energize their life-style by developing a sense of meaning and purpose in their lives.* One's personal values, priorities, and sense of life's meaning inevitably guide and shape one's life-style. For this reason, the continuing growth of one's spiritual and value life undergirds other aspects of high-level wellness. Having an energizing awareness of the purpose and preciousness of one's life is an invaluable resource for increasing physical as well as emotional and interpersonal wellness. A faith or philosophy of life that makes one aware of really *belonging* in the wider scheme of things provides a nurturing context of transpersonal meaning. There is a lively interest within holistic health circles in using the ancient heritage of spiritual healing within the context of medical and psychotherapeutic methods. This is based in part on the recognition that the self-healing, self-protective resources of one's body are somehow linked with one's faith and sense of meaning. As Hans Selye, pioneer researcher on stress, makes clear, it is our attitudes toward events in our lives that turn them into "distress" or "eustress" (good stress), not the events *per se.*[12] A sense of transpersonal purpose can help people cope constructively with enormous stress. The Wholistic Health Centers pioneered by Granger Westberg offer an innovative model of whole-person health care in which the spiritual dimension of healing is integrated with conventional

medical resources. These centers are located in churches and staffed by a physician, a nurse, and a pastoral counselor. (See the book by Robert Cunningham, in the "For Further Exploration" section, for a description of these centers.)

(7) *A wholeness-oriented counselor-therapist should encourage clients to laugh more, have more fun, chuckle at themselves, and enjoy life's simple pleasures.* Abundant laughter apparently has the power to activate the body's own healing powers. This was the discovery that Norman Cousins made when he used old slapstick movies to help cure himself of an "irreversible" deterioration of his connective tissue.[13] The physician author of *Laugh after Laugh: The Healing Power of Humor,* reports that he has encountered a surprising number of persons who seemed to have laughed themselves back to health or have used humor to cope constructively with sickness.[14] A seventeenth-century British physician, Dr. Thomas Sydenham, put it well: "The arrival of one clown has more beneficial influence upon a town than 20 asses laden with drugs."[15]

When doing holistic, growth therapy with male clients, it's well to remember that men have a particularly urgent need to develop wellness life-styles. In America the life expectancy of men is about eight years less than that of women.[16] Two hypotheses have been advanced to explain the widening gap in male-female longevity. The biological explanation attributes men's shorter life expectancy to genetic factors. The psychosocial explanation attributes it to the lethal demands and pressures that men internalize as they learn the male role. After a critical evaluation of both hypotheses, James Harrison of the Albert Einstein College of Medicine concludes: "The best available evidence confirms the psychosocial perspective that sex-role socialization accounts for the larger part of men's shorter life expectancy."[17] In all patriarchal cultures, men are socialized to try to be more successful and powerful than others; to always be strong, competitive, and independent; to not show "weak," women-like feelings like dependency. But to the degree that men fulfill their socially programmed sex roles, they must deprive themselves of the satisfaction of many of their basic human needs. The significantly higher incidence among males of stress-related maladies (e.g., heart attacks, stomach ulcers, suicide, alcoholism) supports Harrison's conclusion.

Growth Resources from Biofeedback

Biofeedback is an exciting development in the contemporary biomedical field. In many parts of the world, psychologists and psychotherapists are using biofeedback to throw new light on an age-old mystery—the relationship between the mind and the body. The evidence from this new technology affirms the deep interdependency of the physical and mental facets of human beings and the fact that whole-person healing and growth involves the harmonious, integrated enhancement of both these dimensions. Biofeedback research also increases our awareness of the mind's remarkable power to participate in enhancing both mental and physical health. Barbara Brown, pioneer biofeedback researcher, reports that the new technology "points straight to the greatest mystery of all: the ability of the mind to control its own and the body's sickness and health."[18]

Biofeedback utilizes various instruments that measure bodily changes such as muscular tension, blood pressure, brain wave frequencies, skin temperature, and heart rate. The instruments feed back this information, via meters, tones, or lights, to the persons whose functions are being monitored, thus making them conscious of changes in their internal states of which they are ordinarily unaware. With practice, people can learn to control the body system being monitored and to continue this control, on their own, without the instruments.

The research on and the clinical applications of biofeedback illuminate the complexities and potentialities of the human mind. Barbara Brown declares: "I am still filled with awe and wonder when I record human brain waves in my laboratory . . . the more we probe, the more marvelous and labyrinthine the world of the mind-brain becomes."[19] Biofeedback research shows that the mind can bring under some degree of voluntary control *any* physiological functions of which it becomes aware. Volitional control can be established, through biofeedback learning, over processes long believed to be totally subject to the involuntary control of the autonomic nervous system.

All this is dramatic evidence that the human will is not only alive and well but that its participation in mind-body wholeness can be much more inclusive than formerly believed. All forms of hard determinism, including those of Skinner and Freud, must now be corrected in light of this evidence. In the new phase of human evolution (described by Teilhard de Chardin and others) humankind is called to take a responsible part in choosing the directions of mental-spiritual evolution. Barbara Brown points out, "Biofeedback may provide the instrument to excise the cataracts of scientific vision that so long have prevented participation of the mind of man *[sic]* in the survival and evolution of his own consciousness and psyche."[20]

The ability to learn to control one's physiological functions is being used to treat many types of psychosomatic stress problems, including tension and migraine headaches, cardiovascular problems such as hypertension, and gastrointestinal difficulties of various kinds. Biofeedback is being used to retrain neuromuscular functioning after strokes. It is also proving useful in anxiety states and stress-related problems such as drug abuse, insomnia, and persistent pain. Brain-wave biofeedback training involving learning to increase one's alpha waves (associated with a relaxed, tranquil feeling state) has been used with some success in treating neuroses, psychoses, and behavior problems.[21]

The applications of biofeedback to emotional, psychological, and interpersonal problems depends on what Alyce and Elmer Green, biofeedback researchers at the Menninger Foundation, call the "psychophysiological principle:" "Every change in the physiological state is accompanied by an appropriate change in the mental-emotional state, and conversely, every change in the mental-emotional state, conscious or unconscious, is accompanied by an appropriate change in the physiological state."[22] Because of this correlation, learned control of bodily functions may help increase voluntary control over the psychological-emotional correlates of these changes. To illustrate, research has discovered that changes in our skin temperature and the degree of skin conductivity of small electrical impulses (both indications of our degree of general relaxation) are correlated with emotional changes. Such messages from our skin often reflect unconscious emotional responses more accurately than what we are aware of consciously. As the various bodily states that are correlated with optimal mental health and total growth become better understood, biofeedback may be used more widely and productively in psychotherapy and life enrichment work, and in precise evaluation of these.

Most psychotherapists who use biofeedback devices regard them only as adjunctive resources within psychotherapy. Once clients learn the simple procedures of monitoring their bodily changes, they can practice controlling these changes on their own. This do-it-yourself aspect can save the therapists' time (and the clients' money). It also can help clients develop feelings of autonomy and self-esteem. To discover that one *can* accomplish significant changes on one's own and that one *can* control one's body and feelings, tends to increase feelings of competence and hope for further growth.

Howard Stone reports on the use of biofeedback in a pastoral counseling center in Arizona that biofeedback is useful in helping people with stress-related problems learn how to relax deeply. The therapist simply loans an inexpensive skin temperature thermometer to such clients (after explaining and demonstrating its use), suggesting that they use it between therapy sessions. By using the machine, clients learn how it feels when they are deeply relaxed and how to achieve this state. They can then relax without dependence on the feedback devices. Stone reports: "Methods such as progressive relaxation, yoga, TM and other meditative techniques have been used to help people relax. Biofeedback does the same thing . . . and does it much more rapidly since from the first session the client is able to see how he or she is actually learning to relax."[23]

Brain-wave biofeedback is described by Elmer and Alyce Green as the "yoga of the West" because it helps people learn to change their consciousness to a state of alert quietness that is like that achieved by many meditative techniques. By learning to increase their output of alpha and theta waves, some people report meditation-like experiences of integration or centeredness.

Some researchers are exploring the relationship between the altered state of consciousness called "reverie" (produced by theta wave training) and enhancement of physical healing, problem solving, and creativity. Elmer Green reports that the gap between conscious and unconscious processes apparently is voluntarily narrowed during reverie and the creativity of the unconscious made more available to the persons.[24] As a tool for exploring the healing-growth potentials of various self-altered states of consciousness, biofeedback may help us develop resources for enriching our spiritual lives.

Biofeedback instruments simply extend the range of the natural feedback from our bodies. A fringe benefit that both biofeedback and the body therapies can help give us is increased awareness of these vital messages from our bodies. Many of us live in asphalt and concrete cities cut off from full body awareness. We tend to insulate ourselves from the healing feedback from nature and from our bodies. Our bodies try to tell us to give ourselves a mini-vacation (five to ten minutes of relaxation) from the pressures of our frantic life-styles in a technological society. The message comes in coded forms such as a tension headache or chronic insomnia. Rather than listening to the wisdom of our bodies and changing our high-pressure life-styles, we pop an aspirin, a tranquilizer, or a psychic energizer.[25]

Growth Resources from the Body Therapies

The "body therapies" are actually a constellation of therapies and growth approaches that emphasize working directly with the body as a way of increasing wholeness. These approaches differ widely among themselves in both theory and methods.[26] They include Wilhelm Reich's orgone therapy; Alexander Lowen's bioenergetics; Ira Rolf's structural integration (called "Rolfing"); Arthur Janov's primal therapy; autogenic training, a deep relaxation method; sensory awareness methods; dance and movement therapies; and such Eastern body disciplines as t'ai-chi, Aikido Zen awareness training, and hatha yoga. Gestalt therapy and some feminist therapies also include a prominent emphasis on body awareness and empowerment.

The primary thrust of these somato-therapies—helping people increase their physical vitality—is one important dimension of any whole person approach to counseling or psychotherapy. According to the body therapy perspective, the basic alienation that impoverishes the health of many people is an inner estrangement from their bodies. In our success-worshiping left-brain society, we overvalue rationality, cognitive knowledge, control, analysis, and work, and separate these from aspects of ourselves that we undervalue—feelings, intuition, synthesis, body awareness, play, and other right-brain functions. To the degree that we are alienated from experiencing and affirming our bodies, our capacity for feeling deeply and for sensuousness, playfulness, and creativity is diminished.

In therapy with body-estranged people, direct work to enhance body awareness and energy is needed to help them reclaim their bodies. The goal of such body work is both to liberate the body's trapped energies and pleasure potentials, and to help awaken those intellectual, creative, and spiritual capacities which have been dulled by body rejection.

Wilhelm Reich (the foreparent of many body therapies) believed that the "body armor" of chronic muscular rigidity incorporates and continues to express the constricting early life experiences that created these somato-psychic defenses. He discovered that when these chronic muscular tensions dissolved during therapy, one of three biologically based feelings emerged into awareness—anxiety, anger, or sexual excitement. Alexander Lowen has modified Reich's theory and methods in various ways.[27] He defines the main goal of therapy as freeing people from their chronic constrictions of breathing and muscular tensions so that their whole organism can experience a flow of life energy. He instructs clients in various body postures, exercises, and emotionally releasing verbalizing by which they can overcome the deadening of feelings and pleasure resulting from blocked energy flow. Lowen reminds us that the blocks and the resources for growth are in our bodies as well as our minds: "Personality is much broader than consciousness. . . . It is an expression of the total being: of its physical vitality, of its muscular coordination, of its inner harmony and outward grace. The magnetism of a personality is . . . the radiance of an alive body in which the mental and physical aspects reflect each other."[28] A strong sense of personal identity involves an integration of the body image and the self image. In Lowen's words: "The ego depends for its sense of identity upon the perception of the body. If the body is charged and responsive, its pleasure function will be strong and meaningful, and the ego image will be grounded in body image."[29] A person with diminished awareness of bodily feeling becomes split into a disembodied spirit and disenchanted body. The ego, divorced from the body, is vulnerable and weak. When rejected, the nonrational, body-feelings side of us becomes "demonic," breaking through in such distorted forms as destructive aggression, depression, compulsions, and feelings of schizoid detachment. Body therapies aim at helping people say yes to their bodies, joyfully and playfully. With the recovery of body-play, the capacity for greater mind-play (creativity) tends to be increased.

It is important to recognize that body alienation and deadening tend to occur in different ways for men and women in our culture. As a boy I was tall and "skinny" as well as shy, fearful, and unassertive. I was easily dominated by stronger, more aggressive boys. I grew up feeling as many men feel—that my body was inferior because it didn't measure up to the image of the all-American male athlete. In my youth I tried various types of body-building in frantic efforts to make my body fit the image. These produced some modest "improvements." I can resonate to Sam Keen's description of his experience of body-alienation: "I had organized my body around the mirror, the opponent and the job. The body I had fabricated looked good, competed adequately and functioned efficiently, but it was tensed against the invasion of tenderness. I told it what to do, and for the most part it obeyed like a well-paid, sullen butler. It was better at work than at play."[30] During my young adult years I drove my body relentlessly, seeking to make it serve my self-esteem needs to be a "successful" competitor in my work. I continued my I-it relationship with my body until it rebelled against the chronic stress I had kept it under. In my early forties, I discovered that I had developed diabetes due in part, I now see, to the chronic stress to which I subjected my body.

Girls are conditioned by our culture to equate their self-worth with being "pretty" and attractive to boys. Their feelings of personal value tend to be limited to the degree to which they can make their bodies fit the superficial Hollywood image of beauty. They tend, as do boys, to feel that their bodies are always on trial, being judged against idealized criteria to which they can never measure up fully.

The "Playboy syndrome" reflects a special problem for women—the tendency within a male-dominated culture for many men *and* women to perceive and judge women first as bodies and second, if at all, as persons. To make matters worse, to be "feminine" in our culture, women have tended to deaden the natural assertiveness of their bodies and not allow themselves to enjoy their sexuality wholeheartedly. This is why feminist therapies emphasize helping women to accept and enjoy the sensuality of their bodies and express their energies assertively.

The efforts of body therapists are directed at helping people learn to experience their bodies, their feelings, their assertiveness, and their capacities for body pleasure. Lowen declares: "As long as the body remains an object of the ego, it may fulfill the ego's pride, but will never provide the joy and satisfaction that the 'alive' body offers."[31]

The quality of one's sexuality reflects the quality of one's general body awareness. Body alienation weakens one's sexuality—the general feelings and affirmation of one's maleness or femaleness—and diminishes one's sexual pleasuring. It also detaches sex from sexuality, making sex a performance motivated by the ego rather than by basic instinctual needs. "A decrease of sexuality leads inevitably to an increased preoccupation with sex. The attempt is made to recapture the lost feelings by exposing one's self to sexual stimulation or engaging in sexual activity. The results are disastrous."[32]

The somatic therapies aim at helping people awaken their dulled senses, recover sensuous awareness in their whole bodies, rediscover the wonder, spontaneity, and playfulness that they have lost under their load of lopsided rationality and overcontrol. When people begin to revive their aliveness, they often reclaim their "forsaken body with all the fervor of the lost child finding its loving mother."[33]

The body therapies have important implications for spiritual enrichment. These therapies see the alive body as the foundation for all other growth, including spiritual growth. Lowen points out that "as long as the ego dominates the individual he cannot have the oceanic or transcendental experiences that make life meaningful."[34] The body therapies reaffirm, by implication, the ancient Hebrew view of body-mind-spirit wholeness (as do holistic health and biofeedback). They reject the splitting apart, in the Greek and much of the Christian tradition, of body and spirit, nature and history, secular and sacred. They emphasize the crucial importance of affirming the deep "animal" roots of our humanness.[35] They call us to what Sam Keen calls an "incarnate existence" in which we affirm the sacred *in* the so-called secular, and thereby gain a new and profound respect for our bodies and for all living things.[36] The heart of vital religion says a resounding "yes!" to all dimensions of our lives including our bodies. Enlivening religion, as Keen makes clear, must be danced and not merely believed!

Although they provide some important growth resources, there is a significant inadequacy in some of the body therapies. This is the tendency toward body reductionism (which is most prominent in Reichian therapy) and the implicit assumption that body work constitutes the whole of therapy. From a holistic growth perspective, the main thrust of the body therapies is an essential, often neglected dimension of counseling and therapy, but it is only *one* dimension. The body therapy methods are used most productively when they are integrated with methods for helping people enliven themselves in all the other interdependent aspects of their psycho-social-spiritual-physical personhood.

Experiencing Body Enlivening Methods

In this section I will present several body-enlivening exercises that I have found helpful, describing them so that you can use them in self-nurture as well as with clients. The slash mark means, "Stop while you complete what has been suggested."

Body Awareness and Grounding

As you sit, become aware of your body position in relation to the force of gravity./ To feel more firmly grounded, straighten your spine and put both of your feet solidly on the floor./ Picture and feel your rear supported by the chair; your chair and your feet supported by the floor; the floor supported by the building; the building supported by its foundation; the foundation supported by the solid earth beneath it./ Let your weight sink toward the earth and be supported by it./[37]

Cross your legs and arms tightly; be aware of your feelings./ Now uncross your legs and arms in an open, free stance./ How have your feelings and your body awareness changed?/ Sit with your hands palms down on your thighs. Close your eyes and tune in on how you experience this position./ Turn your palms upward. Close your eyes again and become aware of any change in your experience of yourself. Recall and relive in your imagination an experience when you felt threatened or rejected./ Be aware of your body's response./ Now relive another experience when you felt safe, nurtured, loved./ What were the body messages you received as you relived that episode?/ During the next few days, practice being in touch with what occurs in your body, how alive or unalive it feels in different situations. Overall self-awareness can be increased by cultivating greater body-awareness.

Whole Body Aliveness

Take off your clothes and stand in front of a full-length mirror./ Start with your head and move slowly toward your feet, looking at each area or part of your body for a while. Which parts feel energized and alive?/ Be aware of how you feel about your body as a whole./ Which parts do you like? Which would you change if you could?/ Has this "body aliveness check" changed your awareness of your feelings in any part of your body?[38]

Shut your eyes and be aware of your center of energy—the place in your body that feels most alive./ Imagine that your energy is radiating from this center throughout your body. Feel its warming flow thawing the parts that feel less than fully alive./ Continue this until your whole body feels energized and alive.

Breathing Exercises

Several body therapies emphasize breathing exercises as a means of freeing body awareness and energy flow. Breathing is our most fundamental means of self-nurture. As Fritz Perls pointed out, we breathe in shallow, constricted ways to block out threatening feelings. But in so doing we also diminish our feelings of excitement, sensual pleasure, and aliveness, In hatha yoga, "complete breathing" is used as a way to calm the mind, let go of stress, and increase the "life force" in the whole organism. Here is a hatha yoga exercise that can increase deep, nurturing breathing:

"Exhale very deeply so that the lungs are emptied of air. Pull in your abdomen as far as possible to help the exhalation./ Begin a very slow inhalation through your nose. As you inhale, also begin to distend your abdomen. . . ./ Continue the slow inhalation. Slowly expand your chest as far as possible. Make this an exaggerated expansion./ Continue the inhalation. Keep your chest expanded and now raise your shoulders [to create more space for air]. . . . This is the completed posture. Hold for a count of five./ Very slowly exhale completely through your nose and simultaneously allow your body to contract and relax. Exhale very deeply and, with a pause, repeat./ Perform the Complete Breath three times."[39]

Here is a way of using your breathing to reduce bodily stress and become more centered in your mind: Tense and then relax all the muscles of your body several times./ As you practice breathing, as described above, close your eyes and concentrate all of your attention on your breathing./ On each exhalation, let your body tensions and your worries flow out with the air./ Focus your whole attention on one point—the slow, rhythmic flow of air in and out of your nostrils. If your attention wanders, gently bring it back to your breathing./ Don't try to make anything happen. Just "be" your breathing./ Let the length of each inhalation, exhalation, and the space between each breath increase as your mind and body grow quiet./ Say the word "one" gently with each exhalation, feeling your basic oneness—within yourself, with all of life and with Spirit./ Continue this focused breathing until you experience the temporary cessation of the usual flow of thoughts, sensations, images, and feelings in your consciousness./ Stay in this clear, serene consciousness for at least ten minutes./ (This centering method is the essential method used in several Eastern approaches to meditation.)

Now, as you slowly exhale, imagine that your breath-energy is flowing out through your pelvic area, gently caressing and energizing your genitals. Let yourself enjoy this for a while./ Imagine that your breath-energy is flowing out through other areas of your body that need enlivening one area at a time./

Energizing Movement

Here is a delightful way to begin your day, described by Anne Kent Rush:

"Close your door. Be in a room you like. Choose some music to play which pleases you. Take off all your clothes. And dance! Dance for yourself. . . . Try not to think about what your movements look like from the outside. This is a chance to allow your inner rhythms and expressions to be. Every now and again stand still and allow any feelings or sensations inside of you to build and spread and move out into your limbs to become a motion. Try to open yourself and let any movements which your body, you, wants to make. . . . Forget your obligations. Forget any other people or thoughts. . . . Dance!"[40]

It is possible to "play" your favorite music in your imagination for a few minutes during the day to reduce stress and raise your energy level. Let the music in your mind envelop you and flow through your whole being./ If you are alone (or with understanding people) let your body do whatever it wishes, moving freely with the rhythms of the music./ When you finish, sit quietly for a few moments and savor the whole experience./

Anger-Releasing Exercises

These exercises aim at draining off accumulated anger through big muscle movement so that pent-up anger won't waste creative energy or produce chronic depression, stress, sexual diminution, or psychosomatic disorders. When you sense a build-up of frustration or anger, get a cardboard box and find a time when you can be alone in your garage or basement, wearing hard-toed shoes./ Close your eyes and picture the persons or situations which are the sources of your frustration or anger./ When you become aware of your negative feeings, open your eyes and express them by kicking the box and shouting whatever words or sounds well up in you as you kick. Let yourself go! Kick the box to shreds if you feel like it! Keep kicking until you experience a sense of release and lightness within yourself./ If you are depressed, but not aware of anger, try kicking violently anyway. You may find that this pulls the plug on repressed anger and lets it drain off harmlessly./ Another anger-releasing exercise is to pound a bed relentlessly with your fists or a tennis racket or kick the bed while lying on it.[41] Do this until the hurt and anger are drained off.

Violent hitting or kicking of inanimate objects brings into consciousness one's fear and guilt about negative feelings and aggressiveness. Expressing these negative feelings (in spite of the fear and guilt) in ways that don't hurt other people helps diminish the blocks that prevent anger from being expressed appropriately (in small installments) as it occurs, rather than building up as potentially destructive rage. Draining off repressed rage frees people to deal more constructively with reality, including changing whatever can be changed about their frustration-causing situation and relationships. The full release of supercharged negative feelings often allows positive feelings of warmth and love, strength and aliveness to flow within us again.

Healing and Nurture Through Touching

Eric Berne observed that the original interpersonal "strokes" we received as small children were the warm satisfactions of being touched. Although we gradually substitute emotional strokes such as recognition and praise as we grow older, our inner Child continues to yearn for physical contact with others. (In TA terms, such health-jeopardizing behavior as overeating and smoking are attempts to comfort oneself and to compensate for feelings of stroke-deprivation.) It is noteworthy that several thousand nurses and physicians have received training in a new technique called "Therapeutic Touch," which is reminiscent of the laying on of hands, an ancient healing practice in the Christian heritage.

To experience the healing-nurturing energies of touching, I invite you to try this exercise with your spouse or a close friend. Ask the person to sit in a chair with eyes closed./ For a few minutes, practice centering, that is, getting in touch with the center of life energy within you. You may find it helpful to form an image of a warm, gentle, healing light entering and filling your whole body./ Gently put your hands on the other person's head. See if you can sense the flow of life energy through your hands to the other person. All during the experience, visualize that person as radiantly healthy./ After ten minutes or so, gently lift your hands, suggesting that the other person sit quietly for a few minutes to stay with the experience./ After sharing what you each experienced, reverse the roles./ In growth groups, a member who feels the need for nurture or healing can sit in the center while the others encircle and touch that person, surrounding her or him with life energy.

A Self-Healing Method

In their work with cancer patients, O. Carl Simonton and Stephanie Matthews-Simonton have discovered that this exercise often helps people mobilize the self-healing forces within their bodies. (Methods like this should be used to augment, not to replace treatment by conventional medicine and psychotherapy.) The Simontons believe that this same approach can stimulate healing in many types of major or minor illness. The first six steps constitute one approach to full-body relaxation. Such relaxation methods can be taught to clients as do-it-yourself ways of coping with stress and anxiety: 1. Go to a quiet room with soft lighting. Shut the door, sit in a comfortable chair, feet flat on the floor, eyes closed./ 2. Become aware of your breathing. Take a few deep breaths, and as you let out each breath, mentally say the word "relax."/ 3. Concentrate on your face and feel any tension in the muscles of your face and around your eyes./ Make a mental picture of this tension—it might be a rope tied in a knot or a clenched fist. Tense the muscles of your face, squeezing tightly, and then mentally picture them relaxing and becoming comfortable, like a limp rubber band./ 4. As the muscles of your face and eyes become relaxed, feel a wave of relaxation spreading through your body./ 5. Move slowly down your body doing the same thing—your jaw, neck, shoulders, back, upper and lower arms, hands, chest, abdomen, thighs, calves, ankles, feet—until every part of your body is more relaxed. For every part of your body, mentally picture the tension, then picture the tension melting away, allowing relaxation./ 6. Now picture yourself in pleasant, natural surroundings—wherever feels comfortable for you. Mentally fill in the details of color, sound, texture, temperature. Continue to picture yourself in a very relaxed state in this tranquil place for two or three minutes./ 7. Create a mental picture of any ailment or pain that you have now, visualizing it either realistically or symbolically./ 8. Picture any treatment you are receiving and see it either eliminating the source of the ailment or pain or strengthening your body's ability to heal itself./ 9. Picture your body's natural defenses and natural healing processes eliminating the source of the ailment or pain. Picture your body's own army of white blood cells coming into the area of pain or ailment, eliminating the infection or the source of the pain, actively bringing healing. Your white cells are strong and aggressive and very smart!/ 10. Picture yourself healthy and free of the ailment or pain and full of energy./ 11. See yourself proceeding successfully toward meeting your goals in life, your purpose in life being fulfilled, your relationships with others becoming more meaningful and satisfying. Remember that having strong reasons for being well will help you get well./ 12. Give yourself a mental pat on the back for participating in your own recovery./ See yourself doing this relaxation-mental imagery exercise three times a day for five to fifteen minutes—in the morning on rising, at noon after lunch, and at night before going to bed—staying awake and alert as you do it./ 13. Let the muscles of your eyelids lighten up, become ready to open your eyes, and become aware of the room./ 14. Now let your eyes open and you are ready to resume your usual activities.[42] (I often add the following step between 9 and 10:

"Picture yourself surrounded by a warm, healing light—the light of the Spirit of love. Let this light flow through your whole body and mind.")

Experiencing Biofeedback

Experiments have shown that stress and anxiety constrict the blood vessels of the hands and thus lower hand temperature. As one becomes more relaxed, hand temperature tends to rise. Many people can learn to raise their hand temperature voluntarily by learning how to relax. To experience a simple biofeedback technique for monitoring your degree of relaxation, obtain a sensitive thermometer and hold the bulb securely in your fingertips./ Note the temperature./ Then use the following technique. Rest your hands comfortably in your lap while you repeat these words to yourself slowly and silently:

"I feel quite quiet. My whole body is relaxed and comfortable. My right arm is heavy and warm. My left arm is heavy and warm. My right hand is becoming warmer. My left hand is becoming warmer. Warmth is flowing into my hands. They are warm. I can feel the warmth flowing down into my right hand. It is warm and relaxed. I can feel the warmth flowing down into my left hand. It is warm and relaxed. My hands are warm and heavy."[43]

Keep repeating the last sentence to yourself every fifteen seconds. Check the thermometer periodically. Psychologists have found that "the secret of voluntary hand-warming is the development of a passive relaxed attitude."[44] If biofeedback from the thermometer is experienced as a challenge by you, it may, like other stresses, actually decrease your hand temperature by keeping you from relaxing. Discovering that you *can* control the "involuntary" response of the sympathetic nervous system (which regulates skin temperature) by intentionally relaxing, can enhance the awareness, "I'm in charge of me, including my body!"

For Further Exploration of Growth Resources in Holistic Health

Ardell, Donald B. *High Level Wellness, An Alternative to Doctors, Drugs, and Disease*. Emmaus, Pa.: Rodale Press, 1977. A discussion of how we can increase our wellness and that of society. Includes a Resource Guide to books in the field.

HOLISTIC HEALTH, BIOFEEDBACK, AND BODY THERAPIES

Benson, Herbert. *The Relaxation Response.* New York: William Morrow, 1975. Evaluates a variety of stress-reduction methods including transcendental meditation, autogenic training, progressive relaxation, Zen, and yoga approaches to meditation. Suggests a simplified method of meditation.

Boston Women's Health Collective. *Our Bodies, Ourselves: A Book by and for Women,* rev. 2nd ed. New York: Simon & Schuster, 1976. A guide to understanding and being responsible for one's own health.

Cousins, Norman. *Anatomy of an Illness as Perceived by the Patient.* New York: W. W. Norton, 1979. A description of his self-healing.

Cunningham, Robert M., Jr. *The Wholistic Health Centers: A New Direction in Health Care.* Battle Creek, Mich.: W. K. Kellogg Foundation, 1977. Describes the centers developed by Granger E. Westberg.

Gomez, Joan. *How Not to Die Young.* New York: Pocket Books, 1973. Shows how your life-style causes your body to obsolesce prematurely.

Illich, Ivan. *Medical Nemesis.* New York: Pantheon Books, 1976. Gives evidence that some aspects of the medical establishment have become a threat to health.

Keck, L. Robert. *The Spirit of Synergy.* Nashville: Abingdon, 1978. Holistic approaches to religion and health, emphasizing "meditative prayer."

Kelsey, Morton. *The Other Side of Silence.* New York: Paulist Press, 1976. A guide to Christian meditation.

Lappe, Frances Moore. *Diet for a Small Planet.* New York: Ballantine, 1975. Critiques our food production, distribution, and consumption patterns from both personal and planetary health perspectives. Gives suggestions and recipes for living healthier, lower on the food chain.

Leonard, George. *The Ultimate Athlete.* New York: Viking Press, 1974. Explores the celebration of physical fitness and suggests new health-enabling forms of exercise.

McCamy, John, and Presley, James. *Human Life Styling: Keeping Whole in the 20th Century.* New York: Harper & Row, 1975. Includes a nutritional guide and a chapter on environmental wholeness.

Pelletier, Kenneth R. *Mind as Healer, Mind as Slayer.* New York: Delta, 1977. Preventing stress disorders by holistic approaches, including meditation, autogenic training, and biofeedback.

Sanford, John A. *Healing and Wholeness.* New York: Paulist Press, 1977. A Jungian analyst discusses healing resources in early

Christianity, the Greek healing mysteries, C. G. Jung, and among American Indians.

Selye, Hans. *Stress Without Distress.* New York: Signet, 1974. Suggests ways of using stress as challenge and pleasure and avoiding stress as frustration, fear, or anger.

Shealy, C. Norman. *90 Days to Self Health.* New York: Dial Press, 1977. A program of stress control, nutrition, exercise, relaxation, and freedom from overweight, alcohol, and smoking.

Simonton, O. Carl; Matthews-Simonton, Stephanie; and Creighton, James. *Getting Well Again, A Step-by-step, Self-Help Guide to Overcoming Cancer for Patients and Their Families.* Los Angeles: J. P. Tarcher, 1978. Explores personality factors in cancer and then describes ways to mobilize self-healing resources.

For Further Exploration of Growth Resources in Biofeedback

Brown, Barbara B. *New Mind, New Body, Bio-Feedback: New Directions for the Mind.* New York: Bantam Books, 1975. A discussion of the nature and significance of biofeedback with chapters on skin, muscle, and brain-wave applications.

———. *Stress and the Art of Biofeedback.* New York: Harper, 1977. The therapeutic uses of biofeedback for a variety of medical and psychological problems.

Green, Elmer, and Green, Alyce. *Beyond Biofeedback.* New York: Delta, 1977. An exploration of volition, creativity, and a new human self-image as these are illuminated by biofeedback research.

Green, Elmer. "Biofeedback for Mind-Body Self-Regulation, Healing and Creativity," in *Biofeedback and Self Control, 1972,* David Shapiro, et al., eds. Chicago: Aldine Publishing Co., 1973, chap. 11. Explores physiological healing and mental creativity as they are illuminated by the findings of biofeedback.

White, John, ed. *Frontiers of Consciousness.* New York: Avon Books, 1975. Includes two papers on biofeedback as well as two on meditation research.

For Further Exploration of Growth Resources in Body Therapies

Fadiman, James, and Frager, Robert. "Wilhelm Reich and the Psychology of the Body," in *Personality and Personal Growth.* New York: Harper, 1976, chap. 4. Discusses and evaluates Reich's major concepts as well as other body-oriented systems of growth including bioenergetics, structural integration, the Alexander technique, sensory awareness, hatha yoga, t'ai-chi, and Aikido.

Fox, Matthew. *Whee! We, Wee, All the Way Home . . . A Guide to the New Sensual Spirituality*. Wilmington, N.C.: Consortium Books, 1976. Explores playfully the mystical ecstasies that can be experienced in nature, the arts, friendship, sexuality, sports, and thinking. One chapter deals with the sensuality of Jesus and the Hebraic prophets.

Gunther, Bernard. *Sense Relaxation*. New York: Collier, 1968. Also *What to Do Til the Messiah Comes*. Collier, 1971. Sensory awakening exercises illustrated by beautiful photos.

Hittleman, Richard L. *Yoga for Physical Fitness*. New York: Warner Books, 1964. An illustrated do-it-yourself book on hatha yoga exercises.

Lowen, Alexander. *The Betrayal of the Body*. New York: Collier Macmillan, 1967. A discussion of bioenergetics' understanding of psychological-body problems and methods of reclaiming the body.

———. *The Language of the Body*. New York: Macmillan, 1971. An introduction to the key concepts of bioenergetics.

———. "Sexuality, Sex and Human Potential," in *Human Potentialities, the Challenge and the Promise,* Herbert Otto, ed. St. Louis: Warren H. Green, 1968, chap. 10. Discusses the bioenergetic understanding of sexuality as this relates to human potentializing.

Reich, Wilhelm. *The Function of the Orgasm*. New York: Farrar, Strauss & Giroux, 1973. Includes a discussion of bioenergy and character analysis and his therapy.

Rush, Anne Kent. *Getting Clear: Body Work for Women*. New York: Random House, 1973. Two hundred eighty-one body enlivening exercises. Useful for men as well as women.

Voices: Journal of the American Academy of Psychotherapists, issue on Psychotherapy and the Body, vol. 12, no. 2, issue 44.

Chapter 9

Growth Resources in Family Systems Therapies

The diverse cluster of therapies whose aim is to facilitate creative change in relationships and in social systems represents a highly significant development in contemporary therapies. These relational-systems approaches reflect fundamental changes in our understanding of both the nature of human growth and the central focus of therapy. The shift in their therapeutic focus is away from a primary concern with what occurs *within individuals* (the preoccupation of the mainstream of therapy since Freud) and toward enhancing *interpersonal relationships and small social systems such as families.* This conceptual reorientation has given rise to therapies that are a veritable gold mine of resources for enriching the quality of relationships and helping institutions, organizations, and communities become more growth-nurturing for everyone.

There are four broad categories of systemic approaches to personal-social change: The first category, *ad hoc group therapies,* includes the many types of group counseling and therapy, growth groups, and self-help groups that are flourishing today. All of these create and use small *ad hoc* groups to help individuals experience healing and growth. From a systems perspective, this is a hybrid category. It retains the primary goal of the individualistic therapies—transforming what goes on within individuals—but also introduces a new systems methodology that uses a growthful quality of group experience to enable individuals to change.

The second category of systemic therapies aims at *changing ongoing, natural systems* such as marriages and families. This category includes the many forms of conjoint marriage counseling and therapy, marriage and family enrichment, and the multiple-family and extended family approaches to therapy and family enrichment. The common goal of these methodologies is to enhance the quality of relationships within these natural systems so that they will become environments of healing and growth for everyone within them.

The third category of systemic approaches includes all those which aim at making the emotional climate of *larger face-to-face systems* (such as churches, schools, industries, and social agencies) more growth-enabling. Included are the therapeutic community approaches and what is called "organizational development." These approaches intervene directly in larger social organisms to increase their growthfulness for individuals. Organizational development seeks to increase the effectiveness of organizations in fulfilling their institutional objectives in ways that also fulfill the needs of individuals.

The fourth category of systemic approaches includes all those which aim at making *larger, non-face-to-face systems* such as governments, institutions, and economic and legal systems more responsive to the real needs of people and therefore more supportive of human development. The radical therapies, which aim at empowering persons to engage in effective institutional-societal change action, belong in this category, as do other social action approaches (which ordinarily are not called therapies). Feminist therapies (chapter 10) combine the goals of the first and fourth categories. They seek to *heal* the psychological wounds of women caused by our sexist society, and (as an essential part of this healing) to *empower* them to work together to eliminate the collective growth-constriction of all women by all our social systems and institutions. The therapies in this fourth category are beginning to bridge the chasm that has existed between most therapies, with their exclusive concern for personal and rational growth, and social action aimed at social-political change.

All the therapies in these four categories, though differing widely, share one guiding motif—*a commitment to the central therapeutic importance of the systemic perspective.* All of them see groups as the place where healing and growth can be facilitated most effectively. All share the implicit assumption that the degree of wholeness that individuals are able to maintain is strongly influenced, if not determined, by the relative wholeness of their need-satisfying interpersonal systems. All four types seek to create growth systems that will provide a nurturing environment within which people will develop more competence, creativity, and power to live effectively.

This chapter will highlight some growth resources in systemic therapies by focusing on the principles of family therapy. (I will not attempt to describe in detail the significant differences among the various family therapies.) Growth groups are the most widely applicable systemic methodology for nurturing human growth. Obviously, they should have a central place in the work of any growth-oriented professional or institution. Conjoint marriage counseling and enrichment offer superb opportunities for nurturing growth in marriage systems. These approaches also should be a prominent part of any growth program. Self-help groups (many of which are modeled on Alcoholics Anonymous) represent one of the most hopeful developments in the whole field of contemporary therapeutic groups. Because I have discussed growth groups, marriage counseling and enrichment, and self-help groups in some detail elsewhere,[1] I will not deal with these important methodologies here. In the next chapter I will explore growth resources in feminist therapies.

The Systems Conception of Growth in Family Therapies

To understand the nature and goals of growth in family therapies, one must understand the *systemic perspective* as a way of perceiving human beings.[2] This perspective in itself is the most important growth resource available in these therapies. Like the growth perspective, the systemic perspective functions like a new set of glasses for growth-enablers. When counselors and therapists put on these glasses, a new world becomes visible as the glasses provide fresh ways of seeing and understanding people. The growth resistances, needs, and possibilities of individuals often are illuminated dramatically as they are perceived in their interpersonal context. As clients are helped to put on these glasses, they sometimes get a new understanding of both the growth problems and the growth opportunities they face. The systems perspective can help all of us be more aware that both our brokenness and our wholeness are the consequences, to a considerable degree, of the quality of our systems of need-satisfying relationships.

For those of us who have invested years of professional training in putting on the intrapsychic glasses, it usually requires strenuous effort to learn to also see people through the interpersonal-systemic glasses. But the glasses for seeing intrapsychic dynamics, which we have learned to wear, provide a much more meaningful picture of human beings when the interpersonal-systemic way of perceiving is added.

As was pointed out in chapter 3, interpersonalism was the central motif of the thinking of Harry Stack Sullivan, the foreparent of systems therapies. The systemic therapies presuppose an interpersonal view of human beings. In a profound sense, we human beings *are* our relationships. The *within* and the *between* of persons' lives are two interdependent aspects of their personalities. Intrapsychic dynamics reflect the individual's pattern of interpersonal relationships and vice versa. Systems theory developed beyond Sullivan's view by showing how individuals can be understood fully only when they are seen in the context of all the social systems—the family, extended family, institutional and cultural systems—of which they are a part and which shape their personal identity, behavior, and relationships. Building on this awareness, systemic therapies took the crucial step methodologically by intervening directly in interpersonal systems to help them become more growth-enabling *as systems*.

Using family systems as illustrative, let's look at the dynamics of social systems and how they nurture or negate human growth. Families are the basic system of "people making" (Satir) in all human societies. A family is a primary social organism with a distinctive identity or "personality" of its own, which is more than the sum of its parts. There is an organic interdependency among members of any primary social system that is somewhat analogous to the parts of one's body. The functioning of any one part of such a system reflects and influences, to some degree, the interaction of all the parts of the whole organism. To illustrate, family therapists have discovered that children who are "identified patients" (to use family therapist Virginia Satir's term for family members who are emotionally disturbed, delinquent, or psychosomatically ill) often are expressing, in their dysfunction, the hidden conflicts in their parents' marriage. The identified patient's dysfunction actually serves a function in the family system in that it allows other family members to avoid facing and taking responsibility for their own pain.

The behavior, attitudes, values, and pattern of relating of individual family members are shaped by the family structure—that is, by the unconscious family rules, expectations, values, taboos, beliefs, patterns of communication, and distribution of power among its members. This dynamic family structure can frustrate or facilitate the potentializing of all its members.

Because of a family's organic interdependency and its unconscious structure, it often is difficult for one person to change and grow unless the whole family system changes in directions that support that individual's growth or the individual leaves the family and establishes a new network of nurture. Those who do therapy in institutional settings with psychologically disturbed persons have long been aware that such persons often regress dramatically when they return to their families. The basic goal of family therapy is to work with the whole family organism to help them change their underlying rules and patterns so that all their members will be free to grow and none will be needed as a scapegoat to bear hidden family pain.

Family therapist Nathan Ackerman suggests that the term "organism" connotes the family's living process, functional unity, and natural life history—"a period of germination, a birth, a growth and development, a capacity to adapt to change and crisis, a slow decline, and finally, dissolution of the old family into the new."[3] The family's collective identity evolves and its joint "ego strength" fluctuates with the stresses and resources of each stage of the family life cycle. Some families cope constructively, for example, with the heavy pressures of the stage when the children are young but develop dysfunction when the children become teen-agers. This often reflects the unfinished growth work from the parents' own adolescence. Many families need help in revising their family patterns of interaction to cope more growthfully with stressful crises and new family stages.

A family system, like other social organisms, is composed of several interdependent subsystems. It is important for family counselors and therapists to be aware of the patterns of interaction within and among these subsystems—husband-wife, mother-children, father-children, child-child, grandparents-parents, grandparents-children, child-pet, and so on. The marital subsystem develops as two newly married persons work out a functional blend (often with severe clashes and pain) of the diverse family patterns that they carry within them from their families of origin. The joint marital pair identity, which the couple evolves through their interaction, becomes the core of their new family's identity. As children are added they alter the couple's and the family's identity to some degree, even as they are shaped by that identity. Young children automatically learn the implicit rules of their culture as these are reflected in their parents' pattern of approval and punishment. Fortunately, parents who become aware of their implicit family rules, values, and expectations may diminish or interrupt the transmission of ungrowthful patterns to their children. Thus, the family systems perspective, as implemented in family therapy, empowers adults to discover and change intentionally the transgenerational transmission of family patterns that they internalized in their own childhood.

Family therapist Salvador Minuchin describes how unconscious family patterns tend to constrict potentializing:

> Family patterns put blinders on people. . . . You are who you are in your context. This means that your relationship to your brother, your husband, your parents, your sister, and your children, causes you and them to focus sharply on certain aspects of your life and let your other skills and possibilities lie idle and perhaps atrophy. . . . Therapy can sometimes facilitate the activation of such unused skills.[4]

The Goals of Family Systems Therapy

What are the characteristics of growth-enabling families toward which these therapies seek to help families move? Virginia Satir, whose approach is thoroughly growth-centered, has identified four dynamics in families in which growth flourishes. First, within those families, people feel and support one another's self worth. One key to unlocking trapped growth in a family is to teach them how to enhance rather than diminish each other's esteem. Second, persons in growthful families communicate in direct, clear, and honest ways. As Satir put this, "Communication is the greatest single factor affecting a person's health and his relationships to others."[5] The most accurate way to diagnose the nature of a family system's problems is to watch their basic communication pattern—who talks? Who talks *to* whom or *for* whom? Third, the implicit rules within growthful families are fair, flexible, human, and open to renegotiation as the family's situation changes and individuals within the family grow. Fourth, such families are open systems that interact in a mutually nurturing way with a considerable number of people, families, and institutions outside their own family boundaries. Thus, a family's identity and wholeness are determined not just by its inner dynamics but also by its relations with the extended family and close friends, with its community and the organizations that effect its members' growth. Satir sees a positive reciprocity between all these factors: "Feelings of worth can only flourish in an atmosphere where individual differences are appreciated, mistakes are tolerated, communication is open and rules are flexible—the kind of atmosphere that is found in a nurturing family."[6]

Like other social systems, families can be either rigid and closed, or open and growing. Open and closed families can be distinguished by the number and quality of their extrafamilial relationships and by their responses to crises and change. Open, healthy families have more persons in their network of mutual-support than do closed families. Closed, rigid families are extremely vulnerable to crises. They resist change and try desperately to maintain the *status quo* by inflexible rules and by psychological or physical coercion. In contrast, open families tend to cope more constructively with crises and change. They are more open to revising, through negotiation, their family's working agreement (family contract) concerning the distribution of satisfactions, responsibilities, decision-making, and power within the family. They are more apt to seek to resolve their conflicting wants and needs by fair compromises or in other win-win rather than win-lose ways. They recognize that in intimate relationships if one person loses, no one really wins because the relationship is hurt thereby.

The research of family therapist Murray Bowen[7] has illuminated another crucial goal in helping families become more growth-enabling. A family is a system of interacting and counterbalancing forces, according to Bowen. Two primary forces in all families are the force toward togetherness and fusion, and the counter force toward differentiation and individuality. The togetherness-fusion force, which is deeply rooted in the biological survival needs of human beings, is the cohesive force that makes for the bonding of family systems (and other close relationships). The autonomy-individuality force is also rooted in a profound human need. Families vary greatly in the ratio of these two needs.

The basic pattern of a family's individuality-togetherness ratio is passed on from one generation to the next. A healthy balance between togetherness and individuality allows family members to be closely involved with one another without losing their sense of autonomy. When a family system maintains its optimal balance between these two forces, it is able to handle heavy stress constructively without family members' developing symptoms of dysfunction. Bowen has discovered that the most disturbed and growth-stifling families are those in which the fusion force far outweighs the individuality force. This creates sticky interdependency, rigidity, and an intolerance of individualism and nonconformity within the family. When heavy internal or external stress strikes such families, they are very vulnerable. Family members are likely to develop emotional, behavioral, relational, or psychosomatic problems as maladaptive responses to the family organism's stress. Although both togetherness and individuality are essential human needs, families that nurture optimal growth and cope-ability among their members are those in which individuality is valued and encouraged. Bowen's therapy seeks to help family members who are symbiotically enmeshed with one another to move toward greater self-definition and individuality.

Here, in summary, are the major operational goals of family systems therapy. Family therapists usually meet with the whole family and occasionally with one or more subsystems within the family seeking to help the family learn:

(1) *To communicate their feelings (both positive and negative), needs, desires, values, and hopes more openly, clearly, and congruently.* The therapist is a "coach" of effective, relationship-strengthening communication skills. (2) *To shift from focusing mainly on the "identified patient" and to deal with the hidden pain, conflict, and blocked growth in all family members that cause the individual's problems.* This may involve a number of marriage therapy sessions with the wife-husband subsystem. (3) *To interrupt their mutually damaging hurt-anger-attack cycles sooner and to gradually substitute self-feeding cycles of mutual need satisfaction among family members.* (4) *To mutually nourish rather than starve self-esteem in all family members.* (5) *To become aware of their family's contract*—its implicit rules, roles, values, expectations, and beliefs—and *then to renegotiate a more*

growthful working agreement that distributes satisfactions and responsibilities, power, and growth opportunities fairly. (6) *To see the positive but abortive growth strivings in much of the frustrating behavior of family members and to learn how to encourage the expression of these strivings in more self-actualizing ways.*[8] (7) *To resolve more constructively the inevitable conflicts of living together,* recognizing that growth often can be activated precisely at the points of conflict. (8) *To develop a healthier balance between their need for togetherness and their need for autonomy,* giving more room for the latter. (9) *To experiment with new behaviors and ways of relating* that are more responsive to the real needs of all family members. This often involves doing family "homework" assignments between sessions. (10) *To make the interaction within and among their subsystem more growth-engendering.* (11) *To open up their family system* by developing more supportive relationships with other people, families, and institutions outside the family. (12) *To create an interpersonal climate of high-level wellness within the family,* thus making it a better growth environment for all its members.

Because the marital subsystem is the dynamic core of a family's evolving identity, growth-oriented marriage counseling (concurrent with family therapy) is sometimes essential for enhancing family interaction. Encouraging couples to commit themselves to a redefinition of "love" as caring about and encouraging each other's fullest possible development, helps them make their marriage a better interpersonal environment of mutual growth. Experiencing both personal growth and a mutually growthful marriage empowers parents to nurture their children's fullest becoming.

A central issue in growthful marriage counseling is how to develop real equality between spouses. This issue has not been emphasized adequately in most of the literature on marriage counseling and family therapy. There is overwhelming evidence that the institution of marriage and the ways in which many couples define their personal marriage contracts is growth-limiting, particularly for women. To illustrate, single women, on the average, are healthier both physically and psychologically than married women. The opposite is true for men.[9] Many of the problems of troubled children and adolescents, which bring families to therapy, stem from the unfulfilling, one-down position of their mothers and the emotionally distant, high-pressure life-styles of their success-driven fathers. Women who have few sources of esteem and power outside of the family tend to overinvest in wifing and mothering roles. They exercise their basic human need for power through controlling their children (and often their husbands) in covert, manipulative ways.

If marriage counseling and family therapy are to be growth-liberating, professionals who work with families must have their own consciousness raised regarding the destructiveness of sexism in the laws and customs defining the institution of marriage. They must actively assist couples to become aware of and correct the areas of injustice and unfairness in their marriages, with respect to the distribution of power, decision-making, and opportunities for self-development. They should challenge and coach couples in developing the skills needed to renegotiate and update their marriage contract (covenant) regularly to provide opportunities for both parties to share fairly in child care, breadwinning, education, personal satisfactions, and household chores. Growthful marriage counseling and enrichment should aim at encouraging couples to relate as two strong, growing individuals who choose to form a relationship of interdependency that respects differences and autonomy.

Our culture's growth-constricting sex roles are learned by children by observing and internalizing the roles their parents act out. The implicit family rules, which shape the self-image, sense of competence, and esteem of children, are usually very different for girls and boys, even in the same family. Different behavior is rewarded and punished. Sexist dual standards and self-definitions are thus internalized and passed on through the generations in family systems. To help break the stranglehold of sexism on the full becoming of both women and men, it is essential that marriage and family therapy and enrichment help parents learn methods of nonsexist child-nurturing.[10]

Some Applications of Family Therapy Approaches

The goals and principles of family therapy described above are equally relevant for use in family life enrichment experiences for relatively functional, "healthy" families who wish to develop more of their unused growth potentials. "Healthy family growth sessions" involve the use of enrichment methods with the whole family.[11] In family enrichment workshops and camps, functional families can support one another's creative change. The growthfulness of many families could be increased significantly if they had such a family growth "booster" once or twice a year.

The systemic philosophy and methodology of family therapy and enrichment can be applied productively to any close, committed relationship. Any close friendship can be made more mutually growthful by applying the principles of marriage and family enrichment and therapy. There is a pressing need also to use such approaches to help the millions of single people in our society to develop family-like support systems. These are needed to nurture their growth in our lonely, urbanized society where "being married" is defined as the norm, making singles feel diminished self-worth.

The systemic perspective offers a valuable orientation for understanding and helping *individuals* to grow. In doing growth-oriented counseling with individuals, it is important to remember that their family-of-origin and present family (or other network of mutual nurture) are always present within them. We all carry within us, throughout our lives, the influence of the family system in which our personalities were created. This inner family tends to shape our present relationships. Individual therapy aims at helping people grow beyond the limitations and claim the latent strengths of their internalized families of origin, and to withdraw the projection of inappropriate attitudes and expectations from those families onto their present intimate relationships. Individual growth is more apt to continue after therapy if a person's growth is accompanied by creative changes in her or his contemporary family system. It often facilitates this process to have a few sessions with a person's "significant others" during individual therapy. Or, in marriage therapy, a few sessions involving the couple's children and/or parents, frequently reveals otherwise hidden dimensions of their marital interaction that prove effective in helping them alter their growth-stifling ways of relating. Seeing the couple's parents interact may illuminate for the couple the sources of their own communication hang-ups and conflicts. In doing individual therapy with persons who still value their marriages, it sometimes becomes essential to integrate marriage therapy with the process in order to prevent the person's growth from alienating him or her from the spouse.

The systemic perspective offers a variety of resources for enhancing spiritual and value growth. In one sense, family therapy is a way of helping families whose guiding values and priorities are not functioning growthfully to reformulate their values and priorities. A family's basic philosophy of life, spiritual orientation and values are "caught" by young children more than they are "taught," as they absorb the spiritual-values climate of that family. Continuing spiritual development throughout adulthood is best nurtured in family-like caring groups in which spiritual values are experienced in relationships. The systemic perspective reaffirms the ancient Hebrew awareness that spiritual growth occurs best in a caring community with a shared commitment to spiritual values. A biblical expression of this systemic awareness is found in references to the early church as the "*body* of Christ" in which individuals are "members of each other."

A vital dimension of an open, growing family system is its openness to the wider spiritual reality whom we call God. This openness provides a transpersonal and transfamilial context of meaning and support. The wholeness of family members can be profoundly nurtured by their awareness of their connectedness with other persons and ultimately with the whole of humankind, with the biosphere, and with the loving Spirit of the universe.

Wholeness in Larger Systems

When one works holistically to increase the growthfulness of intimate systems, it is a natural progression to look beyond their boundaries to the larger systems that deplete or enrich the lives of all individuals and families. Several family therapists have researched the impact of larger social systems on the family. I was first introduced to this orientation during my training in family therapy with Salvador Minuchin. (I recall the impact of spending time, at Minuchin's suggestion, in the homes of client families in the ghetto of Philadelphia.) From his work with ghetto families, Minuchin has developed a keen awareness of the reciprocity between family systems and societal structures. He believes that it is important for family therapists to learn about a family's experiences when they are *not* in the clinic and to become more aware of the socioeconomic oppression which has a profound, negative impact on those families' systems every hour of their lives. He declares:

> Every therapist who works with our population is familiar with numerous instances in which patterns of change within the family are out of phase with patterns of change in the neighborhood. Consider, for instance, the plight of a family attempting to change certain internal patterns while it is living in the midst of a rapidly deteriorating urban neighborhood which seems to require them to retain these patterns. A mother's attempts to modify her hierarchical and punitive relationship with her adolescent daughters may be defeated by the social phenomena outside her door. When her daughters satisfy their understandable heterosexual curiosity by continually glancing out the front door to see if any boys are passing, she is compelled to adopt her old punitive role: "Sure, I want to change. I don't want to yell at them for that, but how can I *not* tell them to stop looking out? The winos are taking over that corner, and pimps are beginning to come around. The girls have got to stay in."[12]

Minuchin also points to the insidious impact on slum families of chronic male unemployment. This produces an overvaluing of the role of "provider" and an undervaluing of the other significant roles of men—husband, father, human being.

Minuchin calls for multiple-leveled intervention in order to help slum families:

> The questions are no longer, "can we introduce change by just working within family systems?" or "can intervention at the societal level alone modify the ecological unbalance in these families?" The false dichotomy implied by such questions and the need for multiple levels of intervention have been acknowledged. The coordination of work within the family with community approaches now raises a new set of questions: How can the use of multiple levels of intervention be made coherently functional?[13]

He sees the need for increased study of the little-understood mechanisms by which family systems regulate their interaction with outside systems. Without this understanding it will remain impossible to devise social change programs (e.g., youth job training, head start) that ghetto families can use fully, in conjunction with family systems therapy, to interrupt the vicious, mutual reinforcement of family and community problems.

Murray Bowen has been examining the forces in contemporary society that increase stress on families and render them highly vulnerable to dysfunction—e.g., the frantic pace of life, the loss of supportive contact with the extended family, the pressures caused by the population explosion and the depletion of nonrenewable resources. These and other social changes have provided a society in which many parents experience heightened anxieties together with diminished awareness and self-confidence. All of this blunts their effectiveness in parenting.

From her perspective, Virginia Satir declares: "I see a need for families to ask to become partners in any institution in which any of their members are involved and to be considered a part of that establishment."[14] As a practical approach to meeting this need she recommends that parents sit down with their children in family meetings so that everyone can get in touch with where everyone else is in relation to outside institutions—school, business, church, boy scouts, the track team, etc. "The family meeting would be the one place where lacks, oversights, injustices, rewards and experiences by individuals would be looked at in the frame of everyone's needs and the adjustment [in the family and in outside institutions] that might have to be made."[15]

Re-creating the Extended Family

The family systems perspective makes it clear that, to cope creatively with the multiple crises and pressures of our world, many people desperately need to find substitutes for the extended family. In our rootless, highly mobile society, millions of individuals and families do not get a sense of support from their extended family or from their neighbors. Without a vital support system their capacity to cope is greatly reduced. To lessen psychological and family disorders and to increase human potentializing, an innovative strategy is needed to provide a variety of easily available networks of caring and mutual nurture for individuals and families within every community. The major growth-nurturing institutions of our society—schools and churches—have a tremendous opportunity to help develop such nurturing networks.

Here are some suggestions for helping religious organizations function as extended family networks of nurture. Similar approaches can be used to revitalize other people-serving institutions: (1) The consciousness of many religious leaders (professional and lay) concerning the urgent need in their community for networks of nurture for both individuals and families must first be raised. (2) Many leaders of congregations need on-the-job training in the skills of facilitating small growth-healing-action groups. Mental health professionals, including specialists in pastoral counseling, are the logical persons to provide this training. (3) Leaders of congregations should develop a smorgasbord of small groups, workshops, classes, and retreats, designed to meet the needs for nurture and growth-support of individuals and families in their congregation and community. The aim of such groups is the prevention of personal and family pathology through mutual nurture of growth. Here are some of the types of growth groups currently being used by churches—grief recovery groups; divorce growth groups; preparation for marriage and early marriage enrichment groups; creative singlehood groups; parenting skills groups; solo parenting groups; mid-years marriage renewal groups; creative retirement groups; parents of handicapped children groups; support groups for families of terminally ill persons. Participants in such groups should be encouraged to reach out to other persons facing similar life situations. (4) Leaders of congregations should recruit, train, and continue to coach carefully chosen caring teams to provide better support for individuals and families experiencing major life crises. To illustrate, the pastor of a church in Minneapolis has trained some twenty young adult and middle adult couples to provide support for the newly marrieds in his congregation. Such "befrienders" can be a rich resource to help young couples (particularly the highly vulnerable teen couples) learn the relational skills to cope with the stresses of growthing a new marriage. Experience has shown that some lay people who have weathered crises and grown as a result, can be trained to co-lead growth nurturing groups effectively. Thus, the leadership pool for a church's nurture-support network can draw heavily on these natural growth facilitators who are available in every congregation. Pastors with training in counseling (including group methods) should take the major responsibility in training and coaching caring teams from which support group leaders can be drawn. Mental health professionals in the congregation and community should be enlisted to provide assistance in the training and also to provide the backup services that are needed when lay persons encounter persons who need professional help. The basic structure of the support-nurture network in a congregation can be modeled on the self-help groups, which represent one of the most dynamic thrusts in the contemporary therapeutic scene. By developing caring teams and a network of nurture groups, church leaders can help enliven their congregations, making them more family-like places of healing and growth throughout the life cycle.

A Unified Systemic Model

This diagram depicts the interdependent dimensions of an ecological model of personal growth and social change:[16]

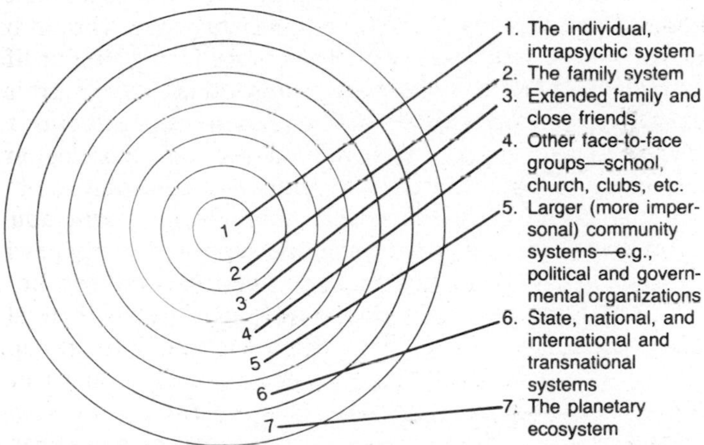

The diagram would be more complete and accurate if it could be three-dimensional. The dimension that integrates these seven interacting circles on the target of growth-change is what Tillich called the vertical dimension. This is the transpersonal dimension of the one Spirit in which all reality has its common roots.

> Which change-growth methods are useful in each sphere of this target? Education, counseling, psychotherapy, and growth groups can produce change in individuals (circle 1). Relationship-oriented counseling methods . . . and growth groups are viable instruments of change within the intimate relationships of circle 2. In circle 3 . . . and circle 4 . . . , dynamic education, group therapy, growth groups [and organizational development] are effective methods. Changes in circle 5 (larger, more impersonal organizations) and circle 6 (the systems beyond the local community) may occur through educational [and] persuasive approaches, but often they require the use of political [and other social action] methods. . . . Effecting

> change in larger systems . . . and between systems usually involves a greater use of confrontation in the form of political and economic power.[17]

Change in circle 7 involves a combination of consciousness-raising education designed to increase enlightened caring for the whole biosphere, and social-political action to produce changes in the institutions of our society that are essential to protect our precious and fragile ecological environment.

> Change within any system depends on interaction with other systems. On the target of systems (above), *change in one circle is more likely to occur and be permanent if the systems on one or both sides also change.* To illustrate, individual growth is more likely to occur and be sustained if the family also changes constructively; family changes are more likely to occur and be sustained if the extended family changes to support them; growth in all three is more likely to occur and be sustained if the institutions of society are growth-oriented. Movement toward a person-enhancing world community requires simultaneous action for change in each sphere on the target.[18]

An ecological-systems orientation to change and growth helps keep one aware, when attempting to effect change in one circle, of the interdependence of that dimension of change with all other dimensions.

The systemic perspective can provide the general principles for developing the sorely needed sociotherapies for the larger groups, institutions, and socio-economic-political systems, which collectively determine the healing-growthing climate of our communities and of our world society. The working concepts and methods of the systemic therapies may well give us resources for fostering the continuing self-renewal which is needed within our people-serving institutions and wider systems.

The urgency of implementing a multileveled systemic approach to personal growth and social change cannot be overemphasized. Perceptive students of the future continue to confront us with the awesome evidence that time may be running out for humankind. At least seven immense, interdependent threats to the quality of life on spaceship earth continue to escalate: the population explosion; the widening gulf between rich and poor nations; massive malnutrition (caused mainly by economic injustice, which produces maldistribution of available food); environmental pollution and degradation; the depletion of the irreplaceable resources of our finite planet; the growing threat of nuclear terrorism and eventual holocaust (with the equivalent of one and a half million Hiroshima-sized bombs in the arsenals of the world); and the worldwide tendency for the fruits of science and technology to be used without ethical responsibility.[19] Before World War II, H. G. Wells asked, "What would a world of human beings gone sane be like?"[20] In our pathogenic societies, life-loving people everywhere long to experience a world of human beings and institutions gone sane! The individualistic growth therapies, no matter how widely they become available, cannot interrupt the deadly momentum of the impersonal forces of massive destructiveness. Only the development of more effective methods of institutional and societal transformation, undergirded by a groundswell of personal and relational growth, can turn the tide toward planetary sanity.

Experiencing a Family Self-Change Method

The Intentional Family Method (IFM) is a do-it-yourself communication tool that can be used by families to move toward greater wholeness (and the goals of family therapy and enrichment described earlier). As a self-help tool, it can be taught to families in family counseling and therapy, and in family enrichment groups, workshops, and camps. Experiencing the IFM can help families feel mutually affirmed; become more aware of their strengths; identify the areas of needed change to make their interaction more mutually growthful; and negotiate a new family contract that will enable these changes to occur and thus reduce the causes of unconstructive family conflict. I have described the use of this tool by couples in detail elsewhere.[21] Therefore, I will only outline the steps here to show how it can be used by families. I suggest that you invite your whole family to try this exercise, setting aside at least an hour for this purpose. Read the instructions for each step and then take as long as you need to complete it:

Step #1: Your family undoubtedly has a lot going *for* it, even though there are things each of you would like to change. In order to become more aware of your family's strengths and assets, do a "go-round," giving each family member a chance to say what she or he likes about being a part of this family./ Now, do a second go-round focusing on one person at a time. Allow everyone an opportunity to say what they like and appreciate about that family member. Start with the person who is feeling "down" or under particular pressures now./ Share how you all feel now about this experience.

Step #2: The purpose of this step, which builds on the first, is to identify some unmet needs or wants of family members. Do another family go-round, giving everyone an opportunity to say what they need or want more of from the family. Give everyone a turn before you discuss the various needs or wants./ Now as a family communication exercise, let other family members tell each person what they heard his or her wants and needs to be./

Step #3: Your family and your relationships will be enriched if you work out together a family change plan to meet at least one of each person's wants or needs. If there are needs that several of you mentioned—e.g., having more family work or fun time together—you'll find that those needs will be the easiest to satisfy as a family. Negotiate a joint plan that is fair and acceptable to all of you. This may be the most difficult step, but it is also the payoff of the whole exercise./ After you have worked out a fair, feasible plan, write it down including the time schedule and each person's part in implementing it./

Step #4: Now, begin implementing your change plan, keeping track of your progress./ As you thus increase the mutual need-satisfaction and decrease the causes of conflict among ourselves, congratulate yourselves! You deserve it. You are becoming change agents who are learning to intentionally improve your family system./ After you implement your first plan, select a new set of needs-wants of each family member and devise and implement a plan to meet those./ If your efforts to change your own relating do not work, I recommend that you join a family enrichment group or workshop, or have some conjoint family counseling, to gain the help of a trained family communications facilitator in developing the rich family potentials you want to actualize./

For Further Exploration of Growth Resources in Systemic Therapies

Ackerman, Nathan. *The Psychodynamics of Family Life.* New York: Basic Books, 1958. A classic by a pioneer in family therapy.

Bertalanffy, Ludwig von. *General Systems Theory: Foundation, Development, Application.* New York: George Braziller, 1968. A basic introduction to systems theory.

Bowen, Murray. "Family Therapy and Family Group Therapy," chap. 11 in *Treating Relationships,* David H. L. Olson, ed. Lake Mills, Iowa: Graphic Publishing Co., 1976. Includes a brief history of family therapy and a description of Bowen's contributions to family therapy.

Clinebell, Howard. *Basic Types of Pastoral Counseling.* Chap. 6, "Role-Relationship Marriage Counseling"; chap. 7, "Family Group Therapy and Transactional Analysis"; chap. 12, "Group Pastoral Counseling."

———. *Growth Groups,* chap. 10, "Training Change Agents to Humanize Society." Describes the use of growth groups in social action.

Guerney, Bernard G., Jr. *Relationship Enhancement.* San Francisco: Jossey-Bass, 1977. Describes relationship skills training programs that can be used in therapy, problem prevention, and enrichment.

Kantor, David, and Lehr, William. *Inside the Family, Toward a Theory of Process.* New York: Harper Colophon Books, 1975. Reports what trained observers discovered about how family systems actually function.

Leas, Speed, and Kittlaus, Paul. *The Pastoral Counselor in Social Action.* Philadelphia: Fortress Press, 1981. Two social action specialists focus on processes and techniques that can be used to facilitate social change, using pastoral counseling insights.

Luthman, Shirley G., and Kirschenbaum, Martin. *The Dynamic Family.* Palo Alto, Calif.: Science and Behavior Books, 1974. A thoroughly growth-oriented approach to family therapy, derived in part from Virginia Satir's approach.

Minuchin, Salvador. *Families and Family Therapy.* Cambridge, Mass.: Harvard University Press, 1974. An introduction to structural family therapy, an approach that seeks to change the organization of the family.

———, et al. *Families of the Slums.* New York: Basic Books, 1967. An exploration of the structure and treatment of disadvantaged families.

Pattison, E. Mansell. *Pastor and Parish—A Systems Approach.* Philadelphia: Fortress Press, 1977. Using a systems approach to increase the effectiveness of a church.

Sanford, Nevitt. *Self and Society, Social Change and Individual Development.* New York: Atherton Press, 1966. Presents a developmental model to help institutions become more growth-enabling.

Satir, Virginia. *Conjoint Family Therapy.* Palo Alto, Calif.: Science and Behavior Books, 1964. A guide to the theory and practice of her communication-centered approach.

———. *Peoplemaking.* Palo Alto, Calif.: Science and Behavior Books, 1972. A book to help parents develop more growth-nurturing families.

Seifert, Harvey, and Clinebell, Howard. *Personal Growth and Social Change.* Philadelphia: Westminster Press, 1974. A guide for ministers and lay persons to help them become change agents.

Stewart, Charles W. *The Minister as Family Counselor.* Nashville: Abingdon, 1979. Describes ways of strengthening families and sees the church as a family of families.

Chapter 10

Growth Resources in Feminist Therapies

Feminist therapies are one type of radical therapy. The common motif in all the radical therapies is the conviction that personal growth and social change are inextricably interdependent. In my view, this motif must be one dimension of any therapy that seeks to maximize human growth. A systemic-political awareness is needed to offset the temptation, besetting every therapeutic and growth approach, to become the luxury of the privileged, a privatized, socially irresponsible form of secularized salvation-seeking. The awareness of the societal roots of every personal problem can help keep us counselors, therapists, and teachers working at the crucial though difficult task of integrating our commitment to personal growth with our concern for helping to create growth-sustaining institutions. The philosophy and the methodology of the radical therapies can help the disciplines of counseling and therapy to transcend their middle-class origins and become channels of liberation and growth for the poor and oppressed who are the vast majority of the earth's people.

There are three major streams of radical therapies. In an early type of radical therapy, R. D. Laing, Thomas Szasz, and others challenged the apolitical belief system and the oppressive institutional practices of conventional psychiatry.[1] A second stream emerged from the impact of the new left (during the sixties and early seventies) on certain mental health professionals including Claude Steiner, Hogie Wyckoff, and Phil Brown.[2] In a paper representing this perspective, Lester Gelb declares, "In the treatment of the individual or group of individuals we must be aware that social change may be the most meaningful therapeutic goal and therefore must be a real part of our professional concern."[3] The third stream of radical therapy, feminist therapy, is the most rapidly growing and influential in terms of its impact on therapists of many orientations.

All three streams share the view that the societal context of an individual's problems is an essential concern in therapy. As the radical therapy manifesto declares: "Liberation from within must be accompanied by liberation from without."[4] All these streams see the traditional mental-health philosophy and delivery systems as unhealthy for patients, especially for the relatively powerless people in a society—including the poor, minorities, and women. All three streams call for the democratizing of hierarchical therapist-patient relationships and of mental health centers. The credo of radical therapy—"Therapy means change not adjustment"—is a motif of all three streams.

I will focus in this chapter on the feminist stream of radical therapy for several reasons. Feminist therapies concentrate attention on the growth-inhibiting ways that half the human family (and their institutions) treats the other half. (What could be more basic for anyone who does therapy or receives it?) It is clear that sexism *is* a massive cause of truncated growth, in both women and men, and a major cause of diminished effectiveness in most therapies. Feminist therapists tend to keep a balance between the goals of personal healing and growth, on the one side, and sociopolitical empowerment to equip and motivate persons to change sexist systems, on the other. Most feminist therapies have a robust sense of the interrelatedness of personal, relational, social, political, and historical factors in liberation. This contrasts with the most radical of the radical therapists, who seem to reduce therapy to social action. Furthermore, feminist therapy tends to be explicitly growth-oriented:

> "Therapy" is not something reserved for desperate and "sick" people—but rather it can be for anyone functioning well who would like to function better. Therapy is viewed as a process of heightening one's consciousness and mobilizing one's personal powers. By learning tools for self-awareness, you can integrate the "therapeutic" process into your life so that you continue to develop and grow consciously.[5]

The feminist vision of human wholeness is an essential dimension of any therapy that is truly liberating for either women or men. In my experience, there is fresh hope and fresh power for growth in this vision.

There is no one body of theory and methods shared by all feminist therapists. A "feminist therapist" is any therapist for whom the feminist perspective is a central therapeutic philosophy and orientation. Such therapists represent a variety of therapeutic orientations and degrees of radicality in their feminism.[6]

My closest relationship is with a radical feminist who is also a skilled therapist. Charlotte Ellen's[7] feminism and her work as a feminist therapist have been a continuing challenge and stimulus to my awareness of the importance of the issues explored in this chapter. My personal struggles with these issues undoubtedly have colored my reflection on them.

Insights about Growth in Feminist Psychology

Feminist psychologists have identified the male biases that have distorted the understanding of "normal" human development, which undergirds the work of growth-oriented professionals.[8] They also have documented the growth-diminishing sexism in traditional psychotherapeutic theories and in the practice of most therapists. They have exposed the need for the "liberators" of growth to be liberated from sexism so that they *can* facilitate the full becoming of both women and men.

The growth possibilities inherent in the feminist understanding of human growth are well stated in Jean Baker Miller's powerful book, *Toward a New Psychology of Women.* Here are some of her salient points:

> Humanity has been held to a limited and distorted view of itself—from its interpretations of the most intimate of personal emotions to its grandest vision of human possibilities—precisely by virtue of its subordination of women. . . . As other perceptions arise—precisely these perceptions that men, because of their dominant position, could not perceive—the total vision of human possibilities enlarges and is transformed. The old is severely challenged.

> Although women have been like a subservient caste, in many ways, "they have played a specific role in male-led society in ways no other suppressed group has done. They have been intertwined with men in intimate and intense relationships, creating the milieu—the family—in which the human mind as we know it has been formed. Thus women's situation is a crucial key to understanding [and changing] the psychological order."

> A dominant group [men] inevitably has the greatest influence in determining a culture's overall outlook—its philosophy, morality, social theory, and even its science. The dominant group thus legitimizes the unequal relationship and incorporates it into society's guiding concepts. . . . In the case of women, for example, despite overwhelming evidence to the contrary, the notion persists that women are meant to be passive, submissive and docile—in short, secondary. From this premise, the outcome of therapy and encounters with psychology and other "sciences" are often determined.[9]

According to Miller, the potentialities assigned in our culture to the dominant group (men) for development reflect only a limited part of the total range of human potentialities. Subordinates (women and others) are assigned potentials that are less valued by the culture. Yet, in our present world value crisis, the very potentials that women have overdeveloped and men have largely ignored, are the key to developing more humanizing ways of living by both sexes. In male-dominated societies, women have had to develop greater awareness of relationships and of feelings, and greater tolerance of these feelings of vulnerability that are inherent in all growth. They have had to develop relationship- and people-nurturing skills, which are not well developed by most men. They have come to recognize the essential cooperative and creative nature of healthy human relationships. The lopsided development of nurturing and serving capacities by women, and their socially reinforced neglect of their many other potentials, contribute to the problems that bring women to therapy. (The same is true, in reverse, for men.) But the value for both sexes of the socially denigrated potentials women have had to develop is real, nonetheless. They have developed the very attributes that the world needs to save us from lopsided values of men, which drive them and male-led institutions and nations to "advance at any cost, pay any price, drive out competitors, and kill them if necessary."[10] Our society must learn to value the strengths women have developed and provide them equal opportunity to participate in reshaping our institutions and our society. Only thus will women and men be able to develop their full potentials in our society.

Growth toward wholeness for women involves developing their strong, assertive, rational potentials and integrating these with the nurturing, relational strengths they have overdeveloped. Growth for men involves developing their neglected nurturing, feelingful, vulnerable, relating, cooperative capacities and integrating these with the strengths that society has programmed them to overdevelop. Miller reflects on how the splitting of human potentials between the sexes impoverishes everyone: "We do not yet talk about how much we are all interdependent and *need* to relate to an equal, how challenging and beneficial that process can be, how often this is thwarted, and how little practice we get in it, and how much of our life is spent at the much more primitive level of learning how to be either one-up or one-down."[11] Healthy growth for both women and men must involve developing and bringing together in creative synthesis the nurturing strengths and the assertive strengths that all human beings possess potentially. This understanding of human growth is an invaluable contribution from feminist psychology to all parents and to all of us in the growth professions.

Feminist thinkers have exposed the ways in which the

effectiveness of traditional therapies has been reduced by sexism in both their theory and practice. Freud, whose theories have been formative in most psychotherapeutic schools until recently, perceived women as damaged men (without a penis). Women, he believed, see themselves as defective and inferior and therefore turn their aggressiveness inward. This produces "normal" personality in them that is passive, dependent, and masochistic. Their innate submissiveness fits them for their "normal" roles as dependently attached to men, serving others as wives and mothers. The general history of psychotherapeutic theory, until the advent of the feminist therapists, has reflected and reinforced the misogynic prejudices of male-dominated culture.[12] Clara Thompson and Karen Horney offered refreshing exceptions to the male distortions of psychotherapeutic understandings. As foremothers of contemporary feminist therapists, they pointed to the sexist misconceptions and blind spots of psychoanalytic theories.[13]

In her classic study, *Women and Madness,* Phyllis Chesler points out that the professions of psychiatry and psychology are dominated by men while the majority of their patients are women. She shows that most clinicians, both male and female, do therapy on the basis of traditional myths about female inferiority and sex-role stereotypes; that most therapists defend as "scientific" and "therapeutic" views of women as innately submissive and dependent; and that the institutions of private therapy (for the affluent) and mental hospitals (for the poor) mirror rather than challenge the general female experience of being treated as inferior in a patriarchal culture:

> For most women, psychotherapeutic encounter is just one more instance of an unequal relationship, just one more opportunity to be rewarded for expressing distress and to be "helped" by being (expertly) dominated. Both psychotherapy and white or middle-class marriage isolate women from each other; both emphasize individual rather than collective solutions to woman's unhappiness; both are based on a woman's helplessness and dependence on a stronger male authority figure. . . . Both control and oppress

> women similarly—yet, at the same time, are the two safest (most approved and familiar) havens for middle-class women in a society that offers them few—if any—alternatives.

Chesler points to the consequence for women of isolating the personal from the cultural dimensions of their problems:

> Both psychotherapy and marriage enable women to express and diffuse their anger by experiencing it as a form of emotional illness, by translating it into hysterical symptoms: frigidity, chronic depression, phobias, and the like. Each woman, as patient, thinks these symptoms are unique and are her own fault: she is "neurotic." She wants from a psychotherapist what she wants—and often cannot get—from a husband: attention, understanding, merciful relief, a *personal* solution.[14]

A revealing study of sex-role stereotypes in therapists was done by Inge K. Boverman and four other psychologists. They developed a questionnaire consisting of 122 bipolar items, each of which described a human characteristic such as "Very aggressive—Not at all aggressive." They administered it to 79 psychologists, psychiatrists, and social workers (46 men, 33 women).[15] One-third of the clinicians were asked to pick the characteristics describing a "healthy, mature, socially competent adult person"; one-third to pick items describing a "healthy, mature, socially competent adult man"; and one-third a "healthy, mature, socially competent adult woman." The researchers found that clinicians of both sexes held concepts of "health" and "maturity" that parallel our society's sex-role stereotypes. The traits chosen to describe a healthy adult did not differ significantly from those describing a healthy man, but they were strikingly different from the traits chosen to describe a healthy woman. Other studies have shown that the characteristics identified with a healthy woman are less valued in our society than traits identified with a healthy adult male. The choices of the clinicians of both sexes revealed a negative conception of a "healthy" woman. They described a healthy woman as more emotional, less objective, more excitable in crises, less competitive, more easily influenced, less aggressive, less independent, less adventurous, more conceited about appearance, having more easily hurt feelings, and disliking math and science, more than a healthy adult or a healthy man.

It seems clear that the clinicians' unconscious sex-role stereotypes must constrict the full potentializing of their women clients. If a woman client accepted and internalized these therapists' criteria of wholeness, she could not develop personality potentials that are most valued by our culture and identified with a "healthy male" and a "healthy adult."

Some Key Concepts of Feminist Therapies

Drawing on the thought of Anne Kent Rush, Jean Baker Miller, Elizabeth Friar Williams, and Charlotte Ellen, let me overview the key concepts in the thought of feminist therapists:

—Contrary to the dominant beliefs of our society, women generally possess strong potentials for autonomy, competency, and leadership. The task of therapy is to help them discover and develop all their rich inner potentials and powers.

—For women to develop hidden strengths is an exciting but risky adventure. When they risk moving out of their subservient "place," they receive flak from both men and from unliberated women. But this is the necessary risk of growth.

*—The societal programming of women is a basic block to their growth which must receive attention in any effective therapy. Their problems in living cannot be reduced to intrapsychic and interpersonal dynamics, for these both are rooted in the wider dynamics of their relative powerlessness and inferiority as defined by society. In contrast to traditional therapies, feminist therapy includes consciousness-raising to help women regain their power and self-worth by redefining themselves. The personal and political dimensions of women's (and other oppressed people's) problems must not be

separated. Personal empowerment (growth) should equip and motivate one to sociopolitical action with others, to change the social sources of diminished growth.

*—Consciousness-raising therapy for women should increase their understanding of the past and present roots of their personal problems in the historical and the contemporary social position of women.

—Women need to develop their own special powers both for their own wholeness and for the wholeness (and perhaps survival) of society. Having been devalued and neglected for so long, female energy and insights must now be emphasized to counterbalance the destructive effects of male dominance.

*—Women in therapy should be encouraged to develop strong, autonomous identities, not derived from their relations with men.

—There is excitement for women in recovering their lost heritage as healers and growth nurturers through the millennia.[16]

*—Therapy for women seeks to enable them to integrate the many splits that they have internalized from patriarchal cultures—splits between mind and body, thought, feeling, and action; the rational and the intuitive; the scientific and the artistic; the objective and the subjective; the individual and her environment. Therapy seeks to restore the essential unity of life.

*—Therapy for women is best done in small groups of women, with a woman therapist. There the energy and powerful mutuality of women can be experienced. In such a reality-oriented community of mutual caring, women can grapple together with inner and relational problems and potentials, and with the impact of the wider society on their lives. A women's therapy group (which must include consciousness-raising) can help women integrate the experience of therapy with their total lives; it can reduce the isolation from other women (in middle-class society) and the hurt of being "helped" by powerful authority figures, usually male.

*—Women in therapy should be encouraged to explore and expand their life options and to move intentionally toward self-chosen growth goals. They should be encouraged to be assertive in satisfying their real needs, choosing life-styles and occupations that they find fulfilling (in the home, in paid employment, or a combination of both).

—Women should be helped in therapy to recognize their appropriate anger at their one-down position in society. They should be encouraged to use this anger to change relationships and social practices rather than turning their anger on themselves in ways that produce depression, masochism, and psychosomatic problems.

*—Women should be free to define "normal" for themselves. Every woman is ultimately the only real "expert" in her own healing and growth. Therapy should help her discover her capacity for self-healing.

*—Only therapists with raised consciousness, who are continuing to work on their own continuing liberation, can function as growth-liberating rather than subtly oppressive therapists. The political awareness of the therapist is a crucial resource in any therapy that is really liberating.

*—Nonhierarchical relationships between therapist and client are essential for therapy to be fully effective. The professional elitism of some mental health professionals increases the inequality and hurts the client's already frayed self-esteem.

—Women in therapy should discover precisely how they make themselves vulnerable to exploitation by others, especially men.

*—Body awareness and empowerment is a vital part of therapy for women since most women have been alienated from both their physical strength and their pleasure potentials. Women should be helped to develop their capacities for enjoying their own bodies and encouraged to derive at least as much pleasure from sex as do their partners.

*—Women in therapy should be freed to enjoy other women as desirable, loving friends.

—Women in therapy should learn to respect and satisfy their own needs. Serving others should be an expression of one's love for them rather than one's sole mission in life; a woman should learn to expect others whom she serves to reciprocate fairly in meeting her needs.

The feminist vision that energizes feminist therapists is releasing a growth renaissance among women today. Jean Baker Miller declares:

> Women have always grown in certain ways despite whatever obstructions were in the path. . . . What is new today is the conscious and explicit search for even further growth by larger numbers of women. . . . Many women are now asking about the prospects and processes of self-development. . . . There is a new and exciting sense of motivation and purpose, a burst of energy and incisiveness among many women.[17]

Feminist Therapy Resources for Therapy with Men

Some of the working concepts of feminist therapy parallel emphases in other growth-oriented therapies—e.g., the affirmation of the riches of human potentials; nonhierarchical therapist-client relationships; the goal of restoring unity within oneself and with one's environment; the emphases on self-healing and body work. Furthermore, the principles of feminist therapies offer valuable resources for the growth of men as well as women. Elizabeth Williams states: "I think of feminist therapy as a way to sensitize people of both sexes to the way in which they use role behavior to keep themselves at a distance from their own and other's realities and from realizing themselves as fully developed human beings."[18] As an experiment, go back and change "woman" to "black" in these principles./ Now, try changing the word "woman" to "man" and vice versa in the principles with the asterisks./ The use of these principles with growth-oppressed people, even those who are subtly oppressed (white males for example), can increase awareness of their need to change constricting social definitions of wholeness for themselves. Feminism and feminist therapies offer new, more whole definitions of healthy "maleness" as well as healthy "femaleness."

For us middle-class white males, it is more difficult to become aware of how our growth is limited by social programming than it is for women and minorities. Our growth-constrictions are sugarcoated and hidden behind the rewards of our one-up position. The payoffs of our privileges and power are so seductive, it's easy to ignore their high costs. Only when men feel anger at the price they pay by sacrificing their full humanity do they begin to free themselves by making radical changes in their values and life-styles.

More and more men are beginning to sense that we can't have it both ways. We can't have the power and comfort of trying to keep women in their "place" without boxing ourselves in with the male mystique—the exhausting one-upmanship; the struggling to always win; the feelings of damaged self-worth when we don't win; the loneliness of never letting ourselves be vulnerably open with another person, particularly a man; the chronic hiding of half our feelings—the vulnerable, fearful, tender, needy, longing, "weak" feelings; the disguised, only half-satisfying ways of getting the nurture we need from others; the always precarious foundation for our self-worth in proving our "manly" value by continuing successes; the chronic stress of feeling ultimately responsible for supporting one's family "successfully"; the pressure to stay on the success-seeking treadmill until one is knocked off by a mid-life heart attack.

It is essential for therapists who work with men to help raise their consciousness concerning ways the chronic pressures to "be a man" spawn both intrapsychic and interpersonal problems. Just as women are dehumanized by being treated as sex objects, men are treated as success objects.[19] Because many of us men have not developed the inner powers of wholeness, we are threatened by the blossoming power that women are discovering in themselves. The fact that we tend to perceive other men as potential competitors means that we must concentrate most of our normal human needs for closeness and dependency on women, often on only one woman. Our unconscious shame about dependency (which feels "unmanly") produces anger and ambivalence toward the woman upon whom we are dependent. Consequently we both express aggression toward her and frighten ourselves with the fantasy (which often proves not to be a fantasy) that she will leave us if she really discovers her strength as an autonomous person.[20]

The glib statement, "Never mind about women's liberation—I'm for *human* liberation!" often indicates that the speaker (usually a man) is ignoring the unique liberation needs of women in our society. The growth-oppression of women overlaps and intertwines with that of men but, in many respects, it is different. Achieving liberation from a one-down position in society is very different from achieving liberation from a one-up position. For women, liberation is like struggling to swim upstream against the powerful current of institutional sexism. For men, in contrast, liberation is like discovering that the current we thought was taking us where we wanted to be is carrying us away from those we love and toward the brink of a waterfall (an early death from chronic male stress). Our liberation as men and as women has separate and unique dimensions, even as it also has many areas of similarity and interdependence. Whatever members of either sex do to liberate themselves and their full potentials makes it more urgent for the other sex to grow freely and fully.

Firsthand encounter with the feminist awareness in a woman therapist or in another close relationship can increase a man's awareness of himself as an *oppressed oppressor*. It can help him see how he is contributing, directly or indirectly, to the diminished growth of women, in his personal relationships and in institutions where he has decision-making power. This confrontation may help a man sense his own need for liberation as well as the need to renegotiate a fair marriage contract or help create equal opportunities for advancement among the women employees of his business.

I had only a vague inkling that I needed to liberate myself from anything (except my personal hang-ups) until Charlotte began to challenge and change her growth-restricting programming as a woman and as a wife. As she moved out of her "box," I gradually became aware of mine. Just as the black freedom movement triggered a chain reaction of other liberation movements (including the reawakening of the women's movement), the feminist awareness and its political consequences are triggering demands for liberation among many men. The emotional intimacy in many women-men relations makes the impact on men of changes in women very powerful. I know from experience that, when a woman who is liberating herself is someone with whom a man has a deep bond of caring, that man's motivation for change can become very strong.

It is essential for both male and female counselors-therapists to be involved in their own continuing self-liberation and to get their consciousness raised (regarding the role of sexism in personal problems). Elizabeth Williams states: "It is theoretically possible for male therapists to be good feminists, but it takes work for them to achieve a real understanding of sexism and its effects on women. Some feminist-therapy referral organizations have a few men on their lists—men who have taken the time and trouble to go through consciousness raising."[21]

Whatever his feminist awareness, a man has two disadvantages as a growth enabler for women. He cannot know the experience of women in a sexist society from the inside, and he cannot serve as a role model, for a woman client, of a strong, competent, caring woman. But if his consciousness has been raised and if he is warm, open, vulnerable, and growing (as well as competent), relating to such a man can be growth-enabling for both women and men. A male counselor who has struggled and grown in his self-liberation has certain advantages over women therapists in working with male clients. He can understand from the inside the pain of a man who is struggling ambivalently for liberation. He also can function as a role model of a man who is on the liberation journey. Women feminists can be effective growth enablers for men as well as women if they have owned their own power, so that they can avoid projecting their anger toward the male-dominated power establishment inappropriately onto male clients.

Here are some characteristics of a liberated and liberating counselor-therapist, female or male:

> Such a counselor: 1. Values being female equally with being male. A woman counselee cannot learn to value herself from a counselor who devalues women. 2. Believes in complete equality between women and men at all levels and in all areas of public and private life, on the job, and at home. 3. Is aware of the fact that deeply embedded cultural stereotypes are likely to have their influence on him or her at an unconscious level, even though intellectually he or she rejects such stereotypes. 4. Is nondefensive, unpretentious, and nonjudgmental. 5. Holds the basic philosophy that it is his or her job to help the client find out who she or he is and wants to be. This may mean raising the issue of other choices and options for persons who are not raising that issue for themselves. 6. Is constantly aware of his or her limitations in working with a person of the other sex. 7. Is in the process of becoming (and encouraging counselee and client to become) a more whole person.[22]

Our society will need many more liberated counselor-therapists in the years ahead. As the speed of change in women's identity accelerates, the epidemic of painful conflict in female-male relationships will increase by geometric progression. This crisis in intimate relationships is fraught with pain but also with unprecedented potentialities. In our times there probably is greater conflict in male-female relationships than during any previous period in history. But there are also greater opportunities for developing the depth and creativity that are possible only between equals. Many couples will need the skills of a growth-oriented, liberated therapist to learn how to use these growth opportunities.

To be fully effective, women's CR (consciousness-raising) and CR-therapy groups must be led by women and men's groups by men. Before they can relate to men and participate in society from a position of equality, many women must mobilize these inner strengths from which they have been alienated by society's programming. This mobilization occurs most effectively in small groups composed of and led by women. Because women therapists have the advantages described earlier, they must be the primary growth-enablers for women clients. Similarly, male therapists whose consciousness has been raised must carry the primary responsibility for facilitating the liberation and growth of male clients.

To meet the increasing need for female growth therapists, more women must be trained for all the counseling-therapy professions, including pastoral counseling. Graduate training and continuing education for therapy professionals should include consciousness-raising experiences that heighten therapists' awareness of sexism and of other societal problems that must be faced in therapy. The training of both female and male therapists should balance the analytical, critical, rational, left-brain, so-called "masculine" orientation (which has dominated most training) with training experiences that foster personal growth and the development of the nurturing, integrative, creative, intuitive, right-brain side of their personalities. Training should make counselors-therapists aware that professional elitism and the hierarchical delivery systems that are still prevalent within the mental health establishment are counterproductive to wholeness and must be changed.

The Process and Methods of Feminist Therapies

Feminist therapists use a wide variety of methods, depending on their therapeutic training, style, and preference. But the feminist orientation is at the center of their work, influencing everything they do. A brochure from a feminist therapy center describes the way in which various approaches are used: "While we rely on and find valuable many of the modalities of traditional therapies, we utilize these in a non-sexist context and strive toward demystifying the power relationship between client and therapist."[23]

An open, nonhierarchical client-therapist relationship is basic in any radical therapy style. One feminist therapist I know well uses these approaches to help demystify therapy and change the "doctor-patient" relationship that many clients expect when they come: She introduces herself by her first name rather than "Doctor"; she feels free to share her own feelings and struggles as these are relevant to the client's issues; she demystifies the therapy process by saying why she is using particular techniques; she affirms the client's capacity and responsibility for self-healing and growth; she does much of her therapy sitting on pillows on the floor.

The central and unique methodology of feminist therapies is the use of consciousness raising in both individual and group therapy.[24] The source of CR methods is the CR groups as these developed within radical therapy and within the feminist movement. Because this model integrates personal growth and social-political change, the CR group is a valuable innovation for the whole field of therapy and growth work. Effective CR groups blend processes that help to restore a sense of personal self-esteem, power, and competency, together with conscientizing processes that help people become aware of the role of societal oppression in their problems and empower them to join with others in social change efforts. The CR group model can be used for therapeutic-growth-liberation work with any oppressed group. It may be the key to creating indigenous socio-therapies among those in pockets of poverty in affluent countries and among economically and politically oppressed people in the developing countries.

In their unmodified form CR groups have no professional "leader" or "therapist"; they are explicitly not "therapy" (with the connotations of privatized sickness, and passivity in receiving help from a one-up professional that that word connotes for many people). But, as the experience of countless women demonstrates, an effective CR group *can* be very therapeutic. CR groups illustrate the remarkable healing-growthing power of lay, self-help groups that are flourishing in many places.

The authors of a manual on setting up CR groups state the philosophy of feminist consciousness raising:

> The key to all that happens in the CR . . . is the phrase "from the personal to the political." In the CR meeting the members will begin by discussing their own experiences, being as personal as they can and wish; but with the guidance of the leader they will recognize the common denominators of their experiences and see the political implications of whatever is happening in their own lives. . . . "Political" . . . in this context refers not to political parties or voting, but to the concept of power in society: who has it, how it is used, how can one get it, how society is managed. Unless the political point is made for each topic discussed in CR, there is a danger that the women will not genuinely have their consciousness raised; they may—or may not—achieve some relief from tension or pain, but until they see the connection between what happens to them as individual women and what happens to all women in a sexist society, they are not experiencing real feminist CR. . . . The other kinds of group activity labeled CR miss the essence of the feminist approach when they concentrate solely on ways the individual woman can improve her situation or beef up her personal "copability"; however valuable these may be, they are at best temporary expedients and at worst illusory, since they coax the woman to work on herself rather than society. There are no personal solutions to social problems—only adjustment, accommodations, temporary loopholes—and pain. Nothing a woman can do for herself alone will solve her basic problem of being female in a society rigged against her.

They conclude with this affirmation of the values of the process:

> Feminist consciousness raising will enrich a woman's personal life with sisterhood, support from other women, intellectual and emotional stimulation; but its most important contribution will be to show her how to work to free herself and other women through feminist understanding and action. Real CR is inevitably tremendously exciting and genuinely liberating. It is worth all the effort it takes.[25]

In an in-depth analysis of CR groups as an alternative to traditional psychotherapy for women[26] Barbara Kirsch cites a study describing four stages in the group process: (1) *Opening up*—Each member tells personal experiences as a woman in a nonjudgmental atmosphere of support and acceptance of feelings; group closeness and mutual trust develop rapidly. (2) *Sharing*—Through deeper expression of feelings, needs, and experiences, the individuals discover that many of their problems are shared by other women; this leads to the awareness that their problems root in society's problems more than in their individual inadequacies. The sense of group cohesion grows stronger with this awareness. (3) *Analyzing*—The group reaches beyond personal experiences and focuses on the devalued position of women in society. This leads to new objective understandings, which are integrated with the member's personal experiences as women. (4) *Abstracting*—The group members evolve a new vision of their potentials as women, and the group begins to see itself as a means for changing social institutions so that the potentials of women can be realized more fully.

Some feminist therapists have discovered that the CR group's philosophy and methods can be integrated with professionally led group therapy in ways that deepen the growth-enabling effects of both. Charlotte Ellen reports these learnings from experiences with small CR-therapy groups:

> I have learned a few things since I first began doing such groups. It is clearly possible to combine therapy with CR. The group members become even more "therapeutic" for each other than the "therapist" has been. It is possible to do gestalt work in a way which really includes and enhances the group instead of just being individual work in a group setting. . . . The group feeling and support, *and* the strengths of the individuals grow much faster when the facilitator becomes a member of the group. My function has become, in such groups, simply that of having up my sleeve possible agenda items and exercises, moving in on those rare

> occasions when the group is bogged down or when someone clearly needs my "more skilled" intervention. My own pain and struggle as a woman are at least as "therapeutic" as my leadership skills.[27]

Charlotte's groups ordinarily run for eight weekly two-hour sessions. Group sessions usually begin with a CR type go-round in which each woman has a chance to share her situation and needs. Sessions may focus, in CR group fashion, on topics suggested by the therapist or group members out of their evolving needs—e.g., developing a stronger sense of self; learning how not to give one's power away; enjoying one's sexuality; career dreams and changes; issues around children; relations with women and men; women's spirituality. A part of each session is spent in a structured CR-growth experience—e.g., assertiveness training, body awareness work, guided fantasies. Group members often take between-session assignments such as journal writing or drawing a self-portrait. The last session is a four-hour mini-marathon ending with a joyful celebration of the growth that group members have experienced.

CR groups, in both their original form and their modified CR-therapy form, can be effective liberation-growth experiences for men as well as women. For over three years, I have been part of a small, leaderless men's sharing group. We try to be both supportive and honest with one another as we wrestle with personal issues and explore ways of liberating ourselves as men. For me it is a refreshing discovery to find that I *can* risk being vulnerable and being nurtured by men. Gradually we are discovering the reward of mutual caring as "brothers."

For men who are living with liberated women, a men's CR group can be particularly valuable. It can help them deal openly with the pain and anger of a changing relationship, in a climate of acceptance, trust, and honesty. It can support them while it also confronts them with their blind spots and their contributions to the problems in their marriage or other committed relationships. It can reduce their overdependency on women and encourage them to develop self-nurture and inner strengths so that they will be able to enjoy interdependency with strong, liberated, growing women.[28]

Weaknesses of Feminism from the Growth Perspectives

As essential as the feminist perspective is for growth-enabling therapy, there are certain strands in some radical feminist thought that are potentially counterproductive of growth. One of these strands is the viewpoint that declares that the entire therapeutic establishment is inherently oppressive to women. In her blanket condemnation of therapies, Mary Daly rejects even feminist therapy. Daly calls for *all* women's healing to occur without the label of "therapy" and outside the therapeutic establishment.[29] Her valid awareness of the growth-oppressiveness for women of many conventional therapies apparently causes her to ignore the fact that many women *do* experience liberating growth as a result of therapy with therapists for whom the feminist perspective is a central and transforming orientation.

Radical feminists who regard sexism as *the* basic cause of all other injustices and oppression fail to recognize the complex, circular causality among all forms of oppression. I agree with the basic feminist view that the inequality of the sexes feeds all other injustices in our society and that liberation from sexism is essential for the full potentializing of women or men. But it seems clear that sexism is also fed by other social evils—racism, economic exploitation, class inequality. Wholeness-enabling counselors and therapists must be equally committed to working for, and to enabling their clients to work for, the elimination of all these intricately interrelated societal problems, which together constitute the swamp in which the malarial mosquitoes of personal problems proliferate.

The position of some radical feminists who advocate separatism of women from men as a long-range strategy cannot provide a basis for either a growth-sustaining society or growth-enabling therapies. It is a psychological illusion that either women or men can develop their full humanity totally isolated from the other half of the human family. The "power of absence," to use Daly's phrase, is a short-term necessity for some women to help them force changes in unjust personal relations with men. Collectively the power of absence may be a necessary time-limited method of forcing changes in the male-dominated institutions of society. But separatism and further polarization of the sexes cannot provide a long-range strategy for a growth-enabling society. There is evidence that most women and men want and need close relations with the other sex. When these are relationships of real equality, they can be environments of mutual growth for both sexes. The full liberation and growth of women and men are deeply interdependent. It will take the best efforts of liberated women *and* liberated men working together as equals to accomplish the difficult but essential transformation of our major institutions which alone *will* free people of both sexes to become full human beings. Separatism as a long-range strategy is counter-productive of the essential climate of mutuality and reciprocity that is needed to motivate men and women to collaborate in this way.

These weaknesses in the thought of some radical feminists are not present in the approaches of most feminist therapists. Nor do these weaknesses diminish the importance of the central thrust of feminist vision for all growth-enablers, including therapists. Think of the mind-boggling gains for humankind that can be actualized as the dream of full human liberation is gradually fulfilled. The leadership and creativity pool of the human family eventually could be doubled, without increasing the world's population, as women free and equip themselves to use their full intelligence, relational skills, creativity, leadership, and growth-nurturing abilities in society, and as men free and equip themselves to use their full relational, nurturing, feelingful, and creative capacities in the home and in society. As women develop more of their other potentials, they will not need to satisfy most of their esteem and power needs by having many children. Thus the threat that we will breed ourselves off a livable planet will be reduced. If the skills and values that women have developed are incorporated into our life-styles and our institutions, the need to conquer, subdue, and exploit one another, other groups and nations, and the earth will tend to gradually diminish. Whether we move in these directions depends on how we respond to the challenges of the feminist critique and vision. The challenge to us as counselors, therapists, and growth enablers is direct and powerful!

Experiencing Growth Methods from Feminist Therapy

Rush's *Getting Clear, Body Work for Women,* and *Feminism as Therapy* by Mander and Rush, offer a rich variety of CR-growth methods, many of which can be used with both sexes. *Responsible Assertive Behavior* by Lange and Jakubowski has exercises for developing constructive assertiveness in one's attitudes and behavior. (Chapter 10 discusses ways of combining assertion training and consciousness raising in women's and men's groups.) *Counseling for Liberation* by Charlotte H. Clinebell describes the "fishbowl," the "sex reversal fantasy" (pp. 68-71), and the "unlived life fantasy" (71-72), all of which can provide powerful experiences of consciousness raising for both women and for men. If you have access to these books, I recommend that you take time to sample and experience several of these growth exercises.

Here are some additional CR exercises that I invite you to try now, to raise your own consciousness and to become aware of which exercises you can use in counseling and in growth groups. Debrief each experience with someone you trust:

> Close your eyes and get in touch with your experience as a woman or a man, being aware of which parts of this feel heavy, constricted, or unalive, and which parts feel strong, buoyant, energized, and alive./ Picture two empty chairs facing each other./ Put the two sides of yourself in the two chairs and carry on a dialogue between them./ See if the alive sides can revitalize the other side of yourself./

> Imagine that you are going for help with a personal problem to a counselor who has been recommended to you by someone you trust./ See yourself walking through the door of the counselor's office and discovering that she is a woman./ What are your

feelings?/ Now, repeat the fantasy but this time have the counselor be a man./ Repeat the fantasy and have the counselor be a black woman./ A black man./

Close your eyes and see yourself relating to your spouse or to your best friend of the other sex./ Imagine that the two of you are utterly free spirits, liberated from your restricting sex-role programming and your sexual hang-ups. Be aware of how each of you feels, behaves, and relates to the other./ Now, compare this fantasy experience with the ways you actually feel, act, and relate./ Decide what you will do to move from your present degree of inner freedom and aliveness to a more liberated state of being./ Ask your spouse or friend to try the fantasy./ Share and compare your two experiences and your decisions about changes, seeing if you can develop a joint plan to support each other's growth and the full liberation of your relationship./

For Further Exploration of Feminist and Radical Therapy

Brenton, Myron. *The American Male.* New York: Coward-McCann, 1966. Explores how the code of masculinity cripples the personality and restricts the enjoyment of men, and suggests how they can liberate themselves.

Broverman, Inge K., et al. "Sex Role Stereotypes and Clinical Judgments of Mental Health," *Journal of Consulting and Clinical Psychology,* vol. 34, no. 1, pp. 1-7. Report on research revealing the sexism of therapists.

Brown, Phil, ed. *Radical Psychology.* New York: Harper Colophon Books, 1973. A collection of papers on radical therapy.

Chesler, Phyllis. *About Men.* New York: Simon & Schuster, 1978. A revealing study of the destructiveness of male dominance and values.

———. *Women and Madness.* New York: Avon Books, 1973. Documents the central role of sexism in "mental illness" in women and the destructiveness of much of their treatment by male therapists.

Clinebell, Charlotte Holt. *Counseling for Liberation.* Philadelphia: Fortress Press, 1976. Describes methods of integrating counseling and consciousness-raising and methods of liberating pastoral counseling and the church.

———. *Meet Me in the Middle/On Becoming Human Together.* New York: Harper, 1973. An autobiographically oriented discussion of the issues facing women and men struggling for more liberated, whole lives.

Daly, Mary. *Gyn/Ecology, The Metaethics of Radical Feminism.* Boston: Beacon Press, 1979. A powerful exposé of male destructiveness to women in Indian suttee, Chinese footbinding, African genital mutilation, European witchburning, and American medicine and psychotherapy. Documents the blindness of male scholarship to the meaning of all these forms of massive male cruelty.

Dinnerstein, Dorothy. *The Mermaid and the Minotaur, Sexual Arrangements and Human Malaise.* New York: Harper Colophon Books, 1976. A depth exploration of the deleterious effects of the prevailing form of emotional symbiosis between the sexes.

Farrell, Warren. *The Liberated Man.* New York: Bantam Books, 1975. Describes male trappedness, what liberation can mean for a man, and how to achieve it.

Fasteau, Marc F. *The Male Machine.* New York: McGraw-Hill, 1974. Explores the destructiveness of the masculine stereotype and looks to an androgynous future.

Franks, Violet, and Burtle, Vasanti, eds. *Women in Therapy, New Psychotherapies for a Changing Society.* New York: Brunner/Mazel, 1974. Essays on the changing psychology of women and the new therapeutic approaches that emerge from this.

Gornick, Vivian, and Moran, Barbara K. *Woman in Sexist Society: Studies in Power and Powerlessness.* New York: New American Library, 1972. A series of papers exploring the experience of women in a male-dominated world.

Jongeward, Dorothy, and Scott, Dru. *Women as Winners.* Reading, Mass.: Addison-Wesley, 1976. Uses TA and gestalt therapy to understand our society's constrictions on the full growth of women and to provide methods of removing these limitations.

Lange, Arthur J., and Jakubowski, Patricia. *Responsible Assertive Behavior.* Champaign, Ill.: Research Press, 1976. Cognitive and behavioral procedures for trainers planning and leading assertion groups.

Malcomson, William L. *Success Is a Failure Experience, Male Liberation and the American Myth of Success.* Nashville: Abingdon, 1976. Explores the bondage of the male success myth and ways of breaking free.

Mander, Anica Vesel, and Rush, Anne Kent. *Feminism as Therapy.*

New York: Random House/Bookworks, 1974. An exploration of feminism as a healing experience for women.

Miller, Jean Baker, ed. *Psychoanalysis and Women: Contributions to New Theory and Therapy.* New York: Brunner/Mazel, 1973. A collection of papers by persons challenging, correcting, and enriching the traditional male-defined psychology of women.

———. *Toward a New Psychology of Women.* Boston: Beacon Press, 1976. A groundbreaking book that sets forth a new understanding of women!

Nichols, Jack. *Men's Liberation, A New Definition of Masculinity.* New York: Penguin Books, 1975. Discusses the need for men to be liberated and shows how the lives of both sexes can be enriched when this happens.

Perl, Harriet, and Abarbanell, Gay, coordinators. *Guidelines to Feminist Consciousness Raising.* Prepared for the National Task Force on CR of the National Organization for Women; published by the coordinators in Los Angeles in 1975. A how-to manual on the philosophy, ground rules, and leadership for consciousness-raising groups.

Rich, Adrienne. *Of Woman Born, Motherhood as Experience and Institution.* New York: Bantam Books, 1976. Explores the two meanings of motherhood—as a relationship of women to their creative powers, and as a male-defined, constricting institution that diminishes both sexes.

Rush, Anne Kent. *Getting Clear, Body Work for Women.* New York: Random House, 1973. Methods of self-growth for women (and men).

Steinmann, Anne, and Fox, David J. *The Male Dilemma.* New York: Jason Aronson, 1974. Analyzes the responses of men to changing sex roles with suggestions for developing more liberated relationships between the sexes.

Weisstein, Naomi. "Psychology Constructs the Female," in Gornick and Moran, *Woman in Sexist Society,* chap. 8. An overview of the blindness of male-oriented psychology to the discovery of the real potentials of women.

Williams, Elizabeth Friar. *Notes of a Feminist Therapist.* New York: Praeger, 1976. Describes feminist therapy and presents feminist issues as reflected in the lives of women in therapy.

Wyckoff, Hogie, ed. *Love, Therapy and Politics, Issues in Radical Therapy.* New York: Grove Press, 1976. Twenty articles from the journal *Radical Therapy.*

Chapter 11

Growth Resources in Psychosynthesis

Psychosynthesis was developed by psychiatrist Roberto Assagioli, who was born in Venice, Italy, in 1888. He had his medical and psychiatric training at the University of Florence, where he also studied philosophy and psychology. Assagioli was part of the original psychoanalytic group in Italy, but around 1911 he began to move beyond Freud, developing his own approach. He continued to change and develop psychosynthesis until his death in Florence in 1974. Until relatively recently, his work was not widely known outside of Italy. But in the last decade his books have been translated into many languages, and psychosynthesis institutes have developed in various parts of the world. In this country his ideas are influencing a growing number of therapists as well as persons in the human potentials movement.

Psychosynthesis is a whole-person approach to healing and growth. It is one of the most productive sources of both concepts and methods for growth-oriented counselors and therapists. Psychosynthesis is explicitly growth-centered. With prophetic insight, Assagioli declares: "Only the development of his inner powers can offset the dangers inherent in man's *[sic]* losing control of the tremendous forces at his disposal and becoming the victim of his own achievements. . . . This is indispensable for maintaining the sanity and indeed the very survival of humanity."[1]

Psychosynthesis is also explicitly spiritually oriented. Many of its methods are useful in facilitating spiritual growth. The impact of psychosynthesis on pastoral counseling theory and practice has been relatively slight, even though it is potentially invaluable as a resource for any spiritually oriented counselor. The full incorporation of this approach is one of the challenges for the future of pastoral counseling.

Until the last few years, I did not sense the significance of psychosynthesis and therefore did not take time to explore this therapy in depth. When I did, I was excited by its riches and struck by the many parallels with the approach that I was by then calling Growth Counseling.

Psychosynthesis' Insights About Growth

In discussing the affinities of his views with those of Carl Jung, Assagioli states his wholeness orientation:

> In the practice of therapy we both agree in rejecting "pathologism," the concentration upon morbid manifestations and symptoms of a supposedly psychological "disease." We regard man *[sic]* as a fundamentally healthy organism in which there may be a temporary malfunctioning. Nature is always trying to re-establish harmony, and with the psyche the principle of synthesis is dominant. . . . The task of therapy is to aid the individual in transforming the personality, and integrating apparent contradictions.[2]

Assagioli has an appreciation for the way in which the intensive study of pathology by psychoanalysis and depth psychology has enlarged and deepened our understanding of the human psyche. But he also declared:

> The pathological approach has, besides its assets, also a serious liability, and that is an exaggerated emphasis on the morbid manifestations and on the lower aspects of human nature and

> the consequent unwarranted generalized applications of the many findings of psychopathology to the psychology of normal human beings. This has produced a rather dreary and pessimistic picture of human nature and the tendency to consider its higher values and achievements as derived only from the lower drives, through processes of reaction formation, transformation, and sublimation. Moreover, many important realities and functions have been neglected or ignored: intuition, creativity, the will, and the very core of the human psyche—the Self.[3]

Psychosynthesis affirms the natural drive of persons to grow by integrating their lives at higher levels. The fact that the growth drive can become conscious in us human beings enables us to cooperate with this drive and thus to accelerate the process of actualizing our potentials.

Assagioli accepted many insights derived from Freud's brilliant exploration of the "lower unconscious." Yet he saw Freud's conception of persons as incomplete and inadequate. When asked about the difference between psychosynthesis and psychoanalysis, in an interview not long before his death, he responded with a striking metaphor:

> In one of his letters Freud said, "I am interested only in the basement of the human building." We try to build an elevator which will allow a person access to every level of his personality. After all, a building with only a basement is very limited. We want to open up the terrace where you can sun-bathe or look at the stars. Our concern is the synthesis of all areas of the personality. This means psychosynthesis is holistic, global and inclusive. It is not against psychoanalysis or even behavior modification, but it insists that the need for meaning, for higher values, for a spiritual life, are as real as biological or social needs.[4]

Here is the "egg diagram," which Assagioli created to show the interrelatedness of the various dimensions of personality:[5]

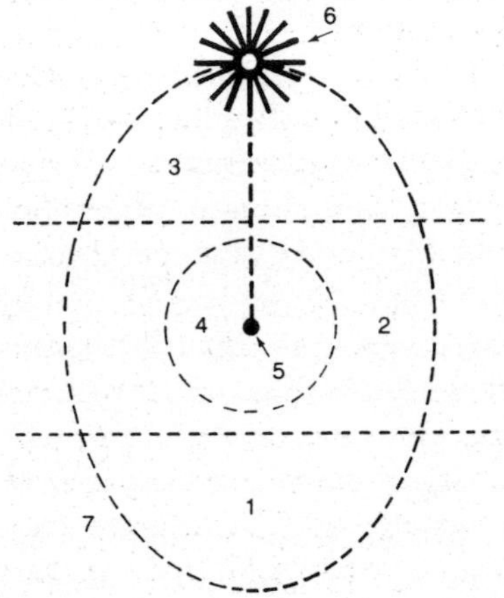

1. The Lower Unconscious
2. The Middle Unconscious
3. The Higher Unconscious, or Superconscious
4. The Field of Consciousness
5. The Conscious Self, or "I"
6. The Transpersonal Self
7. The Collective Unconscious

Assagioli's view of human beings is more complex and richer than Freud's. As the diagram suggests, the unconscious has three levels. In addition to the lower unconscious there is also a middle unconscious, which is accessible to our waking consciousness, and a higher unconscious or "superconscious." The higher Self, our creative center and essence, is within this higher unconscious. The "I," or the self of everyday experience, is not one's ultimate identity. Rather, it is a reflection of the much more creative higher Self. Making our true Self the unifying center of our being is the primary goal of psychosynthesis. The oval delimiting the individual is analogous to the permeable membrane of a cell, which permits active interchange with the whole body. A person is in constant interaction with the wider interpersonal and transpersonal psychological and spiritual environment.

Spiritual Development

Psychosynthesis seeks to combine the objectivity of science with the passion of a seeker for religious truth. "Spiritual" is used in psychosynthesis to include specifically religious experiences but also the whole range of ethical, aesthetic, and humanistic values. Psychosynthesis recognizes and respects the need of many people for formal religion. But its goal is to help people enrich their lives through *direct* spiritual experience.

The basic resources for growth come from the higher Self or superconscious. As do other therapies, psychosynthesis seeks to help people utilize their sexual and aggressive energies creatively. But it also aims at helping them use "the potent superconscious spiritual energies, which have a transforming and regenerating influence on the whole personality." Assagioli emphasized the remarkable potency of these spiritual energies when he declared: "This release may be compared to that of intra-atomic energy latent in matter."[6] The energies of the higher Self exert a continual pull toward the actualization of our higher potentialities.

For Assagioli, the spiritual growth drives are as natural as the sexual and aggressive drives of the lower unconscious:

> May I emphasize the fact that the elements and functions coming from the superconscious, such as aesthetic, ethical, religious experiences, intuition, inspiration, states of mystical consciousness, are factual, are real in the pragmatic sense . . . producing changes both in the inner and the outer world. Therefore, they are amenable to observation and experiment, through the use of the scientific method. . . . Also they can be influenced and utilized through psycho-spiritual techniques.[7]

The *will,* understood as the capacity for decision, planning, and purpose, is regarded as a key resource in all phases of psychosynthesis. The will is a muscle-like part of the personality that can be strengthened and developed by will-training exercises. Decision and action, guided by an effective will, are the main thrusts of growth toward higher levels of integration. Assagioli writes: "The will is like the conductor of an orchestra. He is not self assertive but rather the humble servant of the composer and the score."[8] Among all our potentials, the power of the will should be given priority in striving to create both more complete, integrated selves and a better world. Only by the mobilization of the creative powers of the will can the human family avoid destroying ourselves by our runaway technology.

The *imagination* is another essential growth resource in psychosynthesis. Images and symbols are accumulators and transformers of the psychological energies that empower all growth, whether in therapy, education, or in other contexts. For this reason, the use of guided imaging has a key place in the practice of psychosynthesis.

When one considers the patriarchal climate of the era in which his thinking developed, Assagioli was remarkably liberated in his attitudes toward women. He had a strong emphasis on androgynous wholeness in his understanding of growth. Following Jung's thought (without most of Jung's patriarchal biases) in seeing "masculine" and "feminine" components, he declared: "Only by accepting both the masculine and feminine principles, bringing them together, and harmonizing them within ourselves, will we be able to transcend the conditioning of our roles, and to express the whole range of our latent potential."[9] He emphasized the need in our society for women to be more involved in social and political life and thus to bring greater compassion, altruistic love, and respect for life into the public arena. He affirmed the right of women to combine the public roles with traditional family roles, if they choose, or to give their full energies to social and political roles. He called for a new society that is neither patriarchal nor matriarchal, but a global culture incorporating the best contributions of both men and women. With buoyant optimism, he declared: "All of this is within our reach—for not only is it very beautiful—it is very *human*."[10]

What are the resistances to growth in psychosynthesis? Growth can be blocked by a variety of forces on various levels of the psyche. Assagioli pointed to the conflict between inertia and the craving for security, on the one hand, and the drive toward growth and adventure on the other. Resistance to growth can result from the way emerging needs and drives threaten old securities. Growth also can be blocked by failure to use the will constructively and by overidentification with one of the "subpersonalities" within individuals. The therapist's or client's acceptance of a traditional view of psychopathology can limit growth by causing them to ignore the essential resources for growth in the Self—will, imagination, creativity. Furthermore, inadequate ideals and heroes/heroines can diminish actualization by depriving a person of growth-enhancing goals and models of the good life.

The Process of Growth

A therapist begins psychosynthesis by discovering the particular needs stemming from the unique problems that an individual is facing. If growth is being blocked by unresolved conflicts in the lower unconscious, therapy has an analytic phase in which traditional psychotherapeutic approaches may be used. But *analysis*—"a separating of the whole into component parts in order to understand the nature, function and relationship of these parts"[11]—is seldom more than a minor part of therapy. The primary emphasis, as the word "psychosynthesis" suggests, is *synthesis*—"an integration, a wholeness, a unity, a harmonious use of all your potentialities."

Although there are three phases of the process of psychosynthesis, in actual practice the phases do not necessarily occur in succession or separately. Often they take place in a back-and-forth or parallel manner, depending on the unique growth needs of the individual. If, for example, initial exploration reveals serious ethical and religious conflicts, as is often the case, these may be taken up in therapy immediately.

The first level of psychosynthesis is *personal synthesis*. This phase aims at the synthesis of the conflicted or competing "subpersonalities" around the conscious self or ego (a method for doing this is described later in this chapter). The second level, "spiritual synthesis," aims at integration around the Self, the higher spiritual center. This process seeks to realize the superconscious potentials of personality—the capacities for meaning, values, love, altruism, and for aesthetic, scientific, and spiritual creativity. New creative energies are released in one's life and relationships as synthesis occurs around this spiritual center. The purpose of life, as understood in psychosynthesis, is to manifest this Self as fully as possible in one's everyday life and relationships.

Assagioli saw the process of spiritual development as "a long and arduous journey, an adventure through strange lands full of surprises, difficulties, and even dangers."[12] Disturbing crises often precede and result from a spiritual awakening. But he also saw the joy in growth. Responding to Maslow's call for a "technology of joy," Assagioli defined *enjoyment* as that which results from the satisfaction of any need; *pleasure* he saw as resulting from the gratification of a "basic need" (Maslow's term); *joy* from the satisfaction of a higher need. He declared: "Acts of good will have rich and sometimes amazing results. Altruistic, humanitarian activities give deep satisfaction and a sense of fulfilling one's true purpose in life. As an Eastern sage said, 'World tasks are like fires of joy.' "[13] Self-actualization gives one a joyous sense of power, freedom, and mastery. Full transpersonal Self-realization, involving communion or identification with the transcendent Reality, results in what Assagioli called *Bliss*.

The third level of the process of psychosynthesis, according to Assagioli, is *transpersonal synthesis*. This phase aims at getting one into a harmonious relationship with other persons and with the cosmos. Clearly psychosynthesis is a system-oriented approach. The integration of synthesis of interpersonal relationships, of the individual with various groups, with the whole human family, and with the spiritual reality called God—all may be a part of this third phase of growth. The essential unity of these different relationships is understood as a transpersonal spiritual oneness. Since persons live inextricably in relationships, a "good will" always involves harmonization with the wills of others and with nature. An inclusive ecological awareness is present in Assagioli's understanding of growth:

> Self centeredness is deeply destructive to the cooperation without which a person cannot live a full life in community. This same principle applies to an individual's relation to nature and the universe. No person can take an arrogant stand and consider himself unrelated to the universe. Like it or not, man *[sic]* is part of the universal will and he must somehow tune in and willingly participate in the rhythms of universal life. The harmonization and unification of the individual and universal will is one of the highest human goals, even if it is seldom realized.[14]

There is an outreach thrust in Assagioli's thought which I find refreshing: "Inner experience is not an end in itself but a means to a deeper, more dynamic and effective involvement with and service to humanity."[15] It is significant that Assagioli attempted to launch a "Will Project" aimed at generating good, strong, transpersonal wills to improve relationships in families, between different racial and religious groups, and among nations.[16] In a recent paper in the psychosynthesis journal Donald Keys describes what he calls the "synthesis of the nations," the process by which planetary values and a sense of global responsibility are developed through the "planetization of our consciousness."[17]

The therapist takes an active role in the early phase of psychosynthesis, utilizing whatever methods are needed to actualize that dimension of a person's potentials. Gradually, the individual exercises increasing responsibility, and the therapist becomes primarily a catalyst in the growth process. In the later phases the role of the therapist is gradually taken by the individual's higher Self, of whom the person has increasing awareness and identification. The inner wisdom of one's own higher Self is seen as the most valid source of guidance. Knowing this (as Robert Gerard points out) gives a therapist a sense of both humility and hope:

> If you recognize the existence of a spiritual Self with a capital "S" then you also recognize as a therapist that there is within your patient (within all of us, for that matter) an inner source of love, of intelligence, of wisdom, of creativity, of inner direction and

> purpose. . . . It can help a great deal if the therapist has a conviction, drawn from direct experience, that regardless of how wretched, confused or sick the individual may appear on the surface, there is this inner center of psychological health, of wisdom, of purpose, which is there to be evoked.[18]

The therapist's central task is to help the person become aware of and learn to use this inner wisdom and power for healing and growth.

The nonhierarchical, egalitarian style of psychosynthesis is expressed in Assagioli's view that having a therapist, although an advantage, is not essential: "Psychosynthesis can be applied by the individual himself or herself, fostering and accelerating inner growth and self-actualization. . . . Such self-psychosynthesis should be practiced . . . by every therapist, social worker, and educator (including parents)."[19]

Weaknesses from the Growth Perspective

The weaknesses in psychosynthesis seem to me to be relatively minor, when viewed in the context of its many strengths. Although this therapy has a thoroughly ecological-systemic conception of growth, the lion's share of attention in psychosynthesis circles has been given to intrapsychic growth. Consequently there has been too little effort invested in applying psychosynthesis to interpersonal relationships and to impacting the wider structures of society and the ecosystem. Fortunately, the systemic emphasis seems to have become stronger in recent years. Hopefully it will become an increasingly central concern of therapists who are developing the theory and practice of psychosynthesis.

The emphasis on the will runs the danger of all approaches to growth that highlight intentionality. This is the risk of encouraging what Karen Horney called the "tyranny of the oughts and shoulds." Pushing oneself toward high ideals can produce unproductive frustration and even despair. It is noteworthy that Assagioli warned of this danger. In discussing the use of ideals and action plans in therapy he emphasized that these need to be "authentic," that is, in line with the natural development of the person. Assagioli saw that a "genuine ideal model" can help one tap the resources of the higher Self. Using the power of images, such a model releases the energies of change.[20] Falling into the trap of perfectionism is seen as being prevented by getting in touch with the wisdom of one's higher Self.

Assagioli seems to underestimate the tenacious resistances to growth in us human beings and in society. His enthusiasm for the importance of the will in growth caused him to underemphasize the considerable extent to which the wills of us human beings are "in bondage" (as Martin Luther put it).

Growth Methods from Psychosynthesis

The choice of particular therapeutic methods in psychosynthesis is made in light of the emerging growth needs of each individual. I shall now describe some of these tools which I have found useful. Let me recommend that you try them yourself before you attempt to use them in counseling or therapy or in growth groups:

Disidentification and Self-Identification. This exercise is a way of identifying the "I," or center of consciousness, around which personal synthesis can occur. According to psychosynthesis theory, we are dominated by that with which we are identified. As a middle-class male, I frequently become overidentified with my work and with striving for material security and "success." When I do, my anxieties in that one area of my life dominate my sense of identity and self-worth. To that extent that I *disidentify* myself from my job, my professional roles, and my anxiety about material things, I free myself inwardly from being the captive of my work and of things. It becomes easier to view my job in a more balanced perspective as only *one* important dimension of my life and not the center of my identity or worth.

The first part of this exercise is *disidentification.* Read the following statements a few sentences at a time and then close your eyes and repeat them in your mind silently. Or ask someone to read them to you sentence by sentence while you repeat them inwardly. Sit in a comfortable position, relax, and close your eyes.

I affirm: I *have* a body but *I am more than* my body. My body may find itself in different conditions or sickness; it may be rested or tired. . . . My body is my precious instrument of experience and action in the outer world. . . . I treat it well; I seek to keep it in good health. . . . I have a body, but *I am more than* my body.[21]

In a similar way, disidentify your *self* from your feelings and emotions (I have emotions, but *I am more than* my emotions, and so on); your desires; your intellect and thoughts; your job; your social roles (e.g., father or mother, husband or wife, your job roles); your relationships; your problems. Go through the whole list, taking one aspect of your life at a time. Be aware of those aspects with which you feel overidentified. (I find this exercise helpful when I am investing excessive energy in a part of my body that is giving me trouble—for example, "I have teeth and they are causing me discomfort at this moment, but I am more than my teeth.")

The second part of this exercise is *self-identification*. After finishing the disidentification process, repeat the following:

What am I then? What remains after discarding from the center of my identity the physical, emotional, and mental contents of my personality? . . . It is the essence of myself—a center of pure consciousness and self realization. It is the permanent factor in the ever varying flow of my personal life. It is that which gives me the sense of being, of permanence, of inner security. I recognize and affirm myself as a center of consciousness. I realize that the center not only has a continuity of self-awareness but also a dynamic power; it is capable of observing, mastering, directing and using the psychological processes in my physical body and in my mind. I am a center of awareness and of power.[22]

It takes most people considerable practice before the profundity of this simple exercise is experienced fully.

Getting to Know Your Subpersonalities. Each of us has a diversity of semiautonomous subpersonalities within us. TA emphasizes the Parent-Adult-Child sides of our personalities; gestalt therapy focuses on the Top Dog vs. Under Dog sides. Psychosynthesis has identified hundreds of other subpersonalities. I can recognize many subpersonalities within myself—the Mystic, the Materialist, the Crusader, the Sneak, the Doubter, thc Playful Kid, the Prisoner, the Clown, the Dreamer, the Cynic, the Good Professor. When our subpersonalities are unknown to us, they produce inner conflicts and diffusion in our sense of "I-ness." It facilitates our growth to get to know, understand, and like our subpersonalities. By so doing, our self can learn to direct their expression according to our goals and needs. Thus they become allies and resources for enriching our identity, our life, and our relationships.[23] Here is an exercise for getting to know one's subpersonalities:

"Sit comfortably and relax. After closing your eyes, take a few deep breaths. Imagine a big wooden door in front of you. On the door there is a sign that says SUBPERSONALITIES. Imagine that they all live behind the door. Now open the door and let some of your main subpersonalities come out. Just observe them. Don't get involved. Be aware of them."[24]

Now choose a subpersonality that seems most interesting to you. Carry on a dialogue with this one, finding out what it is like and what it wants and needs./ Now let yourself *become* that subpersonality. Discover how this feels./ Be yourself again and choose another subpersonality with whom to get acquainted. Take all the time you need to develop the best possible relationship with all your subpersonalities one at a time on successive occasions of growth work.

Will Training Exercises. There are six stages of willing, according to Assagioli: (1) the existence of a purpose to be achieved; (2) deliberation on the various goals and their relative importance; (3) making a decision on one important goal and setting aside the others; (4) confirmation of the choice by an affirmation of this goal by will; (5) development of a plan to achieve the goal; (6) directing the implementation of the plan. Will strengthening occurs as one moves intentionally through these stages.

Try this, now. Reflect on the various goals you would like to accomplish within the next week./ Choose one that has high priority and is achievable./ Confirm the choice by affirming that you will invest yourself in achieving this goal./ Devise a concrete, detailed plan and then use your will to implement it. If your goal is to strengthen your body, develop a daily program of physical exercise appropriate to your health. If your goal is to increase your sense of being in charge of your life or to decrease the amont of time you waste, plan and implement a realistic, meaningful schedule for yourself. I recall a client who was plagued by the chronic chaos of trying to accomplish too many things in a given period of time without a prioritized schedule. After a week of implementing a carefully prepared, realistic schedule, he reported: "I feel as though I'm on top of my situation. It's like I'm running my life rather than having circumstances run me!" It is important to become aware of and deal with the subpersonalities that interfere with the functioning of your will—the Self-doubter, the Saboteur, Lazy Bones, and others.

Imagination Training. Images can be used at many points in the process of growth. Some of the common images used in psychosynthesis include seeing oneself walking along a stream, being in a meadow, visiting a house, becoming a lion (to get in touch with one's strong, assertive side), and so on. One's active imagination can provide both motivation and energy for growth. (It activates the energies and creativity of the right hemisphere of our brains.) Assagioli observed that "images and mental pictures tend to produce the physical condition and external acts corresponding to them."[25]

This principle is being used effectively in many areas. The use of imaging by cancer patients, as pioneered by the Simontons (see chapter 8), is one productive application. The next time you have a sore muscle from overexertion of some kind, try relaxing that part of your body and, in your imagination, surround it with a warm, healing energy as you visualize it as well again. Do this several times a day and be aware of the effects. This imaging process seems to release healing energy within the body. If you are worried about some demanding event in the future, try this brief daily exercise: See yourself in your imagination coping with that event in a strong, effective way. Even see yourself enjoying it. Or, if you regard yourself as a shy person, image yourself behaving as a confident and competent person who is obviously respected by others.

Symbolic Identification. This method, developed by Robert Gerard, involves "becoming" an admired person or thing in one's imagination. One identifies with certain qualities in the person or thing and is thus able to "own" resources within oneself that have been ignored. Psychological provincialism is becoming increasingly costly on our shrinking planet. Symbolic identification can help us develop the global consciousness and caring which are needed for survival on a livable planet. Martha Crampton reports: "Symbolic identification may . . . be used to expand our consciousness and to gain a deeper sense of participation in, and oneness with the universe. 'Becoming' such natural symbols as flowers, a tree, a rock, a river, the ocean, the sun, or even the galaxy, can be particularly valuable for this purpose."[26] I suggest you try identifying with a sluggish, polluted river for a while; then identify with a clear, joyful mountain stream./ Be aware of the differences of the impact of these two images./ Or identify with a growing tree or an unfolding flower. Let the images feed your inner life./ Or try symbolic identification with a person or people in great need in your community or in other parts of the world.

Discovering the Self. Psychosynthesis offers a variety of methods for facilitating spiritual growth by opening oneself to the creative energies and wisdom of one's higher Self. I have found one of the most valuable to be the exercise of imagining myself journeying up a mountain path to enjoy communicating with my higher Self at the summit. I invite you to experience this now.[27]

Another approach to increased awareness of your higher Self is to picture and carry on an inner dialogue with your Wise Teacher or the Wise Woman or Wise Man within you, or image and consult with your "inner light," as the Quakers and Mahatma Gandhi refer to the inner source of wisdom. For creative energies to flow it is necessary to relax one's analytical mind temporarily and simply be expectantly open. After the intuitive images or messages are received they must be tested and understood in the fires of the mind through hard, critical thinking. They then can be translated into constructive action. A busy man described his experience:

"I was feeling very speedy, off center and unstable. So I talked with the Wise Old Man about it and at first he said things like, 'You need to rest, to trust the process; everything will take care of itself. If you overwork yourself now you won't be able to do the things you worry about.' But I simply kept waiting for more; opening myself in a kind of silent expectation. After a few minutes, I experienced a quantum jump in understanding. I saw that the worries had a purpose. The Wise Old Man enabled me to see that the worries were a necessary part of the 'process' he had talked about. . . . 'You're irritable and strained, and that's because you're going through a process of learning to work with people and you don't know how to do it yet. But the process is very important in the development of yourself as a person who can give something good to the world. It is, as you well know, the necessary step beyond your sweet but ineffective idealism. It is the step to make your idealism practical and useful in the world. That's why you can be patient with yourself and even take the day off. You're doing fine.' "[28]

In facilitating growth work in counseling and in therapy and growth groups, I find it helpful to invite people to view from the perspective of their higher Selves the problems and growth issues with which they're working. I first experienced the transforming power of this perspective as a client in a relationship with a therapist trained in psychosynthesis.[29]

Erma Pixley, a marriage and family counselor, leads growth groups for women using a variety of psychosynthesis methods. She has the women list the demanding and conflicting roles they play in everyday life and their various subpersonalities—e.g., nurturer, playful child, sensuous lover, counselor. She leads the women in a disidentification, self-identification exercise to become aware of their center of consciousness, which is more than their roles or subpersonalities. She then invites the women to carry on an inner dialogue among their roles and subpersonalities, particularly those which are usurping too much of themselves. She suggests that they bring into this conversation their inner wisdom or higher Self to help them establish balance and integration among their subpersonalities. The women are invited to lift their consciousness to a higher and more inclusive level each day by getting in touch with the essence of all humanity within themselves.[30]

Meditation. Assagioli welcomed insights and methods of enhancing consciousness from the East. (He learned Sanskrit to allow himself to read Eastern mystical texts in their original language.) During the Second World War, he held firmly to his strong convictions about the oneness of humankind. Because of his ideas Mussolini made him a political prisoner. In prison, he worried about his patients in Rome. Quickly he began to observe his own worry, asking himself, "What good can I get from worry? What can I do that is more useful?" This was the answer, which he believed came from his higher Self: "Meditate. You've always wanted to, but were always too busy." Being in solitary confinement, he was not bothered by anyone. He meditated for hours every day. The results surprised him. He never had felt such peace. He recalled that never in his life had he so enjoyed being alive.[31]

Assagioli describes three types of meditation: *reflective meditation* (to acquire in-depth understanding of our ordinary consciousness), *receptive meditation* (to open ourselves to the wisdom of the higher Self), and *creative meditation* (to regenerate and transform our personality). All effective meditation is understood as "inner action" in that it requires will training and results in spiritual energies that produce changes in oneself. Assagioli provides a succinct guide to the uses of the three types of meditation.[32] Receptive meditation is particularly valuable in spiritual growth work. In discussing this, he describes the technique using a mental picture that induces calm, silence, and peace—a tranquil lake mirroring the blue sky, or the starry sky in the silence of the night. He also suggests repeating a phrase such as this one from a hymn of the Greek Mysteries: "Be silent, O strings, that a new melody may flow in me."[33]

For Further Exploration of Psychosynthesis

Assagioli, Roberto. *Psychosynthesis, A Manual of Principles and Techniques*. New York: Viking, 1971. The basic manual on the theory and practice of psychosynthesis.

———. *The Act of Will.* Baltimore: Penguin Books, 1974. A guide to experiencing the strengthening of the will in all its dimensions.

Churchill, Craig M. *Contributions of Psychosynthesis Toward a Growth Oriented Model of Pastoral Counseling.* An unpublished Ph.D. dissertation written at the School of Theology at Claremont, 1973. Available from University Microfilm, Ann Arbor, Michigan.

Haronian, Frank. "Psychosynthesis: A Psychotherapist's Personal Overview," *Pastoral Psychology,* Fall, 1976, pp. 16-33.

———. "A Psychosynthetic Model of Personality and Its Implications for Psychotherapy," *Journal of Humanistic Psychology,* Fall, 1975.

Synthesis, The Realization of Self. The psychosynthesis journal, which includes a Psychosynthesis Workbook with practical techniques for enhancing one's growth. The Synthesis Press, 150 Doherty Way, Redwood City, CA 94061.

The following papers and many more are available from the Psychosynthesis Institute, 3352 Sacramento Street, San Francisco, CA 94118.

- Crampton, Martha. "The Use of Mental Imagery in Psychosynthesis."
- Keen, Sam. "The Golden Mean of Roberto Assagioli." An interview with Assagioli shortly before his death, reprinted from *Psychology Today.*
- Kretschmer, W. H. "Meditative Techniques in Psychotherapy." A description of ways to use meditation in therapy.
- Vargiu, James. "Global Education and Psychosynthesis." The application of psychosynthesis to the development of global consciousness.

Conclusion

The Risks of Growth—Using These Resources for Your Continuing Growth

> I went to a fortune teller with a group of friends. I don't believe in them but this one gave me a valuable tip.
>
> "There is something you want to do," she told me. "You are holding back because there seems to be an obstacle of some kind in your way." (Would apply to the first ten people you meet.) "I'm going to give you some advice. This thing that you want to do—go ahead and start it. If you wait until everything is just right you will never begin at all, for things are never just right. You have to make a start and *put things right* as you go."
>
> The five dollars it cost for this advice was repaid many times. Launch out. Make a break.
>
> Elmer Wheeler, *The Wealth Within You*[1]

This anecdote communicates a simple but dynamic truth about growth that is often overlooked—that a major dream-squelcher which causes us to postpone our potentializing indefinitely is the belief that "I can't do what I'd really like to do because . . ." If you feel some serious inner or outer obstacles to making creative changes in your life, welcome to the human race! So do most people. I can think of lots of "good" reasons for not risking the new scary things that could enable me to develop more of my possibilities. My reasons often (but not always) turn out to be ingenious rationalizations to justify staying in my relatively comfortable cocoon. Liberating the butterfly in you or me to fly is usually risky and often frightening. But the problem with staying in one's cocoon is that, though it's safe and warm and comfortable, the price of staying there indefinitely is very high. The view from a cocoon is very limited, to say the least. One avoids facing one's fear of flying but, by so doing, misses the excitement and joy of flying.

Remember, the most important person for any of us to see through the growth-hope perspective is ourselves. Only as I see myself through the glasses of growth will I be able to see the rich potentialities in you or in the others I meet along the way. Only as I risk letting the butterfly in me out of its cocoon to soar, can I encourage the people whose lives touch mine to risk leaving their cocoons. So let me invite you to see an inner picture of yourself as a butterfly struggling to leave your cocoon. When you succeed, enjoy the freedom and joy of the flight of growth! (Close your eyes and try this now.)/

Of course, as you probably know from experience, our cocoons aren't all that safe or secure, at least not permanently so. Life has a way of kicking us out of our comfortable adjustments, our little havens, sooner or later. Each life stage and each major change in our relationships and in society feels strangely as if someone pushed the ejection button on the cocoon we constructed in the previous stage. So actually we have only two options—to be ejected from our cocoons or to choose to leave them intentionally, even though it's scary, because our longing to fly is stronger (perhaps only a little) than our fear of flying. Leaving each cocoon is, in my experience, like leaving another womb. Unlike the first time we exited a womb, we have some choice in our own rebirthing. Our awareness of both the price and the possibilities of growth gives us the wonderful, though frightening, freedom to choose!

If you followed the suggestion that you keep a journal of your own growth insights and plans as you read the book, I recommend that you look through it now. Or, if you underlined and scribbled notes to yourself in the margin of the book or simply made mental notes to yourself, fine! Take a leisurely stroll through your own responses to what you encountered in this book. Stop to enjoy the things you noted./ Write some additional comments, affirmations, or criticisms of your notes to yourself, as you experience these from the perspective of having finished the book./ Reflect on your notes, picking out the insights and methods of growthing that now raise your energy level most. Trust the barometer of your energy level to suggest that those resources may be crucial ones for your own growth or for your increasing effectiveness as a growth enabler with others. You may find it helpful to make a list of these energy-raisers!/

Now, I suggest that you let your mind relax and *play* with these ideas, one at a time, taking as long as you wish. Let yourself roam among them playfully. Frolic with them, dialogue with them (listening carefully to what *they* say), push against them, arm wrestle with them, or let them caress your mind. See what happens as you stay with them actively and playfully for a while. Let yourself be open to whatever emerges./ Don't say to yourself, "Now I've *got* to implement these good ideas, whether I feel like it or not!" (That's Horney's "tyranny of the oughts and shoulds," which, as she made clear, frustrates rather than facilitates creative change.) See if you can avoid putting that trip on yourself. Just stay among the growth resources that feel most energized./ What do you *want* to do with these? Let your mind play with them as they come back to you and see what happens. Where do they take you? What emerges? What are the next steps? Or jumps? Or flights? Up? Or down? Or sideways? What do *you* really want to do? Let your plans "grow legs or arms"!/ I find it helps me to write out some change plans. See where this process takes you. Perhaps your butterfly will decide to fly in a new place, in a storm or in a serene place. Flow with your experiencing. Trust it. If you do, you'll find that new ways to use these growth resources emerge from your own creativity. You'll not only decide to use them, you'll *enjoy* doing so in your own unique ways!

This "conclusion" didn't go where I expected it would when I started writing it, which is probably just as well. For the only conclusion that will be worth much to you is the one *you* decide to write in your own thought and in your actions and relationships. When you do that, it is really not a conclusion, of course, but a beginning. It's *your* new beginning! (However, if you'd like some more organized suggestions for using the growth insights of a book like this, you'll find these at the end of the companion book to this one.[2])

Whichever or whatever you decide to do or not to do, I had fun writing this non-conclusion. I hope you enjoyed reading it! So, HAPPY FLYING!

Notes

An Overview

1. For an in-depth discussion of these principles see my *Growth Counseling* (Nashville: Abingdon, 1979), chapters 1 and 2.
2. I am building on Abraham Maslow's observation regarding the first, second, and third forces in psychology. What he described as the "fourth force"—transpersonal psychology—is the fifth stream in my schema. (See Maslow's *Toward a Psychology of Being,* 2nd ed. [New York: Van Nostrand, 1968], pp. iii-iv.)

Chapter 1: Sigmund Freud and the Ego Analysts

1. Much of this biographical information is taken from the succinct biographical statement in James Fadiman and Robert Frager, *Personality and Personal Growth* (New York: Harper, 1976), pp. 4-9; for an in-depth biography of Freud see the classical three-volume work by Ernest Jones, *The Life and Work of Sigmund Freud* (New York: Basic Books, 1953, 1955, 1957).
2. Ruth L. Monroe delineates the first four of these generic concepts in *Schools of Psychoanalytic Thought* (New York: Dryden Press, 1955), chapter 2.
3. See Lancelot L. Whyte, *The Unconscious Before Freud* (New York: Basic Books, 1960).
4. In Freud's thought, behavior is seen as motivated by instinctual drives and needs.
5. I am indebted to Rod Hunter for calling my attention to the importance of these points and to a variety of other contributions from Freud's thought.
6. For a discussion of this concept see *Growth Counseling,* pp. 52-55, 63.
7. For a discussion of this issue see "Transference and Countertransference in Pastoral Care," by E. Mansell Pattison, *Journal of Pastoral Care,* Winter 1965, pp. 193-202.
8. For further exploration of this issue see Donald E. Miller's *Wing-Footed Wanderer: Conscience and Transcendence* (Nashville: Abingdon, 1977)

and John Hoffman's *Ethical Confrontation in Counseling* (Chicago: The University of Chicago Press, 1979).

9. Ruth Monroe describes the thought of the ego psychologists as "the mainstream of progress in Freudian psychoanalysis." *Schools of Psychoanalysis,* p. 104.
10. See Freud's *New Introductory Lectures on Psychoanalysis.*
11. Translated by Cecil Baines (New York: International Universities Press, 1946).
12. Hartmann, using an analogy, points out that a full description of a nation must include much more than its conflicts and wars. To understand a nation one must know about all its peaceful activities, the development of its populace, its social structure, economy, peace-time traffic across its borders, and so on. The same principle applies when one is seeking to understand or help people.
13. *Growth Counseling,* pp. 55-56.
14. I have discussed four types of supportive counseling in *Basic Types of Pastoral Counseling* (Nashville: Abingdon Press, 1966), chap. 8.
15. *Generative Man: Psychoanalytic Perspectives* (Philadelphia: Westminster Press, 1973), p. 155.
16. *Growth Counseling,* chap. 6.
17. Erikson, *Identity, Youth and Crisis* (New York: W. W. Norton, 1968), p. 93.
18. See Browning, *Generative Man,* p. 181.
19. For a discussion of religious development, using Erikson's stages, see LeRoy Aden, "Faith and the Developmental Cycle," *Pastoral Psychology,* Spring, 1976; and John J. Gleason, Jr., *Growing Up to God: Eight Steps in Religious Development* (Nashville: Abingdon Press, 1975).
20. *Identity, Youth and Crisis,* p. 106. (*Sic* in brackets is used here and in other quotations throughout *Contemporary Growth Therapies* as a device to call to the reader's awareness the sexist connotations of the generic use of masculine nouns and pronouns.)
21. Browning, *Generative Man,* p. 149.
22. *Insight and Responsibility* (New York: W. W. Norton, 1964), p. 233.
23. *Identity, Youth and Crisis,* p. 260.
24. See *Growth Counseling,* pp. 160-61; also Kate Millett, *Sexual Politics* (New York: Doubleday, 1969), pp. 210-21; Erikson, "Inner and Outer Space: Reflections on Womanhood," *Daedalus,* 93 (1964), pp. 582-606.

Chapter 2: Alfred Adler and Otto Rank

1. The biographical data were drawn mainly from Elizabeth Hall, "Alfred Adler, A Sketch," *Psychology Today,* February, 1970, pp. 45, 67.
2. This list comparing Adler's and Freud's position is from Heinz Ansbacher and R. R. Ansbacher, eds., *The Individual Psychology of Alfred Adler* (New York: Harper, 1956), pp. 4-6.
3. *Ibid.,* p. 115.
4. *Ibid.,* p. 154.
5. *Ibid.,* p. 250.
6. *Ibid.,* p. 248.

7. Heinz Ansbacher, "Alfred Adler, Individual Psychology," reprinted from *Psychology Today* magazine, February, 1970, p. 66. Copyright © 1970 Ziff-Davis Publishing Company.
8. Adler's views on the psychology of religion are set forth in the book edited by the Ansbachers, pp. 460 ff.
9. Ernest Jones, *The Life and Work of Sigmund Freud,* vol. II (New York: Basic Books, 1955), p. 131.
10. Franz Alexander, et al., eds., *Psychoanalytic Pioneers* (New York: Basic Books, 1966), p. 38.
11. Ruth Monroe, *Schools of Psychoanalytic Thought* (New York: The Dryden Press, 1955), p. 576.
12. Rank, *Will Therapy and Truth and Reality* (New York: Alfred A. Knopf, 1945), p. 17.
13. *Ibid.,* pp. 111-12.
14. *Ibid.,* p. 24.
15. *Ibid.,* p. 89.
16. *Ibid.,* pp. 196-97.
17. See Patrick Mullahy, *Oedipus, Myth and Complex* (New York: Grove Press, 1948), p. 198.
18. *Beyond Psychology* (New York: Dover Publications, 1941), p. 267.

Chapter 3: Erich Fromm, Karen Horney, Harry Stack Sullivan

1. See *Escape from Freedom* (New York: Rinehart and Co., 1941), pp. 103-35; 207-39.
2. *Psychoanalysis and Religion* (New Haven: Yale University Press, 1950), pp. 25-26.
3. *Ibid.,* pp. 50-51.
4. Written with D. T. Suzuki and Richard de Martino (New York: Harper & Row, 1964).
5. *Man for Himself* (New York: Rinehart and Co., 1947), p. 250.
6. Fromm, *The Heart of Man* (New York: Harper & Row, 1964), p. 31.
7. *The Anatomy of Human Destructiveness* (New York: Holt, Rinehart and Winston, 1973), p. 290.
8. Fromm, *The Sane Society* (New York: Rinehart and Co., 1955), p. 284.
9. Ralph Hyatt, "Karen Horney, A Tribute," *Journal of Marriage and Family Counseling,* October, 1977, p. 39.
10. Tillich, "Karen Horney, A Funeral Address," *Pastoral Psychology,* May, 1953, p. 12.
11. *Neurosis and Human Growth* (New York: W. W. Norton, 1950), p. 17.
12. *Ibid.,* p. 15.
13. Horney, *Our Inner Conflicts* (New York: W. W. Norton, 1945), p. 41.
14. For a fuller discussion of these three defensive modes, see *ibid.,* chaps. 3, 4, and 5.
15. Gerald Sykes, *The Hidden Remnant* (New York: Harper, 1962), p. 100.
16. *Neurosis and Human Growth,* pp. 377-79.
17. *Our Inner Conflicts,* p. 45.
18. *Feminine Psychology* (New York: W. W. Norton, 1967), p. 116.
19. *Ibid.,* p. 126.
20. *Ibid.,* p. 60.

21. "Horney's Daughter Shares Mother's Early Diaries," *William A. White Institute Newsletter,* Fall 1975, p. 12.
22. Tillich, "Karen Horney, A Funeral Address," pp. 12-13.
23. Robert Coles, "Karen Horney's Flight from Orthodoxy," in *Women and Analysis,* Jean Stouse, ed. (New York: Grossman, 1974), p. 189.
24. Ralph M. Crowley, "Harry Stack Sullivan: The Man," *William A. White Institute Newsletter,* Fall 1970, p. 2.
25. See Mullahy, *The Contributions of Harry Stack Sullivan* (New York: Science House, 1967), chaps. 5, 6, 7.
26. *Conceptions of Modern Psychiatry* (Washington: The W. A. White Psychiatric Foundation, 1947), p. 57.
27. For a fuller discussion of the life eras see Patrick Mullahy, *Oedipus, Myth and Complex, A Review of Psychoanalytic Theory* (New York: Grove Press, 1948), pp. 301-11; and A. H. Chapman, *Harry Stack Sullivan, His Life and His Work* (New York: Putnam's, 1976), chaps. 4 and 5.
28. Donald H. Ford and Hugh B. Urban, *Systems of Psychotherapy* (New York: Wiley, 1963), p. 521.
29. *The Psychiatric Interview* (New York: W. W. Norton, 1954), p. 242.
30. Chapman, *Harry Stack Sullivan,* p. 17.
31. This paper is in *The Fusion of Psychiatry and Social Sciences, Collected Works,* II (New York: W. W. Norton, 1965), 273-89.

Chapter 4: Carl Jung, the Existentialists, Carl Rogers

1. Some of the biographical data in this section are from Fadiman and Frager, *Personality and Personal Growth,* pp. 54-57.
2. Jung, *Memories, Dreams, Reflections* (New York: Random House, 1961), p. 174.
3. *Ibid.,* p. 199.
4. *Ibid.,* p. 297.
5. *Modern Man in Search of a Soul* (New York: Harcourt, Brace, 1933), pp. 110-11.
6. *Ibid.,* p. 117.
7. *Collected Works of C. G. Jung* (Princeton: Princeton University Press, 1967–), 16:355.
8. *Two Essays on Analytical Psychology* (New York: World, 1958), pp. 193-94.
9. *Ibid.,* p. 182.
10. From a letter of Jung dated January 13, 1948.
11. See James Hillman, *Insearch: Psychology and Religion* (New York: Scribner's, 1967), pp. 57 ff.
12. *Collected Works,* 16:454, 448.
13. Letter dated August 12, 1960.
14. "Individual Dream Symbolism in Relation to Alchemy," *The Portable Jung,* Joseph Campbell, ed. (New York: Viking, 1971), p. 362.
15. *The Portable Jung,* p. 167.
16. *Psyche and Soul* (New York: Doubleday, 1958), pp. 49-50.
17. *Modern Man in Search of a Soul,* p. 67.
18. "Psychology or the Clergy," *Collected Works,* 11:330.

19. *Man and His Symbols* (New York: Dell, 1968), p. 76.
20. *The Unconscious Self* (Boston: Little, Brown, 1957), p. 9.
21. Gerald Sykes, *The Hidden Remnant* (New York: Harper, 1962), p. 71.
22. *Modern Man in Search of a Soul,* p. 58.
23. *Two Essays,* pp. 84-85.
24. *Modern Man in Search of a Soul,* p. 229.
25. *Ibid.*, p. 66.
26. *Jung's Letters,* ed. G. Adler (Princeton: Princeton University Press), 1973, p. 456.
27. *Collected Works,* 10:177.
28. *Collected Works,* 7:409.
29. *The Changing of the Gods* (Boston: Beacon Press, 1979), p. 59.
30. The thought of Martin Heidegger, whom Rollo May calls "the fountainhead of present-day existentialist thought," has had a strong impact on the theory of several psychotherapists.
31. *Basic Types of Pastoral Counseling,* p. 263. This statement was written before my consciousness was raised regarding sexist language. It applies equally to clergywomen!
32. Howard Clinebell, "Philosophical-Religious Factors in the Etiology and Treatment of Alcoholism," p. 477.
33. *Psychology and the Human Dilemma* (New York: Van Nostrand, 1967), p. 81 (emphasis added).
34. Søren Kierkegaard, *The Concept of Dread* (Princeton: Princeton University Press, 1944), p. 104.
35. Fred Berthold, Jr., "Anxious Longing," in *Constructive Aspects of Anxiety,* Seward Hiltner and Karl Menninger, eds. (Nashville: Abingdon Press, 1963), p. 71.
36. Tillich, *The Courage to Be,* p. 67.
37. *Existential Psychology* (New York: Random House, 1961), p. 98.
38. *Psychology and the Human Dilemma,* p. 82.
39. *The Doctor and the Soul* (New York: Alfred A. Knopf, 1962), pp. 37-38.
40. *Existence* (New York: Basic Books, 1958), p. 41.
41. *Ibid.*, p. 52.
42. See *Growth Counseling,* p. 48.
43. Bugental, *The Search for Authenticity* (New York: Holt, Rinehart and Winston), p. 31.
44. *Man's Search for Himself* (New York: W. W. Norton, 1953), p. 136.
45. *Existence,* p. 87.
46. *Ibid.*, p. 49.
47. Bugental, *The Search for Authenticity,* p. 15.
48. *The Doctor and the Soul,* pp. 61-62.
49. *Man's Search for Meaning* (New York: Pocket Books, 1963), p. 65.
50. *The Doctor and the Soul,* p. 114.
51. May, *Existence,* pp. 14-15.
52. Frankl's paradoxical intention methods seem to bear little relation to his existential philosophy; his description of how he does therapy with particular persons gives the impression of being manipulative and highly authority-centered.

53. See *Growth Counseling,* chap. 4; *Basic Types of Pastoral Counseling,* chap. 14.
54. Carl Rogers, in *History of Psychology in Autobiography,* eds. E. Boring and G. Lindzen, vol. 5 (New York: Appleton-Century-Crofts, 1967), p. 351.
55. Carl Rogers, "In Retrospect: Forty-Six Years," *The American Psychologist,* 29:122-23; quoted by James Fadiman and Robert Frager in their succinct biographical statement on Rogers in *Personality and Personal Growth,* pp. 279-84.
56. See *Basic Types of Pastoral Counseling,* pp. 27-40.
57. *On Becoming a Person* (Boston: Houghton Mifflin, 1961), p. 181.
58. *Ibid.,* pp. 64-65.
59. *Ibid.,* p. 110.
60. *Ibid.,* p. 35.
61. *Ibid.,* p. 196.
62. *Ibid.,* p. 17.
63. *Ibid.,* p. 33.
64. *Client-Centered Therapy* (Boston: Houghton Mifflin, 1951), pp. x-xl.
65. Harper, *Psychoanalysis and Psychotherapy, 36 Systems* (Englewood Cliffs, N.J.: Spectrum Books, Prentice-Hall, 1959).
66. *On Becoming a Person,* p. 56.
67. *Becoming Partners: Marriage and Its Alternatives* (New York: Harper, 1972), p. 209.
68. *Freedom to Learn* (Columbus: Chas. E. Merrill, 1969), p. 177.
69. See *Growth Counseling,* chap. 1, for a discussion of these six dimensions.
70. See Charles B. Truax and Robert R. Carkhuff, *Toward Effective Counseling and Psychotherapy* (Chicago: Aldine Publishing Co., 1967), p. 25.
71. *Growth Counseling,* pp. 55-56.
72. *On Becoming a Person,* p. 119, p. 22.
73. This is from a dialogue between the two men recorded shortly before Tillich's death.

Chapter 5: The Behavioral-Action Therapies

1. The main points of this historical sketch are paraphrased from a brochure announcing the First Annual Southern California Conference on Behavior Modification, October, 1969.
2. See Joseph Wolpe, *Psychotherapy by Reciprocal Inhibition* (Stanford: Stanford University Press, 1958).
3. Operant conditioning uses rewards to reinforce the learning of desired behavior and withholding of rewards or punishment to eliminate destructive behavior. Operant conditioning is the type used in most behavior therapies.
4. From the brochure described in note 1.
5. See Beck's *Cognitive Therapy and Emotional Disorders* (New York: International Universities Press, 1976).
6. See Albert Ellis and Robert A. Harper, *A Guide to Rational Living* (Englewood Cliffs, N.J.: Prentice-Hall, 1961), and Ellis, et al., *Growth Through Reason* (Palo Alto, Calif.: Science and Behavior Books, 1971).

7. See Bandura, *Principles of Behavior Modification* (New York: Holt, Rinehart & Winston, 1969).
8. These principles are paraphrased from a list of principles developed by H. J. Ehsemch in 1958. See Donald J. Levis, ed., *Learning Approaches to Therapeutic Behavior Change* (Chicago: Aldine, 1970), pp. 12-13.
9. This case was described by G. Terence Wilson and Gerald C. Davison in "Behavior Therapy, A Road to Self-Control," *Psychology Today,* October, 1975, pp. 54-60.
10. *Dr. Knox's Marital Exercise Book* (New York: David McKay, 1975), p. 28.
11. These steps are adapted from "Behavioral Approaches to Marital Therapy," by Robert Liberman in *Couples in Conflict,* eds. Alan S. Gurman and David G. Rice (New York: Jason Aronson, 1975), pp. 207-78.
12. See Jeffrey C. Steger, "Cognitive Behavioral Strategies in the Treatment of Sexual Problems," in John P. Foreyt and Dianna P. Rahtjen, eds., *Cognitive Behavior Therapy, Research and Application* (New York: Plenum Press, 1978), pp. 83-84.
13. See Kaplan, *The New Sex Therapy* (New York: Brunner/Mazel, 1974), and *The Illustrated Manual of Sex Therapy* (New York: The New York Times Book Co., 1975).
14. See Steger, "Cognitive Behavioral Strategies," pp. 91-92.
15. *Reality Therapy* (New York: Harper, 1965), p. 15.
16. *Ibid.,* p. 25.
17. *Ibid.,* pp. 26-27.
18. Crisis theory and methods are discussed in more detail in my book *Basic Types of Pastoral Counseling,* chaps. 8 and 9.
19. For a description of Holmes's stress score, see my book *Growth Counseling for Marriage Enrichment* (Philadelphia: Fortress Press, 1975), pp. 64-65.
20. For a discussion of the power of hope in therapy, see *Growth Counseling,* pp. 48-49.
21. These irrational ideas are paraphrased from Ellis and Harper, *A Guide to Rational Living,* pp. 185-87.
22. *Growth Through Reason,* p. 3.
23. For methods of facilitating spiritual growth, see *Growth Counseling,* chap. 4.
24. *Beyond Freedom and Dignity* (New York: Alfred A. Knopf, 1971), p. 96 and 102.
25. *The Modes and Morals of Psychotherapy* (New York: Holt, Rinehart and Winston, 1964), pp. 121-22.
26. J. Hearndon, *How to Survive in Your Native Land* (New York: Simon & Schuster, 1971), p. 116.

Chapter 6: Transactional Analysis

1. See Claude Steiner, *Scripts People Live* (New York: Bantam Books, 1974), pp. 10 ff. for further biographical information.
2. I first heard Berne at a one-day workshop in Los Angeles around 1962; in 1964, I took part in a weekend training event in the mountains at Idylwild, California, at which he was the principal resource person.
3. Muriel James and Louis M. Savary, *The Power at the Bottom of the Well* (New York: Harper, 1974), p. 14.

4. *Transactional Analysis in Psychotherapy* (New York: Grove Press, 1961), p. 235.
5. *Principles of Group Treatment* (New York: Oxford University Press, 1966), p. 221.
6. *Games People Play* (New York: Grove Press, 1964), p. 48.
7. *Principles of Group Treatment,* p. 310.
8. *Transactional Analysis in Psychotherapy,* pp. 125-26.
9. For a more detailed account of how to present PAC in counseling sessions, see *Basic Types of Pastoral Counseling,* pp. 130-38.
10. *Transactional Analysis in Psychotherapy,* p. 146.
11. "Sex Role Scripting in Men and Women," chap. 13 in Steiner's *Scripts People Live.*
12. See *Scripts People Live,* chaps. 14 and 15.
13. *Women as Winners* (Reading, Mass.: Addison-Wesley, 1971), p. 87.
14. An important TA resource for helping institutions become effective environments of growth is Dorothy Jongeward's *Everybody Wins: TA Applied to Organizations* (Reading, Mass.: Addison-Wesley, 1976).
15. *I'm OK—You're OK* (New York: Harper, 1969), p. 226.
16. *The Power at the Bottom of the Well,* p. 28.
17. Jacque Schuiff discusses the stages of the development of the Child in her *Cathexis Reader* (New York: Harper, 1975).
18. After I wrote this, my attention was called to an article by Janis Litke, "The Spindle—The Teenager in the Adult," *Transactional Analysis Journal,* vol. 3, no. 4.
19. *Game Free: The Meaning of Intimacy* (New York: Harper, 1974), p. 87.
20. *Ibid.*, p. 85.
21. For additional methods of self re-parenting see Muriel James et al., *Techniques in Transactional Analysis* (Reading, Mass.: Addison-Wesley, 1977), chap. 38.

Chapter 7: Gestalt Therapy

1. See *Ego, Hunger and Aggression* (New York: Random House, 1947).
2. See *In and Out the Garbage Pail* (Lafayette, Calif.: Real People Press, 1969) for further information about his life.
3. See "The Roots of Gestalt Therapy" by Edward W. L. Smith in *The Growing Edge of Gestalt Therapy* (New York: Brunner/Mazel, 1976), chap. 1.
4. See my book *Growth Counseling,* pp. 21-25.
5. *Gestalt Therapy Verbatim* (GTV) (Lafayette, Calif.: Real People Press, 1969), p. 2.
6. *Ibid.*, p. 28.
7. Zinker, *Creative Process in Gestalt Therapy* (New York: Brunner/Mazel, 1977), p. 9.
8. *GTV,* p. 31.
9. *Ibid.*, p. 2.
10. Polster, "Women in Therapy: A Gestalt Therapist's View," in Chris Hatcher and Philip Himelstein, eds., *Handbook of Gestalt Therapy* (New York: Jason Aronson, 1976), pp. 557 ff.
11. Zinker, *Creative Process in Gestalt Therapy,* pp. 96-97.

12. See Arnold Beisser, "The Paradoxical Theory of Change," in Joen Fagan and Irma Shepherd, eds., *Gestalt Therapy Now* (Palo Alto, Calif.: Science and Behavior Books, 1970), chap. 6.
13. *Gestalt Therapy Integrated* (GTI) (New York: Brunner/Mazel, 1973), p. 17.
14. *GTV,* p. 63.
15. *GTI,* p. 85.
16. *GTV,* flyleaf.
17. For a fuller description of this experience, see *Growth Counseling,* pp. 21-25.
18. Zinker, *Creative Process in Gestalt Therapy,* p. 5.
19. Lynn Walker, *Body and Soul* (Lafayette, Calif.: Real People Press, 1969).
20. *In and Out the Garbage Pail,* p. 22.
21. See "Present-Centeredness" in *Gestalt Therapy Now,* pp. 47 ff.
22. Zinker, *Creative Process in Gestalt Therapy,* p. 17.
23. *GTV,* p. 76.
24. *Ibid.,* p. 4.
25. Robert Resnick, Gestalt Therapy Workshop, May, 1978.
26. Anica Vesel Mander and Anne Kent Rush, *Feminism as Therapy* (New York: Random House, 1974), p. 48.
27. Reprinted from *Rough Times* by *Journal of Humanistic Psychology,* vol. 17, no. 3, p. 78.
28. Polster and Polster, *GTI,* p. 24.
29. This is adapted from an exercise by Fritz Perls in *GTV,* p. 61.
30. Polster and Polster, *GTI,* pp. 239-40.
31. Paraphrased from a statement by Bob Martin in a gestalt therapy workshop, May, 1978.
32. *GTV,* pp. 68-70.

Chapter 8: Holistic Health, Biofeedback, and Body Therapies

1. "Sing the Body Electric," *Psychology Today,* October 1970, p. 56.
2. These principles are drawn from various sources, the most prominent of which is Ardell's *High Level Wellness* (Emmaus, Pa.: Rodale Press, 1977).
3. For an exploration of the six basic dimensions of wholeness see my book *Growth Counseling,* chap. 1.
4. *High Level Wellness,* p. 293.
5. For more details about the first five strategies, see Ardell's *High Level Wellness,* Part II, from which many of the suggestions in this section were taken.
6. *Ibid.,* p. 98.
7. See the books by Ardell, Lappe, McCamy and Presley, and Shealy and Woodruff for nutritional information.
8. Lionel Tiger, "My Turn: A Very Old Animal Called Man," *Newsweek,* September 4, 1978, p. 13.
9. See Richard L. Hittleman, *Yoga for Physical Fitness* (New York: Warner Books, 1964) for a do-it-yourself approach to hatha yoga.
10. See Herbert Benson, *The Relaxation Response* (West Caldwell, N.J.: Morrow, 1975), pp. 70-71.
11. *High Level Wellness,* p. 166.

12. See Selye's *Stress Without Distress* (New York: Signet Books, 1974).
13. See Cousins' *Anatomy of an Illness* (New York: W. W. Norton, 1979).
14. See Raymond Moody, *Laugh after Laugh: The Healing Power of Humor* (Jacksonville, Fla.: Headwaters Press, 1978).
15. Quoted by Richard Saltus in "Holistic Health Crusaders Seek End to Illness Crisis," *Santa Barbara News Press,* March 6, 1978.
16. In 1977, the life expectancy for white females was 77.7, compared with 69.9 for white males; nonwhite females have an expectancy of 73.8 and nonwhite males 65.0. Information from the National Center for Health Statistics, reported in the *Los Angeles Times,* December 19, 1978.
17. James Harrison, "Warning: The Male Sex Role May Be Dangerous to Your Health," *Journal of Social Issues,* vol. 34, no. 1, p. 65.
18. *New Mind, New Body* (New York: Bantam Books, 1975), p. 11.
19. *Ibid.,* pp. 350-51.
20. *Ibid.,* p. 262.
21. For a review of these applications of biofeedback, see Brown's *Stress and the Art of Biofeedback* (New York: Harper, 1977), pp. 162-65.
22. "Biofeedback: Research and Therapy," in *New Ways to Health,* Nils O. Jacobson, ed. (Stockholm: Natur ock Kultur, 1975), p. 1.
23. Letter from Howard Stone, February 20, 1976.
24. See "Biofeedback for Mind-Body Self Regulation: Healing and Creativity," in *Biofeedback 1972* (Chicago: Aldine Publishing Co., 1973), pp. 152-66.
25. Hazel Henderson emphasized this point in a talk at the School of Theology at Claremont, February 25, 1977.
26. For a summary of the key ideas of several body therapies see Robert A. Harper, *The New Psychotherapies* (Englewood Cliffs, N.J.: Prentice-Hall, 1975), chap. 8.
27. Lowen does not believe, as Reich did, that the sexual orgasm is the only key to mental health. He also makes less use than did Reich of direct body contact by the therapist. His approach to body therapy does not fall into the body-reductionism of Reich's approach, at least to the same degree.
28. "Sexuality, Sex and the Human Potential," in *Human Potentialities,* Herbert Otto, ed. (St. Louis: Warren H. Green, 1968), p. 172.
29. *The Betrayal of the Body* (New York: Collier Macmillan, 1967), pp. 37-38.
30. "The New Carnality," *Psychology Today,* October, 1970, p. 59.
31. *Betrayal of the Body,* p. 209.
32. "Sexuality, Sex and the Human Potential," p. 178.
33. *Betrayal of the Body,* p. 231.
34. *Ibid.,* p. 259.
35. It seems clear that recognizing and respecting our own animal roots is the key to respecting other animals, including the many that are on the "endangered species" list. Respecting our animal roots may even be a key to removing humankind from this list!
36. See the concluding essay of Keen's book, *To a Dancing God* (New York: Harper & Row, 1970), entitled "The Importance of Being Carnal—Notes for a Visceral Theology."
37. Adapted from Rush, *Getting Clear,* pp. 49-50.
38. *Ibid.,* p. 4. For detailed instructions for using this exercise in sexual therapy (and enrichment) see William Hartmann and Virginia Fifthian's *Treatment*

of Sexual Dysfunction (Long Beach, Calif.: Center for Marital and Sexual Studies, 1972), pp. 98-138.

39. Hittleman, *Yoga for Physical Fitness,* pp. 94-96.
40. Rush, *Getting Clear: Body Work for Women* (New York: Random House, 1973), p. 281.
41. See *Betrayal,* p. 223, for Lowen's discussion of this exercise.
42. This exercise is condensed from O. Carl Simonton and Matthews-Simonton, *Getting Well Again* (Los Angeles: J. P. Tarcher, 1978), pp. 131-37.
43. Richard S. Surwit, "Warming Thoughts for a Cold Winter," *Psychology Today,* December, 1978, p. 115. This exercise is a form of "autogenic training," a relaxation technique developed by two German psychiatrists, J. H. Schultz and W. Luthe.
44. *Ibid.,* p. 115.

Chapter 9: Family Systems Therapies

1. See "Role-Relationship Marriage Counseling," chap. 6 in *Basic Types of Pastoral Counseling;* "Enriching Marriage and Family Life," in *Growth Counseling: New Tools for Clergy and Laity,* Part I; *Growth Counseling for Marriage Enrichment; Growth Counseling for Mid-Years Couples;* and "Alcoholics Anonymous—Our Greatest Resource," chap. 5 in *Understanding and Counseling the Alcoholic.*
2. Systems theory, a "general science of wholeness," undergirds the systemic therapies. See Ludwig von Bertalanffy's *General Systems Theory* (New York: George Braziller, 1968).
3. *The Psychodynamics of Family Life* (New York: Basic Books, 1958), p. 17.
4. "The Artificial Boundary Between Self and Society," *Psychology Today,* January, 1977, p. 66.
5. *Conjoint Family Therapy* (Palo Alto, Calif.: Science and Behavior Books, 1964), p. 58.
6. *Peoplemaking* (Palo Alto, Calif.: Science and Behavior Books, 1964), pp. 26-27.
7. For a discussion of his theory see Bowen's "Family Therapy and Family Group Therapy."
8. See Luthman and Kirschenbaum, *The Dynamic Family* (Palo Alto, Calif.: Science and Behavior Books, 1974), p. 5.
9. For documentation of the negative effects of marriage on women, see Jesse Bernard's *Future of Marriage* (New York: Bantam Books, 1973), chaps. 1, 2, and 3.
10. See Carrie Carmichael, *Non-Sexist Childraising* (Boston: Beacon Press, 1977).
11. I have described such sessions and illustrated them by segments from a healthy family growth interview in cassette course IIIB, in *Growth Counseling: New Tools for Clergy and Laity,* Part I.
12. *Families of the Slums* (New York: Basic Books, 1967), p. 374.
13. *Ibid.,* p. 370.
14. *Peoplemaking,* p. 296.
15. *Ibid.*

16. This diagram is adapted from *Growth Groups,* p. 148.
17. *Ibid.,* p. 149
18. *Ibid.,* pp. 149-50.
19. For a powerful discussion of these threats, see *The Seventh Enemy* by Robert Higgins (New York: McGraw-Hill, 1978).
20. From *A Star Begotten;* quoted by Halford E. Luccock in *Unfinished Business* (New York: Harper and Bros., 1956), p. 162.
21. See *Growth Counseling for Marriage Enrichment,* chap. 2.

Chapter 10: Feminist Therapies

1. For a series of papers on these and other radical therapists see *Radical Therapy,* Phil Brown, ed. (New York: Harper Colophon Books, 1973).
2. See Jerome Agel (Producer), *The Radical Therapist* (New York: Ballantine Books, 1971); *Rough Times* (Ballantine Books, 1973); *Love, Therapy and Politics, Issues in Radical Therapy* (New York: Grove Press, 1976); and Hendrick M. Ruitenbeck, *Going Crazy: The Radical Therapy of R. D. Laing and Others* (New York: Bantam Books, 1972).
3. In *Going Crazy,* p. 196.
4. *The Radical Therapist,* 1, p. 1.
5. Rush, *Getting Clear,* pp. 6-7.
6. This is illustrated by the positions of Williams in *Notes of a Feminist Therapist* (New York: Praeger, 1976), and Mander and Rush in *Feminism as Therapy* (New York: Random House/Bookworks, 1974). The authors of both volumes are feminists. Yet the first book reflects a less radical feminist perspective than the second.
7. To avoid confusion, it is important to point out that Charlotte Ellen's earlier name, which still appears on the book cited in this chapter, was Charlotte Holt Clinebell.
8. See *Growth Counseling,* chap. 6.
9. Miller, *Toward a New Psychology of Women* (Boston: Beacon Press, 1976), pp. 1, 10.
10. *Ibid.,* p. 88.
11. *Psychoanalysis and Women* (New York: Brunner/Mazel, 1973), p. 391.
12. Although Jung emphasized the bisexuality of the psyche in both sexes and valued the "feminine" side of persons, he accepted the sexist stereotypes of his culture when he defined the home-centered roles of women as "normal." Alfred Adler recognized that their social powerlessness contributes to the inferiority feelings of women; and Wilhelm Reich identified the interrelatedness of political and sexual oppression. For feminist critiques of Freud and Jung, see Rosemary Radford Reuther's *New Women, New Earth, Sexist Ideologies and Human Liberation* (New York: Seabury Press, 1975), chap. 5; Naomi R. Goldenberg, *Changing of the Gods* (Boston: Beacon Press, 1979), chap. 5.
13. Although Clara Thompson was one of my mentors at the White Institute of Psychiatry, my male programming caused me to ignore this significant thrust in her thought during those years.
14. *Women and Madness* (New York: Avon Books, 1973), pp. 121-22; Chesler further illuminates the role of sexism in therapy in her paper, "Patient and

Patriarch: Women in the Psychotherapeutic Relationship," *Woman in a Sexist Society,* chap. 7.
15. *Journal of Consulting and Clinical Psychology,* vol. 34, no. 1, pp. 1-7.
16. See Barbara Ehrenreich and Deirdre English, *Witches, Midwives and Nurses, A History of Women Healers* (Old Westbury, N.Y.: The Feminist Press, 1973).
17. *Psychoanalysis and Women,* pp. 379-80.
18. *Notes of a Feminist Therapist,* p. 11.
19. Farrell, *The Liberated Man* (New York: Bantam Books, 1975), p. 49.
20. See Phyllis Chesler, *About Men* (New York: Simon & Schuster, 1978), p. 244.
21. Williams, *Notes of a Feminist Therapist,* p. 11.
22. Charlotte Holt Clinebell, *Counseling for Liberation* (Philadelphia: Fortress Press, 1976), pp. 22-23. The author used "androgynous" originally in describing the last characteristic, a term she no longer regards as adequate for expressing psychic wholeness.
23. Center for Feminist Therapy, Los Angeles, California 90064.
24. CR groups are one form of what I call "growth-action groups." See *Growth Groups,* chap. 10.
25. Perl and Abarbanell, *Guidelines to Feminist Consciousness Raising* (Los Angeles, 1975), p. 2.
26. "Consciousness-Raising Groups as Therapy for Women," in Franks and Vasanti, *Women in Therapy* (New York: Brunner/Mazel, 1974), chap. 15. The study she cites is "Free Space: A Perspective on the Small Group in Women's Liberation," by P. Allen.
27. Personal communication, May 7, 1977.
28. For resources for men's CR groups, see Perl and Abarbanell, *Guidelines,* pp. 40-45; *Unbecoming: A Men's CR Group Writes on Oppression and Themselves* (New York: Times Change Press, 1971); and the books by Brenton, Farrell, Fasteau, Malcomson, Nichols, and Steinmann/Fox.
29. See *Gyn/Ecology* (Boston: Beacon Press, 1979), chap. 7.

Chapter 11: Psychosynthesis

1. *The Act of Will* (Baltimore: Penguin Books, 1974), p. 6.
2. Sam Keen, "The Golden Mean of Roberto Assagioli," reprinted from *Psychology Today* magazine, Dec., 1974., p. 98. Copyright © 1974 Ziff-Davis Publishing Company.
3. *Psychosynthesis* (New York: Viking, 1971), p. 35.
4. Keen, "The Golden Mean," p. 98.
5. *The Act of Will,* p. 14.
6. *Psychosynthesis,* p. 8.
7. *Ibid.,* p. 6.
8. *Ibid.,* p. 100.
9. "A Higher View of the Man-Woman Problem" (an interview with Assagioli by Claude Servan-Schreiber) *Synthesis,* vol. 1, no. 1, p. 45.
10. *Ibid.,* p. 49.
11. *Psychosynthesis,* p. 3.
12. *Ibid.,* p. 39.

13. *The Act of Will,* p. 200.
14. Keen, "The Golden Mean," p. 105.
15. *Psychosynthesis,* p. 207.
16. *The Act of Will,* pp. 205-8.
17. "The Synthesis of the Nation," *Synthesis,* vol. 1, no. 2, pp. 8-19.
18. Robert Gerard, "Psychosynthesis, A Psychotherapy for the Whole Man" (mimeographed paper, no date), pp. 5-6.
19. *Ibid.,* p. 9.
20. *Psychosynthesis,* p. 26.
21. This is paraphrased from *Psychosynthesis,* pp. 118-19.
22. Paraphrased from *Psychosynthesis,* pp. 118-19. For further information about this exercise see *The Act of Will,* pp. 211-17.
23. For an illuminating discussion of subpersonalities, see the paper by James G. Vargiu in "Psychosynthesis Workbook," *Synthesis,* vol. 1, no. 1, pp. WB 9-47.
24. "The Door," *Synthesis,* vol. 1, no. 1, pp. WB 50-53.
25. *Psychosynthesis,* p. 144.
26. "Answers from the Unconscious," *Synthesis,* vol. 1, no. 2, p. 145.
27. See *Growth Counseling,* pp. 126-28, for a full description of this exercise.
28. "Dialogue with the Higher Self," *Synthesis,* vol. 1, no. 2, p. 135.
29. See *Growth Counseling,* p. 123.
30. Personal communication, May 1979.
31. This story is from C. W. Henderson, *Awakening* (Englewood Cliffs, N.J.: Prentice-Hall, 1975), p. 170.
32. See *The Act of Will,* pp. 218-31.
33. *Ibid.,* p. 225.

Conclusion: The Risks of Growth

1. (New York: Prentice-Hall, 1955), pp. 149-50.
2. See *Growth Counseling, Hope-Centered Methods for Actualizing Human Wholeness,* pp. 185-90.

Index

INDEX